Black Ethnics

Black Ethnics

Race, Immigration, and the Pursuit of
the American Dream

CHRISTINA M. GREER

OXFORD
UNIVERSITY PRESS

OXFORD
UNIVERSITY PRESS

Oxford University Press is a department of the University of Oxford.
It furthers the University's objective of excellence in research, scholarship,
and education by publishing worldwide.

Oxford   New York
Auckland   Cape Town   Dar es Salaam   Hong Kong   Karachi
Kuala Lumpur   Madrid   Melbourne   Mexico City   Nairobi
New Delhi   Shanghai   Taipei   Toronto

With offices in
Argentina   Austria   Brazil   Chile   Czech Republic   France   Greece
Guatemala   Hungary   Italy   Japan   Poland   Portugal   Singapore
South Korea   Switzerland   Thailand   Turkey   Ukraine   Vietnam

Oxford is a registered trademark of Oxford University Press in the UK and certain other countries.

Published in the United States of America by
Oxford University Press
198 Madison Avenue, New York, NY 10016

© Oxford University Press 2013

Library of Congress Cataloging-in-Publication Data
Greer, Christina M.
Black ethnics : race, immigration, and the pursuit of
the American dream / Christina M. Greer.
pages cm
Includes bibliographical references and index.
ISBN 978–0–19–998930–0 (hardcover : alk. paper); ISBN 978–0–19–998931–7 (pbk. : alk. paper)
1. African Americans—Race identity.
2. Blacks—United States—Race identity.   3. African Americans—Attitudes.
4. Blacks—United States—Attitudes.   5. African Americans—Employment.
6. Blacks—United States—Employment.   7. African Americans—Relations with West
Indians.   8. African Americans—Relations with Africans.   9. Labor unions—United States
10. United States—Race relations.   I. Title.
E185.625.G64 2013
305.896'073—dc23
2012043912

To my grandmother Lillian McCray

CONTENTS

ACKNOWLEDGMENTS

Thanking all of the institutions, scholars, friends, and family who have supported me in this project may be the most daunting task of this entire endeavor. First, I would like to thank the members of Social Services Employees Union (SSEU) Local 371 in New York City. The former president, Charles Ensley (1941–2010), was an inspirational leader in so many ways. I will forever be indebted to Charles for his generosity. I have tried my best to present the story of this dynamic union and truly appreciate the entire union granting me access into their lives.

First and foremost I must thank Jim Glaser for introducing me to the field of political science at Tufts University. I fondly remember our discussions on how to conduct research in new cities, how not to make assumptions about interviewees, and the importance of thinking about a question that excites you to the core. Jim continues to be a diligent mentor and adviser and has laid much of my political science foundation and interest in American politics. Bob Shapiro, Ira Katznelson, and Ester Fuchs have guided me through the dense forest of academia and have each provided their own unique styles in aiding my scholarship. They read earlier drafts of the manuscript and I am grateful for their incisive comments and suggestions. Bob's knowledge of quantitative methods and public opinion has introduced me to a new way of thinking about marginalized populations. Bob has consistently encouraged me "onward" throughout this project. Ira's pointed questions of clarification consistently urged me to think about the larger picture. And Ester continues to remind me that my thoughts have real-world and policy implications. I have been privileged to work with these three groundbreaking scholars and take sole responsibility for any shortcomings in this project. I would also like to thank the anonymous Oxford University Press reviewers who provided substantive suggestions and constructive critiques of the entire manuscript. Their diligent reading of the project helped me to untie certain knots and tie up particular loose ends. I would also like to thank the team at Oxford University Press: David McBride, Sarah Rosenthal, and Gwen Colvin have helped bring this book to fruition. I am extremely grateful to have worked with them for the multiple stages of this process.

I am forever beholden to several organizations and institutions that assisted in the funding of this research. I am thankful for the generous funding provided by Columbia University's Graduate School of Arts and Sciences Political Science Department. I was also supported by the Institute for Social and Economic Research and Policy (ISERP) at Columbia University, the Institute for Research in African American Studies (IRAAS) at Columbia University, the Mendenhall Pre-Doctoral and Mellon Post-Doctoral Programs at Smith College, and a grant from SSEU Local 371. I was able to implement the survey with the assistance of the most dedicated research assistant and friend, Mirembe Nutt-Birigwa. Her excitement, dedication, and countless hours of survey folding and envelope stuffing in the initial stages of the project were more than I could have ever asked for.

I also had the privilege to present iterations of this project at several conferences. I received valuable comments and critiques of this work from scholars during presentations at APSA, MPSA, NCOBPS, CAAR, and ASWAD conferences. I have benefited from the work of several scholars of American politics, race and ethnicity and black politics. I have been influenced by and am extremely thankful for the scholarship of (in alphabetical order) Marissa Abrajano, Bob Erikson, Cathy Cohen, Michael Dawson, Rudy de la Garza, Nancy Foner, Jennifer Hochschild, Vince Hutchings, Kim Johnson, Jane Junn, Philip Kasinitz, Taeku Lee, Robert Lieberman, John Mollenkopf, Melissa Nobles, Diane Pinderhughes, Karthick Ramakrishnan, Reuel Rogers, Mark Sawyer, Lester Spence, Phil Thompson, Al Tillery, and Mary Waters. Their books and articles have been so influential to my professional and intellectual development, and I appreciate their willingness to create innovative paths for future generations of scholars of race and ethnic politics.

I am also extremely thankful for the collegial support and advice of the Political Science Department at Fordham University. Jeff Cohen and Monika McDermott read early iterations of the framework of this project, and Susan Berger, Tom Deluca, John Entelis, and Nicole Fermon have been especially encouraging throughout the book process. The Government Department and the African-American Studies Department at Smith College were also very instrumental during the beginning and final stages of this work. I have benefited tremendously from my conversations with Martha Ackelsberg and Greg White over the years. I would also like to thank Lori Minnite for generously providing the New American Exit Poll data.

At times writing this book felt like a lonely and Sisyphean task. However, it was made so much easier because of the humor, listening ears, and positive energy of colleagues who have become dear friends. They each listened to my ideas and served as enthusiastic motivators. I have benefited a great deal from the exchange of ideas with Joe Bafumi, Robin Hayes, Patrice Howard, Karine Jean-Pierre, Zachariah Mampilly, Kristin Murphy, Kaori Shoji, and Jessica Stanton. During the final laps of this project, I would not have made it without the constant encouragement of Travis Adkins and Dorian Warren. I also could not have asked for three greater writing partners, advice givers, and supreme champions of this work in Sheldon Applewhite, Daphne Lamothe, and Niambi Carter. Each provided invaluable edits and laughter when I needed them most. My success in completing this book has been aided by countless friends and family members who have called, e-mailed, and sent notes and prayers these past few years. These friends and family members helped this goal become a reality, and for them I am forever grateful.

I am most indebted to my mother and father for providing my intellectual foundation as well as an infinite well of support, patience and genuine love. Thank you for your belief in me and for all of the sacrifices you have made to help me achieve so many of my goals. My sister, Dr. Florencia Greer Polite, has been and remains a trailblazer, mentor, best big sister, and constant source of inspiration and reassurance. Last, I can never adequately express my gratitude for the unwavering encouragement I receive from Sam Roberts. I could try to find the words to express my appreciation, but the words just do not exist. There is no other partner with whom I would rather share all aspects of this journey.

Christina M. Greer
New York, NY

Introduction

I maintain I have been a Negro three times—a Negro baby, a Negro girl and a Negro woman. Still, if you have received no clear cut impression of what the Negro in America is like, then you are in the same place with me. There is no The Negro here. Our lives are so diversified, internal attitudes so varied, appearances and capabilities so different, that there is no possible classification so catholic that it will cover us all, except My people! My people!
—Zora Neale Hurston, *Dust Tracks on a Road*, 1942

I entered a university in the mid-1990s in a New England town just outside Boston and discovered I was part of the largest "black class" in the history of the university. I was ecstatic to be among the 60 black students out of roughly 1,200. Before classes began, the school offered the black students a chance to meet one another on a weekend at Cape Cod; to talk about the "racism" we might face in Boston, both on campus and within the community; and to underline the importance of maintaining competitive grades.

One exercise we did that weekend has remained in my memory for over a decade and has informed the roots and genesis of this project: The facilitators asked us to close our eyes and raise our hands if our parents had cautioned us against getting "wrapped up" with the "black kids." As I opened my eyes from what I thought was a relatively odd question, I realized that all but the six black Americans had raised their hands. I was so excited to be with black students for the first time in my academic life that I had never stopped to analyze the nuances that linked and often divided the black populations surrounding me.

After my experience that weekend it did not come as a surprise when members of the Black Student Union lobbied for the name of the organization to be changed to the Pan-African Alliance. What *was* somewhat surprising was the defection of most of the black students from the newly named organization to form two newer groups, the Caribbean Club and the African Student Organization. However, those same students who had "defected" still remained involved in the activities and issues surrounding the Pan-African Alliance. In essence, they established a dual membership in the black organization and the organization that addressed their specific ethnic and cultural needs and wants.

I began to notice that many of the black kids were not "just blacks" or "JBs" like me, a term quickly used by other native-born black Americans and friends when I could come up with no country other than the United States for my racial ancestry. I began to wonder what blacks shared besides color. Many of our experiences were similar while on campus—feelings of isolation in a notoriously segregated city, our interactions with certain professors who saw black students merely as tokens of affirmative action, and the random and sometimes troublesome interactions with campus police, to name a few. In addition, many of the nonblack students saw the entire black population at the university as "just black." Therefore, as much as we were often divided by our cultural, historical, and ethnic differences when interacting on campus, we were also linked by our shared color, a sense of racial solidarity, and the amorphous feelings of what it means to be black, not only in Boston, but in America.

Black ethnic interactions on campus were further complicated by the occasional instances of white students and professors who made distinctions between black ethnic groups by implying that the work ethics and educational pursuits of the children of black immigrants were completely separate and much more evolved than those of the children of native-born blacks. These instances created a multifaceted racial paradigm that, on the one hand, situated all black students outside the dominant "in-group" on campus, and, on the other hand, placed the children of black immigrants more closely situated to the dominant white group on campus.[1]

This complex tension between shared racial identity and cultural ethnic distinction has been a staple within the larger black community for decades and has often gone unnoticed and undocumented by social scientists, scholars of race, and community leaders. This particular struggle between unified identity and cultural and ethnic distinction affects intraracial relationships among blacks and also exposes a different picture of modern-day race relations involving white and other nonblack members of society. Race has become a more complicated phenomenon, and with the influx of millions of immigrants from across the globe, the study of race has evolved: it has become an amalgamation of historical contexts, modern-day experiences, and projections of group dynamics. Many

Americans have been affected by the changing composition of race in neighborhoods, the labor force, the educational system, and the political arena. One need only look at the ever-changing composition of New York City to notice the influx of immigrants into the public, private, and undocumented workforces and the increase in multilingual elementary and secondary schools.

Consider this interaction of native-born black Americans struggling to cope with the emergence of "new blacks" in the United States. In the beginning stages of this project, I often described the research as "a study to unravel the similarities and differences of native-born black Americans and their black ethnic counterparts. Essentially, why do black Americans and Afro-Caribbean and African immigrants sometimes fail to get along, and what political understandings can we garner from this information in order to form a more cohesive racial coalition?"[2] On hearing this brief summary, almost all black Americans from various regions in the United States gave me a puzzled look and quickly pressed me to explain what is *new* about this project. Someone would inevitably say, "Everyone knows we don't always get along. And we know how *they* can be." This blatant yet somewhat coded response from my conversations with native-born black Americans became so common that I began to fear that I had not stumbled on a new and innovative way to analyze race and ethnicity and explain the dynamic black population in the United States. However, I did know that the academic literature, and more specifically the political science literature, had not fully addressed the evolving racial and ethnic relations among blacks in the United States.

Why has the field of political science, and social science more generally, failed to quantitatively assess black populations? Recent surveys have assessed Latino populations and disaggregated Puerto Rican, Dominican, Mexican, and Cuban populations to uncover distinctions within the larger Hispanic population in the United States (Abrajano and Alvarez 2010; de la Garza and Cortina 2008). There is, in addition, a new and expanding literature that quantitatively addresses the ethic, political, and ideological diversity within this country's Asian American populations (Junn et al. 2011; Wong 2010; Lee, Ramakrishnan, and Ramirez 2006; Wong 2006). The absence of black disaggregation thus elicits a larger set of questions pertaining to solidified racial group formation, bloc voting, and generalized self-identification. Perhaps researchers have not seen the need to put financial resources toward disaggregating black populations; but could there be a more positive version of the story, one highlighting the benefits of a larger group solidarity that focuses on shared racial identities without disaggregating potentially divisive differences?

This book explores and seeks to provide a framework for understanding how blacks in the United States negotiate dual identities of race and ethnicity. It also provides a context for the policy issues that could potentially strengthen the political needs of blacks living in cities and urban centers. As black leaders continue to represent increasingly diverse constituencies, diversity among black candidates continues to increase as well. For example, many elected officials in Brooklyn, New York, and Miami, Florida, are finding that the historically "black districts" they represent are actually black and Afro-Caribbean districts with constituencies that need and want differing forms of representation and social services. Similarly, elected officials in Washington, DC, and Atlanta, Georgia, are finding ways to address the needs and wants of their growing number of African constituents.

In many ways, increasingly dynamic black populations have been a difficult phenomenon for political scientists to accept.[3] Scholars have been remiss in their neglect of black ethnic diversity within their models, quantitative data collection, and overall discussion of "African Americans." In contrast, sociologists and economists have provided several theories that attempt to explain black ethnic earnings potentials, assimilation difficulties, acculturation practices across generations, intergroup conflict, and feelings of incorporation in a racialized American society (Djamba 1999; Dodoo 1997; Model 1995; Butcher 1994; Waters 1994, 1999a; Kasinitz 1992; Foner 1987).

So who is African American in the twenty-first century, and how are we defining this individual? Gone are the days of blacks as a monolithic group. Black groups in the United States have expanded well beyond the civil rights generation narrative, where everyone is a descendant of US slavery, the South, and the black Baptist tradition. This lack of a new definition of "black" has been perpetrated by scholars of race, urban politics, and public opinion. If we are to take a snapshot of the steadily increasing and diversifying black population, which has over 5 million foreign-born blacks from throughout the Caribbean and across the continent of Africa and encompasses immigrant political refugee statuses, education visas, and economic pursuits, why not now? Given the interactions of the "new" blacks versus the "old" blacks, or, as some scholars have argued, the "good" blacks versus the "bad" blacks (Rogers 2006), one must ask what the future holds for these groups as they continue to compete for resources, negotiate descriptive and substantive representation, and battle an increasingly solidified "modifier problem"—that is, being "black American" rather than just "American."

Above and beyond black immigration to the United States are the shared ultimate goals and dreams of blacks trying to succeed in the American labor market. Given the economic, neighborhood, and occupational competition experienced within the native-born and foreign-born black communities, one would expect ethnic distinctions to supersede a racial identity, and if this happened, intraracial strife would be an inevitable by-product. Yet despite the sometimes negative perceptions of other black ethnic groups, which would suggest tension, a lack of shared identity, and an overall distrust fueling negative feelings toward the perceived in- or out-group, once in the United States black ethnic groups in fact share a racial identity that extends across ethnicity, generation, and almost all other demographics.

Of course, this shared sense of racial identification among blacks may be solidified by a continued sense of race and racism that has not been erased, even in a "postracial" era.[4] This shared identity, which remains regardless of circumstance (Dawson 1994), is complicated by external and competing factors, yet a sense of racial unity persists in addition to varying groups' solidified ethnic identities. In this book I begin to dissect the interplay between race and ethnicity for blacks in the United States and look at how the negotiations with these dual identities affect participation, partisanship, policy attitudes, and feelings toward the American Dream. The American Dream is the promise of economic, political, and social advancement within the polity and the equitable delivery of these goods to all members, regardless of race or other circumstance (Hochschild 1995). The extent to which individuals and groups subscribe to and invest in the American Dream directly affects their levels of participation, policy stances, and attitudes toward other racial and ethnic groups. This book begins a dialogue regarding the different conceptions of the American Dream by black ethnics.

This book explores some of the reasons black ethnics subscribe to the promises of the polity at different levels, as directly related to integration, assimilation, and expectations of black ethnic groups, both new and old. The simultaneous acceptance of a shared racial identity and preservation of a distinct ethnic identity is the essential element in better understanding coalition building, representation, policy stances, and political participation of blacks as a pathway to the American Dream in twenty-first-century American politics.

Black Ethnicity: Political Participation, Partisanship, and Policy Choices

The logic of this study rests on the assumption that race and ethnicity affect one's attitudes, actions, and abilities to form coalitions that aid black ethnic populations in New York City. There are three primary questions examined in this book. First, due to the varying experiences of immigrants from differing countries, generations, and national origin groups, and the unique histories of countries of origin, scholars contend that political participation is the most important question with respect to understanding immigration (Ramakrishnan 2005). One can more accurately interpret the effects of immigrant status by better understanding the political socialization of new citizens (Tam Cho 1999), the types of political participation newly arrived immigrants undertake (Santoro and Segura 2011), and the obstacles that newly naturalized persons face in exercising the vote (DeSipio 1996). By utilizing national data sources in conjunction with an original survey from the Social Services Employees Union (SSEU) Local 371 labor population, I have been able to observe the effects of union membership on electoral activities.

Second, are there significant pan-ethnic identities among ethnic groups classified as "black," once residing in the United States? If one is to assume that a certain level of pan-ethnicity exists among black ethnic groups in the United States, it raises the question of whether this "groupness" can thereby be used as a potential political resource.[5] In research on Latino pan-ethnic identity, scholars have found that Latinos express significant identification with their national-origin group (Jones-Correa and Leal 1996; de la Garza et al. 1992). However, pan-ethnicity becomes more relevant when individuals reside in relative proximity to one another (Padilla 1984), with shared histories of political and economic exclusion. Gary Segura and Helena Alves Rodrigues (2006: 378) contend that "residential segregation, social distrust, political exclusion, poor-performing public schools and associated rates of educational attainment, poverty, and a variety of social ills affect both immigrants and African-Americans alike." The racial segregation of blacks is evident, particularly in New York City, and more specifically in particular neighborhoods throughout the five boroughs in New York City (Rogers 2006; Kasinitz 1992).[6] Group consciousness for blacks involves a latent solidarity for some issues, and a blatant solidarity for others. Thus, racial group consciousness is contingent on the context and should be thought about in a structural as well as constructed sense.

Finally, when observing attitudes toward policy issues such as government spending, will black populations exhibit significant ethnic distinctions? By distinguishing between "public" issues versus "racial" issues, a clearer understanding of attitudes toward government spending is addressed. Questions pertaining to policy issues also shed light on attitudes among black ethnic groups and expressions of overall feelings of political incorporation and effectiveness.

Black ethnic participatory tendencies, intraracial perceptions, and policy stances directly affect the potential for coalition building as well as scholars' understandings of the attitudes of the diverse group of blacks in the American polity. The questions pertaining to participation, perception, and policy are driven by the larger overarching themes of incorporation, opportunities in the United States, and, ultimately, coalition formation. This book builds on literature that explores immigration, group public opinion and participation, the tensions that exist between diverse populations, and the intersection of race and ethnicity for black populations in America. If Dawson (1994) is correct in stating that an overarching linked fate among black populations exists and that black populations use a collective identity as a shortcut for information in the political realm, to what extent will black immigrants adhere to this concept? If, as

Bobo et al. (2001) contend, blacks evaluate issues in relation to how they affect the collective interests of all black citizens, where does this theory place newly arrived voluntary black immigrants and black ethnics who are adjusting to life as "black Americans," not just "Americans"? The salience of racial identity for native-born blacks and the new understanding of the *necessity* of a racial identity for black immigrants create varying levels of the social and political importance of "blackness" and differing degrees of collective obstacles and pursuits (Bobo and Gilliam 1990; Uhlaner 1989).

Book Overview

The duality of race and ethnicity for foreign-born black populations, in particular, complicates previous theories of in-group and out-group status in that their foreign-born status has allowed foreign-born black ethnics to situate themselves as elevated minorities and move more closely to the dominant in-group. My argument pertaining to diverse black identities and the elevated minority statuses that exist in the United States is expanded and developed over the next five chapters. In this work, black ethnic diversity and ethnic elevated minority status are defined as the dominant in-group treatment of foreign-born blacks, which is distinct from that of native-born blacks. Foreign-born blacks are often perceived by whites and even black Americans as different and "special"—as harder-working and more productive citizens than their black American counterparts. The distinction between foreign-born and native-born blacks by nonblack groups affects the ways in which they interpret and subscribe to the promises of the American Dream.

In chapter 1, I lay out my theory of elevated minority status and linked fate of black ethnics—an extension of Dawson's (1994) black utility heuristic—in order to better understand elevated minority status as an ethnic utility heuristic that incorporates segmented assimilation, political attitudes, and political behaviors of black ethnic immigrants in the late twentieth century and early twenty-first. I utilize previous scholarship from sociologists, economists, and political scientists who have advanced the fields of racial and ethnic politics. My analysis links the research to Asian American studies, Latino politics, urban politics, social identity, and public opinion that have not previously been integrated in a comprehensive analysis pertaining to black diversity. How future scholarship disaggregates the diversity of blacks in America in subsequent works is just one element of the research; therefore, I also focus on how these integrated theories have implications for all "minority" groups[7] living in the United States, and how they use amorphous concepts of race and detailed ethnic identifications as building blocks for larger conversations pertaining to policy, political resources, representation, and benefits. The analyses set forth in this chapter extend the discussion of race and ethnicity to blacks, Latinos, and Asian Americans and lay out larger theories to support the measures used in chapters 3, 4, and 5.

Chapter 2 provides US census data in conjunction with SSEU Local 371 demographic data to better explain the significance of a union population for this particular project. This chapter also explains survey design and implementation and the sample population. Chapters 3, 4, and 5 address how race and ethnicity for blacks affect political participation, intraracial attitudes toward the American Dream, and policy attitudes. They explain how the duality creates overarching intraracial tensions as well as feelings of solidarity, while also showing the shifting significance of race and ethnicity for different groups and at different times. I address the questions of how political participation and partisanship are displayed, whether intraracial coalition building is possible with the widespread range of feelings toward other black ethnic groups, and how attitudes toward racialized and nonracialized government policies are articulated by the different black ethnic groups. Each chapter then provides evidence that there is a cohesive racial identity that is as significant as one's distinct ethnic identity, despite political participation and personal feelings toward other black ethnic groups and contrasting policy stances.

Shared black group racial identity in the United States does exist, alongside and in addition to ethnic identity and individual level concerns and self-interests. I provide analysis about the ethnically diverse black population that not only serves as a political example of the range of participatory behaviors, expectations from the polity, and policy attitudes but also highlights how these important issues can be transferred to other nonblack ethnic groups and contribute to ongoing debates surrounding identity politics, immigration, urban politics, and the future of labor movements. In these chapters, I use transcripts of interviews conducted with the leadership of the SSEU Local 371. The interviews provide an additional layer of individual understandings of the interplay between race and ethnicity for blacks, and how these complex negotiations affect larger coalition building within a social justice–driven union. Each chapter provides a different example of how racial and ethnic duality can engender larger understandings of pluralism, thus bringing together several theories pertaining to identity, ethnocentrism, and complex and continued racial segregation.

Chapter 3 provides an analysis of voter turnout by black union members. In this chapter, high union participatory trends become quite apparent—particularly due to the SSEU's political history and union leadership in New York City politics. In addition to evaluating black union members' participatory trends, this chapter assesses and compares the overall participatory tendencies of black groups using national data sources: the Social Services Employees Union Survey (SSEUS), the National Election Study (NES), and the New American Exit Poll

(NAEP). Participation rates of blacks are also compared to those of nonblack union members within the original SSEUS as well as with nonblack populations from national data sets. This added layer of analysis is critical to extrapolating a larger story of interracial and intraracial participatory similarities and differences among labor populations, and the US population, more generally. Utilizing multiple data sources illuminates the extensive variation that exists in participation rates at the local and national levels, and also highlights the differences between union population turnout rates and participatory tendencies compared to those of the larger US population.

Chapter 4 offers a detailed account of the feelings and perceptions of foreign-born and native-born black union members using the SSEU Local 371 Survey. This chapter argues that black intraracial differences, even subtle ones, elicit attitudes and opinions that greatly influence the US political system. It also includes a qualitative analysis of the genesis of many of these perceptions and feelings of black groups living and working in New York City, and how these opinions affect black perceptions of the American Dream. I find that although there are distinct attitudes among black ethnics regarding modes of success and achievement efforts, there is a significant black racial identity present among native-born and foreign-born populations once in the United States.

Chapter 5 describes the extent to which racial and/or ethnic identity affect policy stances and compares the responses from the SSEU labor members with national data. Using data from the General Social Survey (GSS), the NES, and the SSEUS, the chapter provides evidence that the importance and impact of racial and ethnic identity affects political attitudes and policy beliefs dealing with social spending issues and broader immigration debates. I show that black ethnic groups within SSEU Local 371 exhibited similar attitudes toward government spending issues promoted by the union. There was even an element of racial cohesion regarding issues not promoted by the union leadership. However, black ethnics displayed compellingly distinct differences in opinion toward race-related spending issues. The results indicate that ethnicity does affect policy attitudes, but the evidence also describes a complex overlapping of identities—union, racial, and specific ethnic—when analyzing government spending issues.

Finally, the conclusion summarizes the contributions of this project to the field of political science and the theoretical literature on race, immigration, and labor. It also offers concluding remarks regarding black ethnicity and the future of black political representation and collective participatory engagement. In addition, this chapter also addresses the study's implications for the current immigration debates. In particular, it considers the growing complexities of racial classification, and informs more general policy recommendations for future studies of race and ethnicity in the United States. I find empirical evidence and support for Jane Junn and Natalie Masuoka's (2008: 734) theoretical argument that "the structuring of racial political identity is a complex interaction between policies of the state, political economy, and the stereotypes that result to create incentives for people categorized by race to either adopt or turn away from a group based on identity."

To be clear, this project is not about determining which black ethnic group works hardest, nor is it about which black group is most likely to succeed. It does aim, however, to present the complexity of race and ethnicity for both native-born and foreign-born blacks living in America and to ascertain the possibilities for political coalitions in specific policy areas. This project confirms the importance of a multilayered identity for foreign-born and native-born blacks and examines how racial and ethnic identity directly affects foreign-born blacks' concepts of group racial identity. This work also shows how Afro-Caribbean and African black populations impact black Americans and their perceptions of race, ethnic identity, a collective future, and fulfillment of the American Dream.

CHAPTER 1

A Theory of Black Elevated Minority Status

Before Barack Obama exploded onto the national political scene in 2004, the Republicans, as some may remember, were giddy with excitement over their own special potential candidate for the presidency. In 1992, Colin Powell's name was being thrown around as a possible running mate for then president George H. W. Bush, and in 1995, his name was mentioned as a possible GOP presidential candidate. Powell seemed to have stepped out of a GOP's dream. He was a general in the US Army, and for many whites, he transcended race. Not only had he been quoted on the record as saying, "I ain't that black" (Gates 1997: 84), but he seemed to be the antithesis of Jesse Jackson, the most recent serious black candidate for a party's nomination. Jackson had run for the Democratic nomination for presidency in 1984 and 1988 and was what many in white America viewed as a quintessential African American: descendant of US slavery and the South, a student of the Baptist preaching tradition, a product of a broken home, and a social agitator.[1] General Powell, for many, was a product of arguably one of the most established institutions of American patriotism. He was fair skinned, "articulate," a product of the US military, and a leader in what many viewed as a successful Gulf War. But Powell possessed something else that made him *special*: In the eyes of some of his supporters, he was not African American. For many, it was his Jamaican heritage that made him different, that explained his discipline, professional excellence, and supreme intellect.

Fast forward to 2008, when Barack Obama, the son of a man from Kenya and a woman from Kansas, captivated the hearts of so many Americans. Many of the same conversations began linking Obama and Powell as an ideal presidential candidate, despite not being *really* African American—that is, not a descendant of US slavery and therefore possessing a different relationship with America. I wondered if Obama would have been as attractive to American voters, white voters in particular, if his background were that of a man from Detroit and a woman from Duluth, or a man from Newark and a woman from Nebraska, or a man from Oakland and a woman from Omaha. You see where I am going with this line of thought. The subtle but significant message of his non–African American heritage was a variable both black and white voters initially discussed, debated, and ultimately digested. Many voters saw Obama as black, whether his dad was from Kenya or Kentucky. For some voters, when presented with ethnic diversity, Obama's lack of "authenticity" complicated their sense of racial attachment. For others, though, the comparisons to Jesse Jackson were endless. Whereas Jackson was portrayed as obsessed with race and racial politics, specifically black politics, Obama was presented as a "postracial" candidate. Obama had a racial identity that linked him to the black population, but he was different. For many, he did not have the same "racial baggage" as ninth-generation African Americans—the Jesse Jacksons of the world—thus begging the question, what does racial identity and ethnic distinction mean for blacks living in America?

Although the black population in America has changed and continues to change, race is still relevant. Steady migration of black immigrants continues from small Caribbean islands to large African nations.[2] This book has two aims: (1) to explore the diverse public opinions of black ethnic groups in the early twenty-first century, and (2) to quantitatively analyze the racial politics of black intraracial relationships between black American, Afro-Caribbean, and Africans in the context of the qualitative data that has been used to explain black American and West Indian relationships generally. It has been implicitly acceptable to analyze black groups as homogeneous in social science data while ignoring the dynamic countries of origin, migration patterns, and generational distinctions between black ethnic groups. The central tenet of this book, however, is that both race and ethnicity are factors in black attitudes toward politics, policies, other races, and other black ethnic groups that operate on the individual and group levels. The duality of these attitudes for blacks in America has a strange way of building racial solidarity on the one hand, and reinforcing and re-creating ethnic stereotypes among black groups on the other. Even as the fates of phenotypically black individuals and larger groups are inextricably linked to other phenotypically black people in America, the myth of the monolithic black group persists, as does the myth of the "different, special, and good" black immigrants (Rogers 2006).

The theoretical approach I employ to assist the reader in better understanding black ethnic diversity in twenty-first-century America is one of an "elevated minority status" perspective. This perspective adopts an integrated understanding of one's racial and ethnic identity, as well as their individual and group attachments. In the subsequent pages, I describe the elevated minority status and how it might relate to black ethnics in America. The book establishes its foundation with Dawson's (1994) work focusing on the linked fate of blacks in America, and the integration of race and class for black public opinion and group placement.

I also investigate the "black" modifier that is attached to the American status for black native-born and black immigrants by examining the in- and out-group possibilities for black ethnics in an interracial context. Finally, I show that black ethnics are perceived as an elevated minority group, not a model minority like Asian American individuals and groups (Petersen 1971), but an elevation above their black American counterparts, the widely accepted "last-place" racial group.

My delicate approach to this largely unchartered black ethnic territory integrates several important veins of social science. Dawson's model of linked fate and the black utility heuristic has been critical in providing a theoretical backbone to black group racial identity. However, it provides no road map pertaining to black immigration, specifically first- or second-generation Afro-Caribbeans and Africans who are phenotypically black, and are often characterized as black, but who have different negotiations and allegiances to a larger black group or groups. For an understanding of black ethnic relationships, I largely look to Reuel Rogers's innovative insights on black America and Afro-Caribbean political relationships in New York City, in conjunction with Mary Waters, Nancy Foner, and Phil Kasinitz's social ideas surrounding black immigration and migration patterns. All of these perspectives, when combined with Dawson and Jennifer Hochschild's work on the American Dream, provide a "clearing in the brush" for understanding how black ethnic attitudes and identities in the United States are formed and negotiated. Thus, this work integrates the duality of race and ethnicity for blacks in America as well as individual-level attitudes with larger group identity and attachment. The elevated minority status model allows us to better understand how the individual attitudes of black ethnics affect perceptions of other black groups, and the possibilities for coalition building among black ethnic groups.

More generally, answers to the questions of "What does a shared racial identity mean for coalition building?" or "How do distinct ethnic identities weaken political identification?" are essential in a twenty-first-century polity where blacks continue to define and seek to attain the American dream, political representation, and often limited resources.[3] Thus, I attempt, with the elevated minority status model, to amalgamate our understanding of group conflict, race, ethnicity, group status, immigration, and policies into a single narrative. Other scholars have approached these topics at varying degrees, but this book intends to explicitly integrate these concepts into a single perspective of twenty-first-century black politics.

What is at stake is not just racial or ethnic divisions, or model minority/ elevated minority statuses for black, Latino, Asian American, and even white ethnics in the United States. What is at stake extends to a larger understanding and investment in the American Dream. This collective identity may be political in nature, racial, or coalesced around particular policies. The urgency in determining the root of possible impetuses for coalition building will determine the ultimate course of American political and cultural endurance. By building interethnic coalitions, will black groups in the United States be able to attain more of the promises of the American Dream? Will their collective strategies, policies, and realistic understandings of the inequities and benefits of America, assist them in making increased gains as a group? If we attempt to materialize and qualify the founding principles of American democracy, equity, and ultimate possibility, we must ask more nuanced questions as to how to make these ideals realities. By investigating the issues which foster or prevent coalitions, we can better understand how the potential for an intraracial group cohesion can serve as a pathway for black group attainment of the American Dream—that is, the widely understood promises of the polity. This book is not a naive or vain attempt to solve all democratic inequities; it is an attempt to unravel the factors that prevent substantive black ethnic coalition building in the United States.

Questions about black immigrant integration and interactions with native-born blacks are key to understanding the political orientations and behaviors of blacks in America and the stability of larger black American groups as a cohesive voting bloc within the Democratic Party. Increasingly, black candidates are dipping their toes into politics as Republican candidates on all levels of government. For some, depending on geographic locale, they are leveraging their ethnic status as a new way of introducing the Republican Party to black immigrant groups, as is the case with Mia Love, the Haitian GOP candidates for Congress in 2012. Should we expect new black immigrants to orient themselves to politics in the same manner as native blacks, and will the different histories of new immigrants and native-born blacks lead to different political orientations and behavior, and perhaps even to political tensions and conflict between the different ethnic groups of blacks in America? Despite the importance of these questions, there has been little empirical evidence or comprehensive data collection on the growing diversity among blacks living in America. On the one hand, black ethnic diversity has not grown at the same rates as Latino and Asian American diversity in the United States, even though African migration is steadily increasing each year. Yet, at the other extreme, blacks in America are overwhelmingly analyzed and defined as a homogenous racial group. Observing national-level politics, it appears that black Americans are cohesive voting members within the Democratic Party, and have been for close to half a century. Although Democratic strength does fluctuate slightly on the local level, depending on geographic locale, it is more than likely that those who identify as black in America also identify as Democratic. Thus, attitudes toward racial identity are also, in essence, larger indicators of political identity. If that is the case, the ways in which ethnicity affects and influences racial identity, and therefore potentially alters the political discourse for the larger black group, must be called into question.

Social scientists tend to rely on the broad concepts of race, class, and geographic locale in their models for explaining how black voters participate politically and how they view their statuses as Americans when compared to white Americans (Hochschild 1995; Dawson 1994; Tate 1993; Huckfeldt and Kohlfeld 1989). In essence, current understanding about what motivates black political participation boils down to three questions: (1) How can I improve my own advancement? (2) How does the advancement of my racial group affect me? and (3) How does my advancement—such as political, economic, or social—correlate to how I view my life chances? The approach of this book is that these distinctions between black ethnic groups become blurred because of the intersection of race and ethnicity, both of which are dependent on boundaries that are fluid, subjective, and constantly shifting. Personal identification can include one's concept of self or family, but it could also include one's more distant community—for example, one's neighborhood and ethnic group. Racial group interest, whether used as a proxy for individual self-interest or as a larger call for collective interests, also depends on how one perceives his or her ability to move within the varying boundaries of one's particular group or groups. For example, how and when does Afro-Caribbean identity in the United States extend to all Afro-Caribbeans, or all persons categorized as black? If we use Campbell's (1958) definition of group attachment, we know that individuals need similarity, proximity, common fate, and good figure. By "good figure," Campbell means that individuals resist intrusion and their boundaries are relatively impermeable. One's broad set of beliefs can become constrained by boundaries.[4] Thus, while black ethnic conceptualizations of the interplay between race and ethnicity have profound usefulness, their politicized utility and its relation to advancement within American society serve as the undercurrent of these identifications.

Rather than adding to the volumes of significant scholarship and debates surrounding what exactly race is, this book adds to the very small but growing literature surrounding the interplay of race and ethnicity for blacks in America by using data to explore what it means for native-born and non-native-born blacks in the United States to be black in America in the twenty-first century. Social scientists study concepts pertaining to class, black-white perceptions and attitudes, and socioeconomic status with little attention paid to the intraracial attitudes and relationships among blacks. Black Americans, Afro-Caribbeans, and Africans have been interacting, sharing, and competing in the United States for several decades now. Although ethnic identity has been a visible factor in black communities and neighborhoods, it is still very much uncharted territory in social science research. The relatively small number of these new populations (when compared to Latino and Asian American groups), the geographic concentrations in a few states, their exposure to racism, and the phenotypic similarity to black Americans are just some of the reasons social scientists have only recently begun to explore the nuances within the black population in the United States.

Racial and Ethnic Effects on the Group

In order to consider the differences of black ethnics in the United States, we need to further consider theories of racial identity. Racial identities largely influence group formation, classification, and identification. Because race is not a "natural" attribute but a socially and historically constructed one, scholars are still divided as to whether or not race can actually be used to infer larger group similarities based on physical characteristics—that is, it may be virtually impossible to ignore the similarities of a group based largely on outward appearances (Sipress 1997; Fields 1982). Some scholars argue that race in the United States is a social construction and largely based on physical characteristics (Bobo and Hutchings 1996; See and Wilson 1989). The American construct of race has led scholars to argue that race is a social ideology that has significant historical foundations embedded in the fabric of society, culture, and daily interactions in this country (Sipress 1997). They argue that in American social ideology there is an element of fluidity to racial classification that works in concert with established hierarchies and historical notions. Race has been defined as (1) a constituent of the individual psyche and of relationships among individuals, and (2) an irreducible component of collective identities and social structures (Winant 1994: 52).

Fields (1982) argued that "race rose to meet an ideological need" and that the racial ideological construct persists because people insist on thinking in racial terms. However, Winant (1994) argued that Fields failed to recognize race as a social construct that can serve to reinforce social organization and identity formation throughout the globe. Therefore, race and the social underpinnings of race can significantly affect individuals living in and outside America. In that, Winant believed that an individual without a racial identity is in danger of possessing no identity at all. Due to the systemic racism and discrimination that have been present in America since its inception, there is significance in the binding notion of a black race. Speight, Vera, and Derrickson (1996) argued that individuals who self-label themselves as black do so because they believe their identity is self-evident as well as externally imposed. The current race classification, therefore, affects the myriad of black ethnic groups that currently reside in the United States. Scholars contend that racial space is now global and racial hegemony is worldwide and affects the attitudes and behaviors of blacks living both inside and outside the United States. However, due to conquests, colonization, and migration, the geographic roots of race and racism become more complicated, especially in this country (Winant 1994).

Race is significant for black ethnic populations in the United States, largely because race continues to serve as a fundamental characteristic that influences life chances and circumstances.[5] The prevalence, and what appears to be the permanence of race as a defining characteristic, continues to puzzle scholars, politicians, policy makers, immigrants, and even native-born black populations who have witnessed incremental advances since the beginning of the civil rights movement and the subsequent passages of the Civil Rights Act of 1964 and the Voting Rights Act of 1965. Essentially, race continues to drive the political process, influence social mobility, and complicate normative principles that serve as the foundation of American democracy. As the country strives to maintain its position into the twenty-first century as a democratic world leader, unifier, and freedom advocate, we must better understand the ways in which America incorporates individuals into its democracy. Not only is race important to any discussion of America's fundamental values; it also has political significance in American electoral politics, especially in America's cities. The future of black ethnic coalitions and more ethnically diverse coalitions in urban politics will depend on blacks', and other people of color's, perceptions of treatment, possibilities for advancement, and overall feelings of inclusion.

Race is an organizing principle that assists individuals in their interpretations of the social world. The construct of race is connected to deep-rooted systems of power, control, and varying forms of order (Winant 1994: 2). These principles largely dictate how nations throughout the world organize themselves and continue to subjugate particular individuals within their societies.[6] Slavery has long been abolished in the United States, and Jim Crow ended roughly fifty years ago. Yet, race (and racism) is deeply embedded in American society and affects native-born populations, and subsequently, black ethnic immigrant populations who have never experienced slavery on US soil. Race is in the psyche of oppressors and the oppressed and is manifested in macro- and micro-level relationships (Winant 1994: 2). Therefore, when black populations, both native-born and foreign-born, experience the events of the Rodney King police beatings, the Abner Louima police assault, and the Amadou Diallo police shooting, the effects of race are socialized in the minds of blacks in the United States, regardless of their country of origin.

At the outset, race has dominated political conversations pertaining to US group advancement. However, we cannot ignore the significant effects of ethnicity. The relationship between racial and ethnic labels are linked, not only to racial identity, but to the racial and ethnic socialization of one's membership in a nondominant US group.[7] The socialization of blackness has contributed to the varying levels of importance of racial heritage for individuals, as well as the extent to which individuals perceive themselves as members of a larger racial group (Parham and Helms 1981). Anglin and Whaley (2006) argued that one's black sense of self has been influenced by group socialization and group experiences. The racial and ethnic labels are thus created by the socialization of experiences that bring underlying identities to the surface (Hecht, Collier, and Ribeau 1993). Ethnicity is even more distinctive and specific than racial categorizations in that it is distinct from race and its social categories because it is largely based on culture (Sipress 1997). Our understanding of ethnicity is further complicated when assessing the extent to which one's culture is largely dictated by a racial social classification. Due to the debated definition and construct of race in America, in addition to distinct identifications with one's ethnicity, Anglin and Whaley (2006: 458) argued that ethnic and racial identity are "manifestations of underlying identities that emerged out of socializations and experiences." Therefore, ethnicity is a subset of racial classification, as well as a distinct identity, and contributes to dual identities for several foreign-born black populations who migrate to the United States.

In order to better understand the intersection of race and ethnicity, we must consider similar frameworks used in understanding Latino and Asian populations (de la Garza et al. 1991; Okamoto 2003). Most social scientists recognize the political participatory and public opinion distinctions present among Cuban, Dominican, and Mexican populations, as well as the distinctions between Chinese, Japanese, and Filipino populations living in the United States. Just as these ethnic group populations have overt cultural and historical distinctions and different experiences of incorporation and assimilation (or lack thereof) into US society, they have also been ascribed an overarching racial identity. Incorporation obstacles for Latino and Asian immigrants are often attributed to weak pan-ethnic attachments (Segura and Rodrigues 2006). Due to the vast heterogeneous populations that exist within the larger racial classifications of "Latino" and "Asian," the groups largely remain associated with their specific ethnic group (Jones-Correa and Leal 1996).

Some scholars have argued that blacks in America are no more of a racial group than Latinos due to the trans-Atlantic slave trade, which brought diverse populations of blacks from Africa (Fields 1982). Scholars have argued that it is virtually impossible to think of Latinos as a racial group, or even as a group of individuals with a "linked fate," due to their diverse countries of origin, histories, and linguistic differences. They have maintained that the same argument can be made for blacks in America, who share physical characteristics but hail from varying and quite diverse nations with often drastically different histories, languages, and vehicles of incorporation.

Scholars have contended that racialized hierarchies based on a racial phenotype, immigrant status, ethnicity, and nationality contribute to the development of stratification and complex definitions of black and white groups. They argued that these stratified categories establish life chances and future prospects of success for groups living in the United States. They contended that immigrant groups who were categorized, or who defined themselves, as black experienced subsequent discrimination and segregation that affected their efforts at incorporation, economic gains, and geographic and social mobility (A. Torres 1995; Massey and Denton 1993).

The definition of black ethnic relations that I use in this book extends Reuel Rogers's (2006) substantial work on Afro-Caribbean and black American political relationships and incorporation into the political system. Rogers describes the relationship between Afro-Caribbean and African Americans in New York City, and the complex negotiations that arise for both groups:

> Afro-Caribbean's distinctive ethnic background and immigrant status make for differences in how they and their native-born counterparts perceive and participate in the political process.... Immigrants' home country ties and experiences serve as a kind of cognitive frame or lens through which these newcomers make sense of American political life and the challenges of incorporation. (Rogers 2006: 11, 17)

This ethnic background can be applied more broadly as well. Although Rogers's central analysis is between African Americans and Afro-Caribbeans, it also extends to Africans in America.[8] While it may be possible for all black ethnic groups to incorporate and assimilate into dominant American society,[9] the levels and speeds at which these processes occur will have particular distinctions for each group. While one black ethnic group may interpret particular aspects of the promise of the American Dream as positive, another black ethnic group may interpret it as a limitation or restriction not afforded to them fully; and still another black ethnic group may see both the pros and cons of this particular aspect of the polity and maintain a neutral perception of the ability for America to provide true economic, political, and social equity. Beginning conversations of this multilayered level of integration and segmented assimilation for black ethnics is reflected in the small amount of scholarship detailing black diversity. However, much of the emerging and cutting-edge scholarship pertaining to today's nonwhite populations has largely centered on Asian American and Latino groups (Wong 2010; Junn and Haynie 2008; Lee, Ramakrishnan, and Ramirez 2006; Jones-Correa 1998a; de la Garza 1992; de la Garza et al. 1991).

The incorporation process for black immigrants continues to be a unique journey for black migrants. As African immigrants spend greater periods of time in the United States and transfer from first generation to second and even third generation, what will become of their electoral activities or investment in the

American Dream? Scholars contend that Afro-Caribbeans have an "exit option" and that their disillusionment with the American Dream and maintenance of a "foreign reference point" (Rogers 2006; Bashi Bobb and Clarke 2001) all contribute to their decision making as they live in the United States. African immigrants, however, may not have the same exit option as their Afro-Caribbean counterparts. Significant numbers of Africans have migrated and continue to migrate to the United States for educational reasons, while substantial numbers have entered as refugees. For Nigerians, the primary African respondent group in the SSEU Local 371 sample, recent migration has been attributed to both educational pursuits and distance from political strife. Some fled Nigeria in the mid-1970s, in the aftermath of the Nigeria-Biafra War and the subsequent military dictatorships that followed. Therefore, the reasons for US migration coupled with the increasingly diverse black ethnic groups entering the United States contribute to a more complex makeup of blacks in America than ever before.

The Blurred Color Line

Herein lie buried many things which if read with patience may show the strange meaning of being black here in the drawing of the Twentieth Century. This meaning is not without interest to you, Gentle Reader; for the problem of the Twentieth Century is the problem of the color-line.
—W. E. B. Du Bois, *The Souls of Black Folk*

The issue that W. E. B. Du Bois (1993 [1903]) labeled "the problem of the twentieth century" has not disappeared. The soil has been tilled, but several elements of the soil remain unchanged. Du Bois wrote in a time of colonial empires of European powers, rigid caste societies, and virtual racial dictatorship (Winant 1994). Although white supremacy is no longer overt, Du Bois's words ring true in evolved forms. Blacks and people of color in the United States, for the most part, are no longer rejected outright from job opportunities or housing choices, nor are they physically threatened when trying to vote.[10] However, more nuanced forms of racism, injustice, and inequities are now prevalent in American society that affect both native-born and foreign-born black individuals. American-born blacks continue to discover that the problem of the color line is engrained in the fabric of American democracy and in the pursuit of the American Dream.

Over one hundred years ago, caste systems were recognized as "natural" ways of organizing individuals in American society. Rigid castelike systems no longer exist in the United States, but a new type of caste system threatens the country today. It is not one imposed by overt white power subjugating people of color into slave and indentured servant positions; rather, the new caste system that now threatens American democracy comes from within the deeply seated mind-sets of those who were once held in subservient positions. This mind-set is even shared by newly arriving immigrants who possess a knowledge of America's past practices and who strive to position themselves as far from the "bottom" caste as possible. The modern-day caste struggle is most poignantly played out in some of the interactions between native-born black Americans and their black ethnic counterparts who understand the continued burden of the color line and the weight of race in the United States. The United States that Du Bois articulated so eloquently over one hundred years ago has evolved; however, the residual effects of oppression, distrust, and injustice remain. The new problem facing the twenty-first century is not just of the color line, but how the stratification of this line creates more complex tensions for groups struggling against the notion of "last place" in American democracy. Robert Lieberman (1998) is correct in his assertion that the color line has shifted. However, the blurring of these lines has evolved into a much more complex negotiation with one's race and place in the United States.

At the core, all discussions of race and ethnicity for blacks in America must emphasize the duality that exists for these diverse groups of blacks. Afro-Caribbean and African immigrants living in America have experienced forms of oppression, racism, and subjugation as blacks, even by blacks. For example, residential segregation of blacks has often swiftly introduced black immigrant ethnic groups to the inequities still faced by blacks in the United States. However, this forced integration of native-born blacks and foreign-born blacks, due to segregation, has also produced tensions, mistrust, and competition among black groups (Kasinitz, Battle, and Miyares 2001; Massey and Denton 1988). The historically racist black-white paradigm has extended to black immigrants in many ways. However, this black-white paradigm has also manifested itself in more positive ways for foreign-born blacks. The historical racism and oppression in the United States seems to have either placed Afro-Caribbean and African populations with black Americans, both literally and symbolically, or have treated Afro-Caribbean and African immigrants as different, that is, harder working, smarter, and/or "better" than native-born blacks, what Rogers (2006) defines as "good blacks."

The understanding of race for black newcomers is that racial formation and construction is a largely unique phenomenon applicable to the United States. New immigrants may not easily or readily accept or adhere to the racial categories ascribed to them upon their arrival in the country and therefore cannot (or should not) be expected to automatically accept or identify with the larger black American racial category or group as a whole. Studies have documented Afro-Caribbean populations expressing disillusionment with assimilation in the United States and thereby becoming "black Americans" as opposed to just

"Americans," like their white immigrant counterparts (Rogers 2000; Waters 1994; Foner 1987).[11] Du Bois argued that poor whites received a "public psychological wage" by being "not black" in the United States, which proved their fitness for membership in a free community (Roediger 1991; Ignatiev 1995). This "psychological wage" does not fully extend to black immigrants once they arrive in the United States. Once black immigrants arrive in the United States, they become black American, not just American. The concepts of race, identity, and national origin have created a complex set of issues for the individual and for the larger group. Junn and Masuoka (2008: 731) argue that "racial group identity may not necessarily be a stable psychological predisposition, but instead a perception that may be cued by outside contexts." This is definitely the case for black ethnic groups who are negotiating their relationship with black Americans—how whites perceive them in relation to black Americans, how their American status with a mandatory modifier is solidified by outside contexts and perceptions, and how ethnicity is further negotiated by placing ethnicity as a primary and not secondary identity when the situation arises.

Many immigrant groups share similar obstacles when arriving in the United States. Some scholars have argued that African and Caribbean immigrants may have more in common with other immigrants from across the globe than with native-born black Americans (Portes and Rumbaut 2001). First-generation black immigrants in the United States have faced overwhelming pressures to identify only as "blacks" (Kasinitz 1992; Foner 1987). In fact, they have been described as "invisible immigrants" (Bryce-Laporte 1972), because rather than being contrasted with other immigrants (for example, evaluating Jamaican successes as compared with Chinese), they have been compared most often to black Americans.[12] Because racial phenotype seems to link black ethnics into one racial group, can and will substantive coalitions form? Black groups are clearly grouped together in the United States. However, whether their fates are ultimately linked is part of a larger and constantly changing black ethnic puzzle.

Linked Fates and Coalition Building

Over the past several decades, significant strides have been made by blacks achieving educational success, attaining occupational advancements, and being incorporated into the middle class. However, dark skin is still correlated with poverty in the United States and throughout the globe (Segura and Rodrigues 2006); therefore, class position, societal status, and opportunities for political and economic advancement are in many ways racially assigned in the United States. Race is obviously a physical characteristic that has been used in this country to distinguish a certain group of people with similar phenotypes. This color distinction has led to widespread discrimination and inequities, as Rogers (2006) analyzed, thus lumping phenotypically similar individuals together based on outward identity, without accounting for the existence of differing self-identifications and belief systems.

The racial socialization of people of African descent living in the United States has had distinguishing effects on black populations, one of a "blended" cultural heritage (Larkey, Hecht, and Martin 1993) that emphasizes and connects to African ancestry and representation, as well as subjugation in American culture (Anglin and Whaley 2006). Due to shared skin color with native-born populations, foreign-born black phenotype serves as a basis for discrimination in America (Deaux et al. 2007).

New black immigrants also discover the inequities present in America and the subsequent negotiations with race and identity that directly affect their pursuits of becoming "American" without the mandatory modifier "black." For foreign-born blacks, their American status has a permanent "black" modifier attached to it. The permanent prefix aids in preventing native-born and foreign-born populations from attaining the same American incorporation experienced by other nonblack immigrants. Black racial classification has affected first and second-generation black ethnics in that they did not experience the same processes of assimilation as previous white immigrant populations (Waters 1998; Kinder and Sanders 1996). Cordero-Guzman, Smith, and Grosfoguel (2001: 6) argue that immigrants, once in the United States, quickly learn that "only whites are fit for citizenship, for full membership in the polity and society, so make sure that when your group's ethnicity and race are defined, they fall on the 'white ethnic' and not the 'native minority' side of the color line" (see also Ignatiev 1995; Roediger 1991). Thus, black immigrants seek ways to reduce and possibly diminish the negative effects of the minority status imposed on their American status. It is because of this linking of black immigrants to native-born blacks that in-group fighting and competition decreases opportunities for substantive coalition building. As Afro-Caribbean and African black populations are occasionally promoted to elevated minority status over native-born black populations by whites, coalitional efforts are severely jeopardized and undermined within the larger black group. In that, one group is promoted and their interests are advanced at the expense and exclusion of others.[13] Okamoto (2003: 815) argued, "Competition among pan-ethnic groups will increase the rate of pan-ethnic collective action, whereas competition within pan-ethnic groups will decrease the rate of pan-ethnic collective action."[14] One proposed way to circumvent some of the obstacles that prevent inter- and intraracial ethnic groups from forming coalitions was to organize the various ethnic groups around political issues that were explicitly racial (Guinier and Torres 2002). The data in subsequent chapters show how black ethnics express limited shared opinions regarding racial policy.[15] However, feelings of competition between blacks and whites contributed to more cohesive black ethnic attitudes.

Race, and not necessarily other individual characteristics, structures black American worldviews (Dawson 1994). The formation of black linked fate is based on a shared common history by blacks as a subjugated racial group and the collective identity that is formed a proxy for individual status. However, this idea of black linked fate is "strained" when black ethnic groups are included. If using the definition that these groups share a history as a subjugated group, as a phenotypically similar group within the larger African diaspora, then Dawson's definition and theory hold. However, when observing black ethnic groups in the United States, their histories and modes of voluntary versus nonvoluntary migration drastically affect and contribute to differing histories among black groups. Dawson argues that blacks continue to link their life chances to other blacks, even as their socioeconomic status improves.[16] So what do racial links mean to recent immigrants or groups that see their primary identification through a black ethnic lens? And how do black ethnic groups in the United States form a cohesive group for their political advancement?

Dawson (1994) has thoroughly described the benefits of collective solidarity or "linked fate" for black Americans. He argued that black individuals have perceived their successes as linked to the successes of the larger group as a whole. Dawson's theory of the "black utility heuristic" explains the strong racial group identity that exists among blacks.[17] However, Dawson's analysis largely extends to class dynamics within the larger black community and does not parse out the extensive ethnic variety within the growing black community. Unlike other ethnic groups who migrate to the United States and assimilate into the American social and economic mainstream, for black immigrants, the assimilation and integration process comes with some unique race-based obstacles. Black immigrants have not been able to fully shed the "black" modifier that is added to their new American status. To be clear, black Americans have not necessarily "chosen" their black identity either. As the nations only involuntary immigrants, their black status has historically been imposed on this group, therefore black Americans have adopted, politicized, and expanded this categorization.

ALL OF THE BLACKS ARE AMERICAN. ALL OF THE IMMIGRANTS ARE LATINO. BUT SOME OF US ARE . . . ?

Black Americans have largely been categorized in comparison to whites, based on region, political affiliation, class, and education levels. Segura and Rodrigues (2006: 376) argued that the "historical construction of a racial dynamic that is almost exclusively binary, i.e., black and white ... [and] racial and ethnic interactions between Anglos and other minority groups are assumed to mimic—to some degree—the black-white experience." Simply put, Segura and Rodrigues argued that the "black-white paradigm is no longer sufficient to provide genuine understanding of the political circumstances and experiences of all nonwhite groups" (ibid.: 391).

With the increases in immigration of black ethnic populations to the United States, one cannot necessarily assume that the interactions of black immigrant populations will be the same as those for native-born black American populations. However, the extent to which the interactions between black immigrants and whites differ from native-born black American and white interactions are still called into question.[18] The historically tenuous relationship between blacks and whites cannot be assumed to automatically extend to immigrant populations. On the other hand, the complex racial element that often exists for black immigrants, in that black immigrants are viewed as phenotypically "black," dictates how particular relationships with whites can and will be formed. Although black-white interracial divisions have largely dominated the landscape of American political thought, the complexity of the black populations and negotiations in the American polity raise new questions surrounding incorporation, assimilation, and acceptance.

Several nonblack and nonwhite immigrant groups have expressed feelings of an "in-between" status in which they are "not Black but not White" (Perlmann and Waldinger 1997: 905) or "native born, and not black" (Cordero-Guzman, Smith, and Grosfoguel 2001: 6; Smith 1996). This in-between status for nonblack and nonwhite immigrants extends to black immigrants as well, thereby creating a complex duality in defining race, place, and status in American society.[19] Relationships pertaining to electoral behaviors, partisanship, group mobilization, and other group politics cannot necessarily easily translate into similar black immigrant experiences and relationships with whites and other nonblack populations (Leighley and Vedlitz 1999). According to the US census, the face of black America now includes over 1.5 million immigrants from African nations and over 3.5 million black immigrants from the Caribbean, representing close to 10 percent of the total black population (US Census Bureau 2010).

How blacks in America imagine and create black ethnic coalitions directly relates to how scholars can apply these multifaceted relationships to numerous other ethnic communities. The physical characteristics that seem to link native-born and immigrant blacks and the inequities of resources that continue to affect black peoples in America have led to what Bobo and Hutchings (1996) label as in-group superiorities, elements of ethnocentrism, and overall group hostilities. The limited access to larger political and economic goals creates intraracial tensions and resentments between native-born and newcomer populations. However, the competition among black groups jockeying for anything but last place in the social order has also created a link, bond, or even an understanding of the role of blackness in American society. Descriptive representation—that is, shared characteristics along racial and ethnic (and gender) lines—helps promote feelings of "solidarity, familiarity, and self-esteem among members of that respective group" (Junn and Masuoka 2008: 731; see also Dovi 2002; Mansbridge 2003; Pitkin 1967). The jockeying for economic and political placement in civil society is intraracial (between black ethnic groups) as well as extraracial (between other minority, immigrant, and ethnic groups). It is because of the systemic racism that has occurred, and (to the surprise of many black immigrants) still occurs, that a sense of black racial alliance can be measured.

Incorporation and the "Forever Foreigner"

The differences in past experiences of black ethnic groups extend beyond how these groups view themselves, but also include how they view one another and how other nonblack groups view them. The "forever foreigner" concept that is so readily attached to Asian Americans is manifested differently for African and Afro-Caribbeans, who actively attempt to remain foreign. Junn and Masuoka (2008) argue that the "untrustworthy perpetual outsider" status of Asian Americans serves as a glass ceiling preventing full social integration for Asian Americans. However, for Afro-Caribbeans and Africans, their desire to remain an outsider or foreigner actually precipitates a stronger sense of inclusion into American society, especially by whites and economically privileged groups (Bashi 2007; Portes and Rumbaut 2001). Scholars further argue that Asian American identity is forged by several factors—the diversity of the population, the history of anti-Asian racism in the United States, and the contemporary bias within immigration policy that favors particularly high-skilled workers, producing a selection bias among Asian Americans and further reinstating the competing stereotypes of Asian Americans as a simultaneous model minority and perpetual outsider (Tuan 1998; Yun 1989; Osajima 1988). Rogers (2006: 5) argues, "Newcomers will follow the same path as their native-born black counterparts. In short … African Americans [serve] as a kind of 'model minority' group for other nonwhites in American society." As Rogers and other scholars have poignantly noted, black immigrants do not necessarily want (or need) to adopt the black American model in its entirety. I extend previous theories applied to black immigrants to better understand how these groups assimilate in the United States as elevated minorities. The most frequently referred to "model minority" label has largely been exclusively assigned to relations between Asian Americans and whites. Although black immigrants are not considered models in the same ways as their white and Asian counterparts, they *are* sometimes considered "above" black Americans by white, nonwhite, and even black individuals. Therefore, the concept of elevated minority status is an extension of the model minority, in that Afro-Caribbean and African immigrants are seeking to attain elevated minority status by remaining perpetual outsiders and forever foreign so as not to ever fully incorporate themselves into the black American populace.

Black immigrants as elevated minorities are able, at times, to distinguish themselves from their native-born black counterparts and move closer toward "in-group" status.[20] These racial tropes have implications for the incentives and the costs people face when identifying with a particular racial or ethnic group. The term "model minority" is applied to Asian Americans as a whole, but is perceived as an individual-level trait. The individualistic nature of this set of stereotypical characteristics makes it such that Asian Americans' model minority status provides fewer motives to form a group racial identity (Junn and Masuoka 2008). As the numbers of black immigrants continue to increase, and if their status as elevated minorities persists, will we see tensions rise between an individualistic versus group identification for elevated minorities? Persistence or permanence of an elevated minority status for Afro-Caribbean and Africans in the United States calls into question the possibility for intraracial coalition building.

Black Americans are often classified as a racial group based on phenotypic attributes and are too often linked to negative stereotypes (Bashi Bobb 2001; Dawson 1994; Ho 1991). Many blacks who identify as Afro-Caribbean or African prefer to keep their immigrant status so as not to be associated with black Americans and the negative attributes often ascribed to the racial group (Portes and Rumbaut 2001; Stepick et al. 2001). This particular decision made by some black ethnic groups has led to, whether real or perceived, white promotion of a racialized social hierarchy that lays a foundation for potential intergroup (black versus white) conflict. African and Afro-Caribbean blacks are also situated within this complex binary that does and does not affect them in the same ways it does for black Americans. This, in turn, creates a multiracial environment and intragroup (native-born versus foreign-born black) conflict (Segura and Rodrigues 2006; Kim 2003). Therefore, for similarly racial yet ethnically distinct groups, a multi-multiracial context exists. Du Bois was correct in that the duality of the Negro exists where he or she is both American (where whiteness as the definition is implied) and black. Black immigrants face an additional layer of complexity in negotiating the black-white binary. Indeed, black immigrants face both the black-white binary and the binary of native-born versus foreign-born that exists within the black community living in the United States. Therefore, black ethnics have a Du Boisian tripart Negro experience.

Native-born black Americans have also felt the real and perceived distinctions between themselves and their black immigrant counterparts. Due to the perceived notions of superior black immigrant educational and occupational motivation and mobility, covert tensions have arisen between native-born black Americans and the black immigrant groups they feel are able to more easily assimilate into dominant society, ostensibly enjoying the benefits and not the burdens.[21] Depending on particular factors—time of migration, age, geographic locale, and sending nation—black immigrants may apply racial and ethnic identity differently (Wong 2006; Lein, Conway, and Wong 2004; Hero 1992) and the benefits (or burdens) may be distributed inequitably.[22]

Whites versus Nonwhites and Blacks versus Nonblacks

In the early and mid-twentieth century, Jewish, Irish, Italian, black, and several other populations were historically categorized as nonwhites because they did not fit the White Anglo-Saxon Protestant classification. Ethnic identification for European ethnics was decreased or erased as white ethnics became more assimilated into American society and attained higher socioeconomic status (Jacobson 1999; Dahl 1961). With greater resources, European ethnics did not rely as heavily on their ethnic identity or ethnic community. Some scholars argue that this is occurring within Asian American communities today (Junn 2007; Omi and Winant 1994). This also elicits further questions surrounding whether or not we will observe this behavior with African and Afro-Caribbean blacks over the course of future generations. In other words, will increased economic resources lead to even less reliance on ethnic identity and/or ethnic community? There is a fundamental difference between being excluded and striving not to be included within a particular group. Previous decades and centuries represented a "white versus nonwhite" classification of groups. However, presently, the new classification for many groups is a "black versus nonblack" classification in the twenty-first century. Therefore, black immigrant populations, new to the United States and the nuances of racial hierarchies and incorporation, at times find themselves working to stay out of the "black" classification. The former example, white versus nonwhite, is an exclusion of a majority of people from a dominant group, and the latter example, black versus nonblack, is an effort by diverse groups not to be included in what they perceive as "last place."

Essentially, the racial paradigm in the United States has shifted, and the racial groups that were once distilled into "white versus nonwhite" groups have now evolved into "black versus nonblack" categories. Racial identities are not created equally and distinct historical circumstances, migration patterns, and government policies influence and affect the politics of any racial group classification in America. I theorize that there is a significant difference between (1) keeping populations out of a group, as in the historical case of "white versus nonwhite" identification where no ethnic group was fit for white membership, and (2) populations seeking to remain outside of a particular group, as in the case of blacks versus nonblacks where no ethnic group wants to be placed in membership with blacks.[23]

Through qualitative interviews, Waters (1994) discerned that foreign-born black immigrants attempt to circumvent racism and racist practices in the United States by maintaining native accents, encouraging their children to do the same, and in general, maintaining their foreign identity so as to separate themselves from native-born blacks—and, as a consequence, assimilating more easily into American society. By doing so, she argued, West Indian immigrants have attempted to prevent the downward mobility of being classified as black. This book adds to Waters's theories and argues that it is the inability of blacks, both native-born and foreign-born, to exist as Americans without the modifier "black," that is critical to understanding their positions in American society. As black immigrants struggle to integrate and assimilate into US society and distinguish themselves from their native-born counterparts, they are merely becoming elevated blacks among blacks, and the "black" modifier still remains. Because of the historical context of race within the United States, Waters (2001) argued, national identity has contributed to relevant and significant distinctions among blacks living in America.

Historically, relationships with white Americans, slavery, imperialism, colonialism, tourism, and immigration have vastly affected black Americans and African and Caribbean immigrants in differing ways. This historical background directly affects the ways in which these three groups seek to achieve economic and political goals, as well as how they interact with the other two groups. Again, in agreement with Waters's conclusion that national identities matter in the lives of black immigrants, this work theorizes that nation and identity do not negate the powerful permanence of racial classification for phenotypically black people living in the United States. Thus, foreign-born blacks may be able to distinguish themselves as elevated blacks from native-born blacks in ways Waters (2001); however, the *dissolution* of their black status is not possible. It is impossible to remove the black phenotype that serves as the fundamental distinction between black immigrants from Africa or the Caribbean and the assimilation narratives of Irish, Italian, and Jewish immigrants, or even current immigrants and Latin America or Asia.

Black Immigrant Incorporation Tactics and Obstacles

Previous studies of Afro-Caribbean population's beliefs, attitudes, work ethics, and interactions with black Americans (and whites) show that subtle tensions and distinctions between black American and Afro-Caribbean populations exist in particular contexts. African and Afro-Caribbean immigrants did not follow in the same pattern of political incorporation as their native-born black American counterparts; and largely due to past experiences in their home countries (Portes and Rumbaut 2001 Waters 1994), black ethnics are reluctant to forgo their ethnicity and melt into black American culture (Sowell 1994).[24]

If African and Caribbean immigrants are often seen as elevated minorities[25] who did not experience race-based slavery on American soil,[26] this status allows them to differentiate themselves from native-born black Americans in order to achieve greater acceptance in conventional society, and possibly increased occupational and economic opportunities (Freeman 2002). Waters (1994) has done extensive work on first- and second-generation immigrants and has argued that, due to the "black" modifier on the American status of black immigrants, they prefer to identify as black immigrants rather than as black Americans. She also found that black immigrants believed US racism could be overcome or circumvented through hard work. This belief has often been reinforced by white populations articulating West Indian cultural superiority and the dangers of downward assimilation with black Americans. Because of the fear of downward social mobility, African and Caribbean immigrants have found ways to circumvent notions of black racial group association and promote their own personal, cultural, and economic interests.

So how can we explain the perceptions of overarching West Indian success? There are selectivity effects (Portes and Rumbaut 2001) that directly affect Afro-Caribbean populations who are able to migrate to the United States. The development of community and social networks (Portes 1995; Tilly 1990), preferences of foreign-born blacks by whites over native-born black populations (Kasinitz and Rosenberg 1996; Waters 2001), and cultural differences between West Indian and native-born black populations (Reid 1969) all contribute to intraracial tensions and distrust. Bobb and Clark (2001) found that first-generation West Indians did not believe racism should be an obstacle to mobility. Similarly, Waters (1994, 2001) found that Afro-Caribbean immigrants believed discrimination could be overcome through hard work and belief in the American Dream. She stated that her respondents believed it was their decreased sense of racializing in their life experiences that allowed them to interact more positively with whites. She also stated that Afro-Caribbeans have had a long history of fighting individually, and not collectively, for their rights (2001). Their view of individual agency is consistent with their home country experiences. And in addition, individuals who achieved social mobility and realized aspects of the American dream were more likely to be "racially aware."

This awareness was developed by Afro-Caribbean populations who were socially mobile and had elevated class statuses yet, despite their wealth, were still subject to interpersonal racism. Vickerman (1999) argued that the best way for Afro-Caribbean populations to deal with racism was not through collective organizing, but by working within the system to extract one's personal benefits. Similarly, Bobb and Clark (2001) reported that their Afro-Caribbean respondents did not let racism serve as an obstacle to achieving their dreams. Waters (2001) argued that because Afro-Caribbeans, unlike native-born black Americans, were voluntary US immigrants, their voluntary status allowed them to see racism, prejudice, and discrimination as isolated instances, not as permanent barriers symbolizing American inequity. Through her interviews, Waters found that West Indians believed that structural racism could keep a *group* down but that it could not prevent *individuals* from succeeding. However, Rogers (2006) did not believe that ethnic exceptionalism applied to Afro-Caribbean populations, due to their knowledge of the systemic racism that limits opportunities and achievement for black groups and individuals in the United States. It is the racial consciousness and de facto attachment with black populations that creates a larger racial group identity for native-born and foreign-born peoples. The structural racism that affects groups versus individuals is further complicated when prejudices and discrimination on the structural level begin to affect the individual lives of black populations (i.e. housing, employment, and educational discrimination).[27]

Segura and Rodrigues (2006: 378) contend that "residential segregation, social distrust, political exclusion, poor-performing public schools and associated rates of educational attainment, poverty, and a variety of social ills affect both [immigrants] and African Americans alike." The racial segregation of blacks is evident, particularly in New York City, and more specifically in particular neighborhoods throughout the five boroughs in New York City (Rogers 2006; Kasinitz 1992).[28] In addition to relative residential proximity, or residential segregation, depending on the city, there are other factors that contribute to black ethnic populations' possibilities for pan-ethnic coalition building. The primary factor is racial classification. The strength and organizing principle of phenotype and the mandatory "black" modifier for black immigrants assists in creating a more solidified pan-ethnic identity for black populations, compared to Latinos and Asians.

Often native-born and foreign-born immigrant blacks are subject to the same structural racism in the United States. Waters (2001) argued that native-born and immigrant blacks were all subject to poverty-stricken neighborhoods that had supar schools and occupational and labor market discrimination. However, West Indians, as she referred to her population of study, also faced interpersonal racism at the hands of African Americans. Therefore, with the existence of structural forms of discrimination and inequality present in the lives of black immigrant and native-born black populations, a sense of intraracial tension, distrust, and distinction developed. Waters (1994) stated that black ethnics, and

Afro-Caribbean ethnics in particular, behaved in culturally distinct ways and sought to assimilate and acculturate into American society in ways that distinguished them from their native-born counterparts.

Afro-Caribbean populations utilized "foreign markers," such as accents or style of dress, to distinguish themselves from black Americans, to demonstrate their ethnic distinctiveness, and to thus avoid the racial stigma associated with black Americans (Waters 1994, 2001). Rogers (2006) found that these options were not always available to Afro-Caribbean populations. Many of Rogers's respondents believed whites could not differentiate between native-born and foreign-born populations; they were all "black" to white populations. Kasinitz (1992) and Vickerman (1999) argued that those who celebrated West Indians as more upwardly mobile than their black American counterparts celebrated prematurely. Due to the housing and educational racialization and discrimination second-generation West Indian populations face, scholars expect that they may soon adopt similar native-born black American negative attitudes toward larger society (Cordero-Guzman, Smith, and Grosfoguel 2001: 17–18). Alba and Nee (1999; see also Cordero-Guzman, Smith, and Grosfoguel 2001) stated that the greatest barriers for immigrants and their children was their connection to the African American group as a whole and extended beyond their black skin.

Due to black immigrants' fear of becoming "black Americans," they also distinguished themselves in politically relevant ways. Black immigrant populations formed political subcultures that addressed specific issues facing their particular ethnic communities (Rogers 2006). In recent New York City local elections, Afro-Caribbean and African candidates and elected officials have made their race *and* ethnicity key principles in their platforms in order to, on the one hand, relate to the larger black community, and on the other hand, to distinguish and highlight their specific ethnic background.[29] According to Rogers (2006), group identification implied a level of group membership and psychological attachment to its members. However, he stated that the level of group consciousness differed according to the distinct positions of each group's status in society. For blacks living in America, the psychological attachment—a common fate and emotional interdependence to the group—varies across groups and is often issue-dependent.[30]

To understand the puzzle of race, ethnicity, and identity, we must figure out how relatively separate groups of blacks coming to America from across the globe exhibit shared yet distinct identities once in America. Dawson's notion of linked fates provides a framework for understanding the relevance and impact of being labeled as "black" once in America. Dawson (1994) did not directly observe foreign-born black populations, but he clearly articulated that despite upward mobility for a particular segment of African Americans, racism still remained prevalent—so much so that upwardly mobile African Americans encountered racism and prejudice at similar rates as African Americans in lower social classes.[31] His black utility heuristic stated that life chances for African Americans were linked to the entire racial group, and individuals considered the group when making political choices. By extending Dawson's claim, I argue that individuals are cognizant of their racial group identification when particular racialized incidents occur. For foreign-born populations, their group status is either elevated as ethnically superior or amalgamated into a larger black racial classification. The attitude shifts in 1.5- and second-generation Afro-Caribbeans are attributed to their adoption of black American racial attitudes in conjunction with their own ethnic identities.[32] This incorporation of black American ideas and ideals stems from their placement as "blacks" in American societal ordering, because of their black skin.

The concept of elevated minority status of black immigrants, whether real or perceived, is also helpful in analyzing intra- and interracial perceptions of black immigrants. A better understanding of New York black populations has implications for policy and scholarly debates. On the local and national levels, the intersection of race and national identity, for blacks in America, and for the increasing numbers of immigrants who have migrated to the United States, placement into racial categories often creates new and foreign identities in addition to one's personal self-identification.

Ethnic identity is both categorical and subjective. It is categorical in that you are the ethnicity that your parents are. It is also subjective in that identification can often be a personal choice and can change over one's lifetime (Ashmore, Deaux, and McLaughlin-Volpe 2004; Deaux 1996, 2006; Waters 1990). Scholars have found that whites drop their specific ethnic identifications during the course of their lifetime (Waters 1994, 2001; Kasinitz 1992). However, ethnic identification for black immigrant populations is not abandoned and is maintained alongside their racial identification. As subsequent data throughout this book will show, depending on the issue at hand, one's ethnic identification will shift from the primary to the secondary identification, or vice versa. This research contends that foreign-born black populations will maintain their specific ethnic identities in order to differentiate themselves from the larger black population when "necessary."

Afro-Caribbean populations were not conditioned to see race through the same racial lens as native-born black Americans (Vickerman 1999). In previous studies, Afro-Caribbeans interviewed did not subscribe to the limiting notions of race; they believed it was their access to capital that most directly and significantly affected their chances for upward mobility (Bobb and Clarke 2001). In addition, Afro-Caribbeans' decreased racial consciousness stems from their lack of a "direct claim" to the history of racial subordination. Afro-Caribbeans had an "alternate frame of reference" that lessened their ability to directly address racism through collectivist political responses (Rogers 2006: 189). There is a "foreign reference point," one that aids Afro-Caribbeans in avoiding the American culture of racism (Bobb and Clarke 2001). They are aware of the varying US racial structures, but ultimately return to their home country for their identities. However, the Afro-Caribbean Local 371 members interviewed presented a more complex understanding of their placement in the US polity and their realistic chances for success due to their skin color.

Moving beyond Intraracial Perceptions and Misunderstandings

The historical duality of black immigrant and native-born relations has created, on the one hand, a foundation for transnational social movements and relationships founded in black solidarity struggles, and on the other, deep-seated resentment and distrust of foreign-born blacks, once they migrate to the United States. There is a shared history of the relationship between African and Caribbean freedom fighters, black power movements, and historically black educational institutions in the United States during the 1950s and 1960s.

There are also deep chasms in cultural understanding between native-born blacks and the new African immigrants seeking permanent residence, refugee status, or asylum in the United States. As for Afro-Caribbean relationships with black Americans, there have been well-documented analyses of Afro-Caribbean and native-born black relationships, particularly the large numbers of Afro-Caribbeans as participants and leaders within the civil rights movement struggles (McAdam 1988; Gordon 1998). However, the relationship between black Americans and Afro-Caribbeans has been fraught with misunderstanding.[33]

Scholars have contended that foreign-born blacks are often described as different, harder-working, and overall more ambitious than native-born blacks, thereby implying (or clearly stating) that black Americans do not participate in the labor force at comparative rates, do not have the same level of educational aspirations or achievements (Model 1991, 1995), do not obtain the same prestigious occupations (Kalmijn 1996), or possess the same employment advantages (Model 1995). If this perception is adopted by black Americans, then black immigration would be perceived as an immediate threat to native-born blacks.

Scholars also contend that immigrants challenge the majoritarian status of black Americans. Rogers (2006) argued that the narrative of the hard-working Afro-Caribbean immigrant who is disciplined and dedicated to achievement has seeped into how white Americans view foreign-born black populations. As black Americans seek to enter into the "in-group," the presence of black immigrants threatens black American claims to a potentially higher status (Winant 1994). Bobb and Clark (2001) argue that Afro-Caribbean populations stand to gain by investing in the narratives of "cultural difference stereotyping" that posit Afro-Caribbean populations as educated and hard-working and that highlight laziness and overall failure in black Americans. They state that it is easier for whites to accept black success if it is achieved by individuals who are ethnically different from, and thus culturally superior to, black Americans. Ethnicity in this instance trumps race. As the data in the subsequent chapters shows, the perception that other groups have toward black Americans presents a complexity surrounding one's identification as black American.

This work will explore the seeming contradiction of black immigrants seeking to maintain their own ethnic distinctions from black Americans, while also adopting their political strategies, collective action tactics, and similar policy positions. Foreign-born and native-born blacks have a shared history of balancing racial identity with national identity, whether it is a foreign or American national identity. Because of the uncertainty of allegiances and alliances of migrating blacks as perceived by native-born blacks, a complicated set of linked identities and overall distrust has emerged. This distrust, however, does not dissolve black ethnic populations' linked racial identity. The feelings of distrust do, however, directly affect the formation of a unified intraracial black population on participatory and policy levels.

Dawson and Cohen (2002: 490) argued, "So much of the literature dealing with the process of racialization and categorization in the United States has centered on how people of color have been ascribed behaviors and attributes meant to justify their secondary position." By making black participants the primary focus of this analysis, this research adds to the social science literature that analyzes race and blacks within the political system.

So why are black citizens and migrants so essential to American politics? Why is a black comparative analysis necessary? And why disaggregate black populations at this moment in time? First, historically, black populations have had a unique experience in the United States over its centuries of "peculiar institutions." As the only nonvoluntary immigrants to US soil, the native-born black population provides unique insight into current attitudes of incorporation, inclusion, and equity. When examining political institutions that have adapted to include white and other nonblack immigrants over time, the lasting impressions of America as a nation of unequal opportunities has remained in the minds of native-born black Americans, despite socio-economic gains (Tate 1993).[34]

Second, the union population used in this work allows us to test the extent to which black ethnic populations view racial, ethnic, and/or dual identities as factors in determining their attitudes toward politics, policy, and one another. The union also provides a specialized population in which to compare to national data samples. The Social Services Employees Union-Local 371 has a long-standing history of political involvement and member issue education, as well as black immigrant membership. Observing union members provided a way to illustrate the significance of labor group attachment, policy preferences, and participation rates for black ethnic populations and other nonblack groups. The union has a unique blend of highly educated and participatory members who share similar occupations, yet their distinct opinions are affected by political capital that comes from union membership.

Last, this study examines questions surrounding black ethnic distinctions and provides the context in which these differences arise. This framework primarily addresses black racial and ethnic relations in the United States, while theories of other racial pan-ethnic group interactions and relations are also incorporated. This framework helps us better understand how diverse populations form coalitions and pursue the American Dream. It also enables us to identify the underlying factors that prevent and/or promote collective action. The central question driving this project is how black ethnic differences will aid or deter coalition building as each group seeks to receive the promises of the American polity. Original survey data and national data sources show that the unexpected consequences of increased migration have had significant effects on the native-born black population with respect to interethnic perceptions and attitudes toward black voluntary immigrants. The data also show that, although Afro-Caribbean and African populations express feelings of solidarity with native-born black populations, they also distinguish themselves as immigrants and at times subscribe to notions of an elevated minority status or disillusioned outsiders. While the primary focus of this book centers primarily on the diversity within, distinctions between, and divisions among black ethnics in America, my arguments apply much more broadly to other racial and ethnic communities in the United States.

Studying diversity among blacks in America using these three parameters allows me to integrate three separate research disciplines—public opinion, race relations, and immigration— and bring together new ways of organizing and theorizing black politics (as well as race and ethnic politics more broadly). Although different goals, theories, and populations exist for these three research traditions, I show that in the diversifying black populations in the United States, core similarities exist, as do new and interesting possibilities for extended scholarship and research. Recent public opinion research has focused on how individuals view their placement in the American polity; driving this research is the argument that one's placement in society is directly linked to one's racial group and is affected by members of one's other racial group (Kinder and Dale-Riddle 2012; Bonilla Silva 2010; Dawson 1994; Espiritu 1992; Bobo and Gilliam 1990; Conover 1988).

One final implication of my particular concept of the "black" modifier is how members are defined as black, even if they themselves do not define themselves as black. How one "becomes black" is both from the perspective of the individual and also from the person who perceives that individual based on descriptive characteristics. There is no assumption that all blacks will have the same negotiations with race and ethnicity at the same or similar points of time during their tenure in the United States. The external observer's perspective is often not objective, but subjective, and embodies that particular observer's interactions and understandings of black groups in America—that is, whether that person has preconceived notions of Afro-Caribbeans' and Africans' perceived levels of success or whether that person is assessing all black individuals as one large race-based group. Although the modifier "black" remains for non-native-born blacks having emigrated to the United States, the amorphous definitions of "black" and "American" still remain.

CHAPTER 2

"Where did you come from and what should I call you?"

HOW A NEW YORK CITY LABOR UNION
EXPLAINS CHANGING DEMOGRAPHICS

Racial identity in the United States is as salient today as it ever was. The recent fascination with the term "postracial" in America is, in many ways, a democratic wish rather than a democratic destination. The very declaration of the statement "postracial" is evidence that race, racial identity, and racial guilt and forgiveness are ever-present in the minds of Americans. What does it mean to be postracial in a country where income and wealth divides are greater than ever and have clear racial and historical foundations? What does it mean to be postracial when urban public schools warehouse black and Latino students with minimal educational resources? What does it mean to be postracial when the penal system is overcrowded with black and Latino men and women who have committed nonviolent crimes and are serving decades-long sentences? These events do not occur in vacuums. And even when black individuals do not live in urban centers, do not have children who attend public schools, or have any relation to the prison industrial complex, the effects of these circumstances directly affect the group—the racial group—because of linked fate.

The ramifications of these collective "events" affect all members of the polity (in varying ways), even newcomers. However, a quandary arises when immigrants are inculcated into these debates, discussions, and circumstances because they may not share the same identity or sense of belonging with the larger group. Immigrants may not feel the same levels of membership, shared identity, or linked fate, and may not want to (Jones-Correa 1998a). The problem does not arise when individuals question their membership statuses and affiliations; the unsettling situation, for many black immigrants, is the lack of choice in the processes of membership and incorporation.

This chapter presents US census data and considers the increasing numbers of African and Afro-Caribbeans to the United States in the past decades and makes the case that, although immigrants from Africa and the Caribbean are nowhere near the numbers of immigrants arriving from Latin America, it is still necessary to include phenotypically black immigrants from black countries in discussions surrounding immigration. Africans are among the fastest-growing immigrant groups to the United States and have even surpassed Afro-Caribbean immigrant rates in recent years (Capps, McCabe, and Fix 2011). Aside from the propensity for many scholars to group all blacks together as one homogenous entity, the failure to include black immigrants in current debates surrounding people of African descent living in America has some very unsettling consequences: it assumes collective histories and the same life chances, it fails to address concerns surrounding adequate representation and incorporation into the polity, and it encourages a lack of accountability when addressing coalition-building concerns. This chapter also provides a framework for the Local 371 union. By providing background information about the labor leadership, history, and employee demographics, it offers a clearer picture of the survey sample.

Black Immigrants to America

This bill we sign today is not a revolutionary bill. It does not affect the lives of millions. It will not restructure the shape of our daily lives.
—President Lyndon B. Johnson, *October 3, 1965, on signing the Hart-Celler Immigration Bill*

In order to understand the intricate balance of race and ethnicity for blacks in the United States, in the twenty-first century, we must first ascertain the complex negotiations and frustrations of people of African descent in America and their processes of integration, segregation, and assimilation. The history of black Americans is often described by social scientists as involuntary migration, a largely academic way of defining chattel slavery, brutal living and work conditions, and physical and mental subjugation for over three hundred years. This long history in the United States is filled with incremental political gains, regional migration, slow economic progression, and the ultimate prize—a person of African descent in the White House. Many of the postslavery and post–Jim Crow gains that were made during the civil rights movement altered the institutional structure of the American government on both the state and national level. These gains also positively affected nonblack groups residing in the United States. Strides in the post–civil rights movement altered and increased access for all nonwhite individuals throughout the country and extended well beyond the scope of black American southerners.[1]

Substantial numbers of immigrants migrated to the United States with the passing and implementation of the 1965 Immigration Act.[2] People of Caribbean and African ancestries have resided in, and have continued to migrate to, the United States; thus, the increasing number of African and Afro-Caribbean immigrants has led to substantial questions surrounding the levels of political involvement and partisan attachment of these new black populations. Africans and Afro-Caribbeans have made their presence known in their overall social, cultural, and political advancement for many decades.[3] However, their political presence and policy preferences have largely been muted or amalgamated into that of black public opinion, more commonly understood as African American public opinion by social science scholars. While Afro-Caribbean and African immigrants have largely been folded in with the larger black American population, distinct Caribbean and African debates, policy agendas, and issues of concern have operated on multiple levels within the larger black political discourse. Thus, the duality of Caribbean and African preferences, in respect to their home country and the United States, as well as their incorporation into mainstream America while simultaneously being "new blacks" in America, has created multilayered policy choices for black immigrants. These policy choices involve race, ethnicity, length of time in the United States, and perceptions of home country and other groups.

Significant changes in the level of black immigrants to the United States occurred as a consequence of the 1965 Immigration Act and its subsequent implementation in 1968. Specific principles present in the 1952 McCarran-Walter Act concerning quotas and labor clearances for particular groups were amended, and increases in black ethnic populations began. In 1970, no fewer than fifty thousand blacks had immigrated to the United States, thereby spawning significant increases in the numbers of blacks migrating from Africa and the Caribbean in subsequent years. Afro-Caribbean populations began migrating to the United States at a significant pace after the passage of the 1965 Immigration Act, while African migration swelled during the early 1980s.

The number of black immigrants to the United States represents another important shift. A result of the increase in immigration from various African nations stemmed largely from the implementation of the 1965 Immigration Act, and over a twenty-year period, beginning with 1968, African immigration increased sevenfold.[4] Many members of Congress did not predict this shift, nor did they predict the increase in immigration from the Caribbean and Africa (and Asia) to America. Many members of Congress did not view the 1965 Act as an impetus for change, but rather more of a symbolic act in which civil rights sentiments would be extended beyond the borders of the United States. Many senators and representatives did not believe that full-scale immigration to the United States would be fully utilized. Rep. Emanuel Celler (D-NY) argued to his colleagues:

> With the end of discrimination due to place of birth, there will be shifts in countries other than those of northern and western Europe. Immigrants from Asia and Africa will have to compete and qualify in order to get in, quantitatively and qualitatively, which; itself will hold the numbers down. There will not be, comparatively, many Asians or Africans entering this country.... Since the people of Africa and Asia have very few relatives here, comparatively few could emigrate from those countries because they have no family ties in the United States.[5]

However, the 1965 bill led to over 18 million legal migrants to the United States, thirty years after the Hart-Celler Act was passed. The 18 million immigrants totaled more than triple the number of admittants in the previous thirty-year period.

Afro-Caribbean and African immigration has increased significantly over the past four decades (see table 2.1). The waves of African immigration were largely ignored by social scientists until relatively recently when significant numbers of diverse populations, most specifically Nigerians and Ethiopians, settled in urban and suburban areas of the United States. Possible explanations for the deemphasis of African migration could be attributed to the fact that influxes of African immigration has largely occurred over the past twenty-five years, unlike Afro-Caribbean immigration, which largely began in the mid-twentieth century. In addition, African immigrants have not solely settled in major cities like their Afro-Caribbean immigrant counterparts, but have settled in nontraditional yet budding urban centers such as St. Louis, Pittsburgh, and Minneapolis (Leslie and Peterson 2002; Dyer 2003), and not just the New York City area.

The significant increase in African migration to the United States has contributed to the influx of blacks from a diverse set of African nations. What is also of import are the substantial numbers of black immigrants from regions not in Africa or the Caribbean. We know that for many black immigrants, the journey to the United States is often a multicountry process as individuals work to attain visas, money, and proof of financial and social networks. Therefore, the total number of black immigrants from Africa and the Caribbean is likely even larger than the data suggests. The debates surrounding blacks in America have evolved and now include diverse sets of racial and ethnic groups, issues and problems that extend beyond urban centers, and analyses of blacks as heterogeneous members of American society (Price and Hampton 2010; Sawyer 2006; Swain 1993). The recent increases in black migration to New York City, as

Table 2.1 **Black Immigrants to the United States 1980 to 2008–9**

	1980 (thousands)	1990 (thousands)	% Change 1980 to 1990	2000 (thousands)	% Change 1990 to 2000	2008–9 (thousands)	% Change 2000 to 2008–9
All Black Immigrants	816	1,447	77	2,435	68	3,267	34
African Immigrants	64	184	188	574	212	1,081	88
Afro-Caribbean Immigrants	453	897	98	1,428	59	1,701	19
Black Immigrants from Other Regions	299	366	22	433	18	485	12

Source: Capps, McCabe, and Fix 2011.

well as other cities throughout the United States, signal an important period of diverse incorporation into American society. African migration from countries such as Nigeria and Ethiopia, and Afro-Caribbean migration from Jamaica and Haiti, made America's black population more diverse, with a more complicated understanding of identity. The regional and national diversity is clearly apparent in the number of countries of origin in the Caribbean and Africa over the past ten years.

What's in a Name for Blacks in America?

The nomenclature assigned to blacks in American has been ever changing: blacks in America have been referred to by many names over the past century, from "colored" to "Negro" to "black" to "African American."[6] Scholars assert that the name change to African American suggested a progression from other groups' self-labeling. They argued that a shift from names that were imposed upon the group to "self-naming" occurred for African American populations (Hecht, Collier, and Ribeau 1993; Smitherman 1991; Gates 1989). Much like the debate over the meaning and significance of "race," "black American" and "African American" are large categories that encompass all people with a shared phenotype living in the United States, without allowing for the cultural nuances, distinct histories, and varying migratory narratives that exist. In larger political discourses, these distinctions are rarely brought to the fore. Unsurprisingly, though, once social scientists begin peeling back the layers of racial labeling, they find debates and disagreements over these terms.

Throughout this work, the term "black American" is used to refer to populations most commonly referred to as "African American" in political and social science literature. The decision to call this particular population "black American" is twofold. First, by labeling the group "black American," it decreases the potential for confusion when comparing black American and African populations living in America. Second, this population is referred to as black American so as not to presume links to African identity. Initially, the term "black" or "black American" was associated with a radical identity representing the Black Power movement and struggle of the 1960s. The term "black" has also had negative connotations as a "repudiation of whiteness and the rejection of assimilation" (Smitherman 1991). Although the term "black" has evolved from its radical associations, the usage of the term does signal past associations and identification with the solidarity and unity of the black movement of the 1960s and 1970s (Fine and Bowers 1984). Larkey, Hecht, and Martin (1993) reported that that the terms "black" and "African American" express differing views of one's ethnic identity. They find that the term "African American" represents a blended heritage for respondents, as compared to the term "black," which provides a sense of unity and acceptability. They find a trend in individuals shifting their usage of "black" to "African American" and argue that this represents a move toward self-determination and progress in combining two cultures.

Scholars argue that the usage of the term "black" urges a recognition of race as well as skin color and thus embraces a positive racial consciousness in the face of the dominant group (Larkey, Hecht, and Martin 1993; Goldberg 1990; West 1990). The interplay of racial classification and skin color significantly affects both native-born black populations and black immigrants who are racially classified as "black" solely due to phenotype. My use of the term "black American" attempts to combine the two cultural elements of this work: that is, the ethnocultural, most commonly defined as the heritage and ancestry of a people, as well as the racial, the effects of skin color on a people (Larkey, Hecht, and Martin 1993). Essentially, this project begins to reassemble the concept of diaspora and the extent to which black ethnic groups understand themselves as descendants of people who were removed from Africa during the trans-Atlantic slave trade and share a commonality with other black individuals despite their distribution to other nation-states spanning various periods of time (Edwards 2003; Kelley 1999a).

Throughout this book, I classify black populations into three categories: black American, Afro-Caribbean, and African. These classifications may seem problematic. Africans and Afro-Caribbeans are not monolithic groups, and neither are black Americans, but this initial categorization into two general ethnic groups is a way, initially, to compare these black ethnic groups broadly. The broad categories of "Afro-Caribbean" and "African" provide large enough sample sizes for study. As previously stated, there are significant cultural, historical, and linguistic differences and distinctions between and among African and Afro-Caribbean populations. However, there are also common cultural practices and traditions among populations from Africa and the Caribbean. By "common culture," I mean what Chandra (2006) describes as a similar framework to understanding another group. She argues, "It does not matter whether they subscribe to an identical set of symbols, values, codes, and norms, or whether they speak the same language . . . a common culture means not that the group share all symbols, values, codes, and norms, but that they share some *key symbols, values, codes, and norms that distinguish them from members of other groups*" (Chandra 2006: 411; emphasis added).

The literature explaining diasporic links of black populations throughout the world as a consequence of the international trans-Atlantic slave trades makes these initial categorizations plausible. Diverse national origin groups are collapsed into the "neat" categories "black American," "Afro-Caribbean," and "African." Because of these categories, there are some limits to this data that are important to recognize. Although this book presents data and findings on three distinct black populations, it does not suggest or presume that this represents the attitudes and opinions of all black ethnic populations. In many ways, this book is a snapshot of a unique population of the labor sector in New York City, with a radical and progressive leadership structure. It is also the beginning of an important conversation that has often occurred within and between black ethnic groups, but has had limited discussion within the political science literature. The inclusion of African immigrants to the substantive academic conversations that have generally pertained on the African Americans and West Indians is a necessary step in better understanding all of the new blacks in America.

Why Choose a Labor Population?

The racial and ethnic populations included in this project are black Americans, Afro-Caribbeans, and Africans, as well as Latinos and whites.[7] Currently in New York City, Afro-Caribbean and African individuals account for 39 percent and 5 percent, respectively, of black New Yorkers—44 percent in total (US Census 2010). Focusing on a union population controls for class and occupation in this study. Of course, surveying the increasing number of black ethnics in various professional and service industries throughout New York City would provide diverse and unique sets of opinions and attitudes. However, such large-scale data collection at this time was not possible.

The Social Services Employees Union (SSEU) Local 371 was chosen due to the increasing number of immigrants who have joined the union over the past two decades, especially black immigrant populations. New York's racial composition has changed and expanded over the past fifty years (Cordero-Guzman, Smith, and Grosfoguel 2001), and the economies in which newly arrived immigrants are now integrating have changed from largely manufacturing industries to industries based on services and related fields (Waldinger 1996; Mollenkopf and Castells 1991; Sassen 1991, 1988). There has been an intersection of race and unions since the mid-1960s, as labor unions have been a source of economic and occupational stability for marginalized workers, largely workers of diverse racial and ethnic backgrounds. Unions have also served as a central organization for assisting in the development of immigrant social networks, and have aided immigrants in defining, incorporating, and adjusting to the US labor system, as well as aspects of the US racial system. Foreign-born populations now use labor unions as an entrée into the middle class, similarly to how black Americans from the mid- to late twentieth century utilized labor memberships as a means of middle-class economic security, as well as political and social advancement.

With the addition of foreign-born populations into labor unions, not only have immigrants contributed to the growth of service sector jobs in skilled and unskilled occupations, but these jobs have produced a relative diversity of incomes within the service sector.[8] This book presupposes a certain level of social capital that levels the playing field for native-born and foreign-born populations. Union membership is often used as a measure of political capital, which is different from memberships in other social or political organizations. Currently the most densely unionized state in the country is New York, where unions are actively involved in politics and exist as distinct organizations (Fuchs, Minnite, and Shapiro 2001; Master 1997). Although the percentages of the population belonging to labor unions have declined since the latter half of the twentieth century and the overall future of organized labor seems unclear, unions are important locales in which to examine marginalized groups in American society. Union membership can provide a collective identity derived from members' common interests and solidarity (Taylor 1979). And over the past ten years, the number of foreign-born union members has reached one out of ten among wage and salary workers. Although the aggregate percentages of labor members in the national population have decreased, the actual numbers of foreign-born workers who are union members has increased more than 50 percent in the past two decades (Migration Policy Institute 2004).

As figure 2.1 shows, although there was a steady decline in black labor union membership from 1994 to 2000 figure, there were signs of a resurgence of black

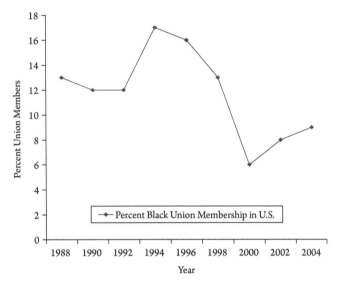

Figure 2.1 Percent of Black Respondents Who Are Union Members (National Sample)
Source: Migration Policy Institute 2004.

membership at the turn of the twenty-first century. Scholars believed that the decreases in organized labor have had direct repercussions resulting in increased inequalities that have disproportionately affected marginalized and historically disadvantaged groups (Warren 2005). Historically, labor unions have been notorious for exclusionary practices involving marginalized groups based on race, gender, and class.[9] However, social justice unions, such as SSEU Local 371, although not always common, have served as a bastion for the underrepresented and disadvantaged groups (Levi 2003). In my interviews with President Charles Ensley, I asked him to explain what has made SSEU Local 371 a social justice union, as opposed to a purely occupational union. He replied:

> We are a progressive activist union that encourages rank and file par-
> ticipation. If we describe ourselves in addition to that, we are a bottoms
> up union, fiercely democratic, with members in control of their own
> union. There is a long history of activism. We involve ourselves in social
> movements. We have a history of civil rights involvement and we are
> active politically, endorsing and supporting progressive candidates. We
> are a labor *movement* whose leaders come from rank and file. It's not
> about the money; it's about working empowerment.

Labor unions traditionally serve as economic and political forces within American society (Levi 2003; Seidman 1994) and help combine varying race-, class-, and gender-based inequalities into one unified voice (Verba, Schlozman, and Brady 2004). Social activist labor unions affect election turnout rates for members because of top-down leadership and provide a stabilizing institutional force within the US democratic system.[10] In addition to these necessary principles, SSEU Local 371 has also served as a continuation of social justice movements in addition to providing economic advancement and political involvement. Because of the activism and history of activism within Local 371, I hypothesized that the levels of electoral participation of members would be higher than national averages. Because of the growing prevalence of foreign-born individuals joining labor unions, SSEU Local 371 was an especially appropriate organization to survey.

The Survey Sample Population

SSEU Local 371 in New York City has been the union of welfare workers for over six decades. For many years Local 371–AFL-CIO was the sole collective bargaining agent for social service staff, and welfare administrators were members of the SSEU. SSEU members were staff members, individuals who were rank-and-file members who worked in welfare centers throughout the city. Local 371 members were administrators who represented supervisors at welfare centers. These two distinct and sometimes divided unions joined forces in December 1964 during one of the largest "No Contract, No Work" strikes of civil servants in the history of New York City. The strike lasted for twenty-eight days, and although it did not end with an immediate contract, the collective bargaining efforts in many ways set a tone of solidarity for the future of the union membership and leadership.

The members of SSEU Local 371 are a core group of social service providers whose jobs range from the protection of children, to addiction counseling and the provision of aid to seniors. SSEU Local 371's members are caseworkers for the protection of children and victims of neglect and abuse; providers of services to people with AIDS and of protective services to adults; addiction counselors; home attendants for seniors and the disabled; early childhood education consultants; fraud detectors in public assistance programs; collectors of money from insurance companies for the Health and Hospitals Corporation; and groups of workers who attempt to move people from welfare to work (job training). These particular union occupations serve as social service delivery systems for New York City residents. By surveying the leadership and rank-and-file members of the union, there was consistency across occupation, relative class, and educational attainment.[11] (See appendix 2B for union member income, class, and education demographics.)

Comparisons of the national and local level were easily done because labor union membership is often asked in national surveys. Also, much of the SSEU survey was modeled after national surveys and includes similar participation, spending, and racial incorporation questions.[12]

One of the unintended benefits of the SSEU Local 371 sample population is the overwhelming number of Nigerian respondents within the African immigrant population.[13] Of the survey participants who identified as African immigrants, 90 percent also classified themselves as Nigerian.[14] Nigerians have immigrated to the United States in the greatest numbers, compared to individuals from other African nations.[15] However, the rates of migration have not been significant enough to warrant a uniquely separate classification, separate from other African populations. Although Nigerians possess a unique cultural identification, their motivations for migration are similar to those of other African groups: the pursuit of increased education opportunities, the attainment of economic security and stability, and a desire to participate in a credible electoral system (Ogbaa 2003).

Similarly, Afro-Caribbean respondents possess distinct histories and cultures pertaining to their specific islands. However, 75 percent of the Afro-Caribbean respondents hail from English-speaking nations that formerly were British colonies. By placing Afro-Caribbeans from various islands into one ethnic category of "Afro-Caribbean," I am adhering to the theories set forth by Fearon and Laitin (1996) that argue that members who subscribe to an ethnic group need only "accept the claim to be immediately descended from other members of the group" (Chandra 2006). In order to reflect "Afro-Caribbean" and "African" opinions, the diversity of one's specific island or country of origin was amalgamated into a larger diasporic categorization.[16]

The SSEU Local 371 survey provides new evidence pertaining to black ethnic group attitudes, but there are limitations to these results. This examination of one union population in New York City does not provide national comparisons with black ethnic populations in other occupational sectors or unions. However, the benefits of conducting a survey in New York City include the diverse black ethnic population and a historical tradition of immigration to the city. There are currently over 8 million people in New York City, of which 2.1 million, or 26 percent, are classified as black (US Census 2010). Of the 2.1 million blacks living in the five boroughs, 39 percent are Afro-Caribbean immigrants, and roughly 5 percent are African immigrants.[17] Although New York City provides substantial black ethnic populations, the inclusion of broader national data helps to generalize my statistical findings.

Why Choose New York City?

New York City was an ideal location to administer the survey due to its influx of black immigrants. New York City has historically been the port for

Afro-Caribbean migrants and has recently witnessed increases of African immigrants as well. Fuchs, Minnite, and Shapiro (2001) argued that New York City is an ideal location to observe the relationship between social capital, community building, and political participation. Because of the economic and entrepreneurial opportunities present, ethnic social networks, and the abundance of native-born black populations in close residential proximity, New York City has been a significant and historically relevant location.[18] All the purposes of my research are served by choosing a locale that receives the most diverse immigrant populations of any other city in the United States (Cordero-Guzman, Smith, and Grosfoguel 2001) as well as having a native-born and foreign-born black union population in a politically active social service industry.

Table 2.2 shows the number of black immigrants who now comprise close to 10 percent of the black population nationwide and 44 percent of the black population in New York City.

One of the many factors contributing to the importance of New York City as a place for this study is the history of immigration and continued immigration. Between 1980 and 1996, New York City received over 1.5 million immigrants (Rivera-Batiz and Santiago 1996). It has been an important site for home country and diasporic politics, where immigrants have been able to instigate nationalist and other struggles (Cordero-Guzman, Smith, and Grosfoguel 2001). But because New York is America's oldest immigrant city and is one of the most important historical ports of entry for immigrants, its political institution and population dynamics have evolved in more progressive ways than in other US cities (Cordero-Guzman, Smith, and Grosfoguel 2001). For many new immigrants, New York is a site for transnational migrant activity and serves as a center

Table 2.2 **Demographics for Black Populations in the United States, New York State, and New York City, 2005**

	Total Population		
	US	*NY State*	*NY City*
Total US Population	308,747,508	19,378,104	8,175,133
Black Population	38,624,000	3,294,277	2,088,510
	Total Foreign-Born Black Population		
	US	*NY State*	*NY City*
African	1,252,020	81,198	101,410
Afro-Caribbean	2,247,999	1,004,344	793,997

Source: US Census 2010.

for the global economy and capitalist development (A.Torres 1995; A. Torres and Bonilla 1993).

This is not meant to depict a city that routinely enjoys racial harmony or even stayed equity. New York City also has a long-standing history of racism and anti-immigrant sentiments; much of the current immigrant politics, policies, and debates revolve around historical negotiations with immigrants, competing national identities and cultural needs, and the conflicts that arise when the lives of diverse populations intersect (Cordero-Guzman, Smith, and Grosfoguel 2001). The integrated black ethnic neighborhoods, which are often racially segregated from other populations in the city and sometimes have substandard housing conditions, serve to further reinforce and solidify inter- and intraracial stereotypes; they can also contribute to hostile policy stances among native-born and foreign-born black populations (Rogers 2006; Soss 2002). The residential segregation by race in New York City positions black ethnic groups in residential negotiations that further complicate their perceptions of one another.[19]

SSEU Local 371 Survey Design and Implementation

The goals of the 2005–6 SSEU Local 371 survey were to unravel the fundamental underpinnings of racial and ethnic group unity and difference and to provide a clearer framework for possible racial and ethnic coalition building. The survey sought to better understand black ethnic cohesion, or a lack thereof. The study consisted of a mail-in survey in which 1,500 questionnaires were initially sent to Local 371 members, 415 of which were successfully completed (a response rate of 31 percent).[20]

The rolls of the Black History and Caribbean Heritage Committees, as well as the informal African Heritage Committee, were oversampled. There is a long shared history of black Americans communicating and working with Afro-Caribbeans and Africans in their respective home countries during the beginning stages and throughout the civil rights movement and African independence movements that clearly support theories of linked fate. However, the way the linkage is expressed by nonactivists over forty years later on US soil presents interesting questions for the present day.

This contributed to a total of 274 surveys completed by members identifying as native-born black American, Afro-Caribbean, or African, 66 percent of the final sample: 135 black Americans, 47 Afro-Caribbeans, and 92 Africans (see table 2.3).

A respondent was defined as a member of one of these groups if they identified racially and ethnically as such and indicated that their parents were also of that ancestry. The survey also included 41 whites, 54 Latinos, and 46 individuals

Table 2.3 **Union Sample Survey**

	Number of Respondents	%
White	41	10
Black American	135	33
Afro-Caribbean	47	11
African	92	22
Latino	54	13
Other	46	11
N	415	100

Source: 2005–6 SSEU Local 371 Survey.

defined as "other." The individuals in the "other" category self-identified as Asian, Native American, or varying biracial identities and were placed in this category because there were too few in each group to analyze. The remainder of the sample consisted of 13 percent Latinos, 10 percent whites, and 11 percent classified as "other" nonblack individuals.

SSEU Local 371 does not keep specific records on the racial and ethnic composition of the roughly 17,000 union members. During our interview with President Ensley, he gave rough estimates. He explained:

> We do not have numbers [on race]. I think the numbers are 60 percent people of African descent, around 20 percent white, and around 20 percent Latino. The union is predominantly women, easily 75 percent. [The] union is getting young, over 50 percent under [the] age of 40. It's getting younger each year because of retirees and new hires.

The data available for the general union population reports that roughly 30 percent of union members are men and roughly 70 percent of the union

Table 2.4 **Gender of Local 371 Survey Respondents (in percentages)**

	Black Amer	Afro-Carib	African	White	Latino
Male	30	30	73	61	38
Female	70	70	27	39	62
N	135	47	92	41	53

Source: 2005–6 SSEU Local 371 Survey.

population is female. Fifty-five percent of the respondents from the SSEU Local 371 survey were women. Because ethnic breakdowns are not available for the entire union, it is only possible to compare the gender percentages of the ethnic samples to the overall union gender composition. In table 2.4, the black American and Afro-Caribbean gender percentages in the sample are the same as those for the overall union population. The gender percentages for African members are the inverse of the overall union gender percentages.

In addition to collecting data on the reported political attitude and behavior of black ethnic, white, and Latino union members, the survey also included detailed demographic information about respondents, including the home country and the ethnicity of the respondents and their parents. The survey also asked questions about racial identification to provide precise measures in distinguishing black ethnics.[21] For example, respondents first indicated which racial and ethnic group they most generally align themselves. Respondents were then asked from what country their relatives hailed, whether they were born in the United States, whether they grew up in the United States, and in what country their mother and father were born. By asking this series of questions, the SSEU Local 371 survey could distinguish first- from second-generation immigrants.[22]

The survey is also able to distinguish black Latinos from other black ethnic Caribbeans. I chose to treat black respondents from Spanish-speaking nations as distinct, when compared to the three primary black ethnic groups, due to the complications of cross-identity with Latino issues. Because Latino populations are more likely to separate themselves by nationality than by skin color, a cohesive black Latino identity is less likely to be formed from within the Hispanic community (Fears 2003; de la Garza et al. 1991). Scholars contended that race matters for Hispanics, but not in the same ways that it does for blacks. In order to identify black Latinos in the sample, the variables used to measure this distinction were race, respondent's country of origin, and parent's country of origin. Most importantly, the survey specifically asked whether the respondent was raised in a Spanish-speaking household. These variables aided in distinguishing black ethnics and black Latinos.

The SSEU Local 371 survey was thus designed to answer the following five questions:

1. Does a pan-ethnic identity exist among black ethnic groups in the United States?
2. How do these groups view one another?
3. How do these groups conceptualize their placement in the American polity?

4. Do policy distinctions exist?
5. What influences the attitudinal and behavioral similarities and differences among these groups?

The survey was initially distributed in mid-October 2005 and ended in March 2006. The survey provided both general racial and ethnic-specific measures of group solidarity. These responses facilitated the comparisons of black ethnic groups and the analysis of intraracial linked fate hypotheses based on class, gender, other demographic variables, evaluations of feelings and perceptions of particular groups, attitudes toward immigrants and potential for success once in the United States, and racial-ethnic partnerships.[23] The uniqueness of the SSEU Local 371 population does not negate what can be learned from these data, including comparisons with results from national surveys.

I also conducted qualitative interviews with members of SSEU Local 371 and with the late Charles Ensley, who served as the group's president for twenty-six years. In-person interviews were conducted from October 2006 to January 2007. The in-person interviews were conducted in English only and encompass in-depth interviews of twenty-two Local 371 members. The interviews were conducted with union leadership[24] and rank-and-file members and lasted from approximately thirty to ninety minutes and were conducted at Local 371 union headquarters in New York City. The interviewees all identified as black American, Afro-Caribbean, or African. The interviews are meant to provide context to many of the quantitative findings presented in subsequent chapters. Many of the anecdotes that arose from the interviews help to fill in some of the "gaps" left by a purely quantitative analysis. Having conducted interviews from previous social scientific research, and also wanting the most honest nature from some of the respondents, I chose not to tape-record my interviews. Many of my respondents stated that they are much more candid when not looking at or thinking about a recording device. Having spoken to several social scientists before embarking on this research, I devised a shorthand to use in interviews and also asked respondents to repeat particularly poignant statements in order to record direct quotes accurately. For many respondents, this was the first time they spoke openly about their feelings, both positive and negative, toward other black ethnic groups either (1) with someone of a different black ethnic group, or (2) with someone who was not a family member or close friend.

As I began interviewing members of the union, many had little resistance openly speaking about their own experiences with race and ethnicity, both in the United States and abroad. The interviews usually began with general questions about the union, its membership, and any current debates circulating within the organization. With the union leadership, more time was dedicated to their observations and frustrations trying to organize and motivate so many different (and sometimes competing) agendas within the local. With rank-and-file members, more time was spent more broadly discussing their experiences with race and ethnicity in their families, in New York City, and in the United States. Many rank-and-file members suggested I speak to other colleagues of theirs who had either similar or quite different experiences negotiating race and ethnicity in their personal and professional lives. Throughout the interview process, I was able to conduct detailed interviews that often came in the form of long discussions and conversations.

In-depth interviews have primarily been used quite effectively by social scientists who have attempted to ascertain the nuances in black intraracial attitudes. There are obvious advantages to conducting interviews with Local 371 members. First, as Local 371 continues to change, I have captured the ideas and opinions of a select group of members and leaders within the organization. Second, the strength of open-ended, in-depth interviews is what Sawyer (2006) argues is the ability to explore the experiences and information that shapes attitudes and opinions. Because of the amorphous nature of race, as well as ethnicity, the complex perceptions, opinions, and even behaviors can be an amalgam of distinct and sometimes contradictory ideas (Sawyer 2006: 104). Through the process combining surveys and in-depth interviews, I am able to use representative samples to ascertain information and utilize in-depth interviews to help us understand *why* respondents express particular attitudes and opinions.

The quantitative analysis in subsequent chapters is based on data from the 2005–6 SSEU Local 371 survey, in addition to qualitative interviews with Local 371 executive and rank and file members. It also compares the SSEU Local 371 union respondents with other New York City and national survey samples. These additional data come from the National Election Study (NES) Cumulative File 1948–2004 focusing on the years 1984–2004,[26] and the New Americans Exit Poll (NAEP) 2005 and 2006 data. The 2004 NES and the 2005 US Census Current Populations Survey are also used to make other comparisons.

As the following chapters discuss, once in the United States, African and Caribbean immigrants encounter racial barriers similar to the ones facing their native-born black American counterparts. Because of the identifiable phenotype of native-born blacks and African and Caribbean immigrants, one might draw conclusions regarding similar ideological and political outlooks and inevitable coalition building. The subsequent chapters show that shared racial attitudes among black ethnics do exist. However, ethnicity remains a significant determinant of intraracial attitudes and policy stances for black populations, especially for the newly arrived groups.

CHAPTER **3**

Political Participation and the Socialization of Blacks into Unions and the Polity

I just moved here from Jamaica and all of a sudden I am "black." Will you please explain to me why I am supposed to be a Democrat?
—Jamaican college student, *New York, NY, 2005*

When observing and interacting with members of Local 371, the role of race within the union played out in a multilayered and continuously evolving manner. Because of the changing nature of union membership, demographics within New York City, and ultimately the populations served by the social service providers, race and its ever-present counterpart, ethnicity, remain a complex, intricate, and shifting aspect of the union's identity.[1]

The ethnic composition of black America has changed over the past several decades. The increasing numbers of marginalized groups in the United States have changed national and local demographic levels.[2] Increased black immigration has also had significant effects on the production of labor in the United States. The increases in immigration have had direct effects on formal and informal labor markets, as well as unions. Black members, both native-born and foreign-born, have affected labor organizations from its rank-and-file membership to the executive and leadership positions. Historically, labor groups have gone through great pains to prevent nonwhite workers from becoming members of unions. Today, however, unions rely on marginalized groups for membership (Warren 2005). With the incorporation of marginalized workers

into the various organized economic and labor sectors, the membership composition has shifted to include more foreign-born members, as well as members in
leadership positions.

The Decline of the Union and the Rise of Black Ethnic
Political Entry and Participation

According to Tate (1991), voting, like other forms of participation, is costly to
individuals, and subsequent political participation is linked to both material and
psychological individual resources. Those possessing certain political skills and
resources can more easily bear the cost of voting. One of the primary resources
that Tate indicated as a determining factor in overcoming the costs of voting is
experience in the political process and education. Those familiar with the electoral process, usually older and better-educated individuals, are more inclined
to vote. According to Verba et al. (1993), the workplace and other nonpoliti-
cal settings are extremely valuable in assisting individuals in developing skills
necessary for political participation. Union membership contributes to political
activity: individuals who are members of a labor organization are more likely to
vote than nonmembers (Delaney, Masters, and Schwochau 1988; Radcliff and
Davis 2000; Rosenstone and Hansen 1993; Leighley and Nagler 2007).

Union membership has been on the decline for the past several years, while
immigrant and foreign-born population membership has been on the rise
(Warren 2005), thus providing foreign-born workers with an entrée into the
middle class. Because newly arrived immigrants are largely unattached to politics
(Garcia 1982) and have a limited interest in political life, a union with an ethos
and history of militant and progressive approaches to public service and social
justice introduces them to participatory acts beyond the traditional act of voting. New immigrants, particularly poor African Americans, Latinos, and Asian
Americans, are the least likely to engage in the political process (Lee 2011; Junn
and Haynie 2008). In addition, immigrants involved in organized labor activities
are more likely to participate in traditional and nontraditional forms of electoral
activity within their new home country (Fuchs, Minnite, and Shapiro 2001).

THE IMPORTANCE OF UNION LEADERSHIP, MEMBERSHIP,
AND EDUCATION

The significant levels of turnout among black Local 371 members can be attributed to three factors: (1) dynamic union leadership, (2) the highly educated
union body (both academically and politically educated), and, most significantly, (3) union membership. Attachment to the union and a strong sense of

group consciousness was the stimulus for political participation for black ethnics in Local 371 (Bobo and Gilliam 1990; Guterbock and London 1983; Shingles 1981; Verba et al. 1972). In many ways, organized labor serves as a primary "mobilizing institution" and has substantial effects on an election and turnout (Rosenstone and Hansen 1993).

For many black immigrant groups, membership within a union serves as an institutional foundation and an entrée into political and even policy education. Many of the native-born and foreign-born black survey responses made specific mention of the dynamic leadership of President Ensley. Ensley was consistently unanimously reelected president of the union for a total of twenty-six years, largely due to his leadership style. He understood and amalgamated the roots of the civil rights movement and national labor struggles and incorporated them into the SSEU Local 371. During the 1960s, the current SSEU Local 371 was divided into two unions, the SSEU and Local 371. Even when the SSEU and Local 371 were two distinct organizations, the traditions of rank-and-file participation, representation of social justice issues, and coalition building were established. President Ensley's union leadership and his incorporation of civil rights struggles with larger social service goals contributed to high levels of rank-and-file electoral mobilization and participation.

In my interviews with President Ensley, I asked him to explain the relationship between increased black membership (both native-born and foreign-born) in unions and the civil rights movement, and how, if at all, the two factors affected him as a labor leader. He explained:

> In my generation, many of us are of a generation who were foot soldiers or leaders in the civil rights movement. Struggle is what we grew up with, struggling to achieve. So since we were involved in that struggle, we identify with working poor and in [the] 1960s we attracted that type of worker to the union and that type of worker gravitated to the union, ones who worked for social justice and working class people.... The impact on me and the union is that I have a sense of what's right and rage when we see injustice. You need a sense of outrage if you're to do this work successfully.

Over the past forty years, there has been a noticeable incorporation of black members as well as foreign-born populations into the labor movement.[3] In many ways, once black immigrant populations arrive in the United States, they have the potential to use labor organizations as entrées into the middle class. Similar to black populations in the post–civil rights era, black foreign-born groups can utilize the benefits of union membership to enhance occupation specialization, financial security, and organizational resources. Labor organizations provide jobs, occupational security, and varying levels of community.[4] Both native-born and foreign-born blacks face racial challenges in the United States; unions serve as organizing agents to assist in the integration of individuals and groups within the political system. In many ways, unions represent groups in an occupational and political sphere (Wong 2006; Jones-Correa 1998a). Black populations continue to find themselves as shared recipients of discrimination and prejudice, therefore many black foreign-born groups negotiate their new racial identity, along with extended group attachments and opportunities to fulfill the American Dream, within the mobilizing context of the SSEU Local 371.

The members of the SSEU Local 371 are the primary sample population for this study. Local 371 is an activist union that promotes unity and intra- and interracial education that focuses on new racial and religious groups within the union. There is no doubt that Local 371 fits the description provided by Kriesi (1995) of a mobilizing organization.[5] In 2006, President Ensley highlighted some of his efforts to promote racial and ethnic understanding throughout the union population. I asked the president to explain the role of the racial and social committees within the union.[6] His replied:

> They are presidentially established committees. We have various heritage nights, to make a stronger union, not at the expense of each other.[7] Therefore, a union is a common ground where we could become stronger to promote solidarity because sometimes people are afraid of what they do not know. So we have heritage committees to promote unity. It is important to me that our workers understand that we have far more in common than our differences. Despite our backgrounds, we're in the same boat as workers. If our interests are to be advanced we must minimize differences just like the mine workers. It's about vision.

President Ensley's approach to solidarity supports Bernstein's (1997) description of the political strategy for cultural goods that deconstructs racial categorizations and identity at the collective level. In essence, President Ensley believes that the culture organizations within the union serve to promote unity, highlight cultural similarities, and illuminate the shared histories and struggles of the diverse members in the union as they work toward common goals. Based on this response from President Ensley, one may expect to see relatively positive intra- and interracial responses that promote his and the union's concepts of solidarity. Because of the racially and ethnically organized social committees, a level of racial and ethnic acceptance was promoted and presumed to be widely embedded in the ethos of union members. However, as the data show, there are sometimes significant ethnic opinion differences found within the union population.

Political Participation and Labor Leadership in a Post–Civil Rights Context

To begin to assess the importance of labor leadership on labor mobilization and political participation, I examined Local 371 member attitudes toward voting to see if members were active participants in traditional forms of political participation. Almost all data, both quantitative analyses and the in-depth interviews, reveal the significance of union leadership and membership on increased propensities to vote in elections. Local 731 members continuously contributed their increased participation levels to their affiliation with the union (Leighley and Nagler 2007). One member stated, "I never voted before joining the union." Another explained, "It is the union that gives us the activist spirit to participate." One member explicitly stated the importance of race and voting, saying, "It is important for black people to vote [especially with all of the police brutality out there]."

According to Tate (1991), there are problems with the race-conscious view of participation. Based on Verba and Nie's 1967 data (Shingles 1981), Tate argued that the effects attributed to race consciousness may actually have been more indicative of the 1960s black protest atmosphere and nonconventional protest tactics that later transferred into conventional forms of political activity (Piven and Cloward 1988). She also asserted that there were residual effects of ad hoc local institutions that operated well before the passage of the Voting Rights Act of 1965. These institutions helped register and mobilize black voters. Therefore, when analyzing participation rates of Local 371 members, it is necessary to consider the effects of organizing within an institutional body, the prevailing effects of the voting rights and civil rights legislation, and the activist history of Local 371, as well as the salient issues that surrounded the 2004 election.[8]

So how can we explain the increased participation and turnout rates of black union members? Pinderhughes (1995) suggested that several factors contribute to increased turnout rates of minorities, including aggressive voter mobilization organizations. SSEU Local 371 and its leadership have addressed national issues and linked them to local issues that directly affect its membership. In several interviews, union members linked the practices of international multi-billion-dollar corporations to the plights of labor union members and nonunion workers. In several of the interviews I conducted with members of the union, they repeated the belief that the overall mission of labor unions is under attack by the right wing and multinational corporations. Therefore, while Democratic Party affiliations and the overall hostile electoral and political climate may motivate black labor members, it is apparent that their union affiliation and attitudes, beliefs, and the behaviors of their executive leaders have been a significant catalyst in participation rates in local and national elections.

President Ensley used his knowledge and relationships with members of the civil rights movement to infuse the spirit and level of political ethos into the union and larger New York City labor politics (Maier 1987). As a result, black SSEU Local 371 member participation in the electoral process has been unusually high compared to that of blacks in the general population. Observing the national data over a twenty-year period, union membership positively affects blacks' propensities to vote.[9] Seventy-two percent of black union member respondents participate in the voting process, compared to 62 percent of black nonunion members.[10] Thus, there are reasons to consider the union as a mobilizing and organizing institution that contributes to a group sense of participation, an individual level of motivation, and an issue educating institution (Levi 2003).

At the same time, there are important top-down features of Local 371 that contribute to the increases in political participation. It is likely that the presence of a long-standing and dynamic leader of Local 371 has contributed to the ethos of participation and turnout. The presence of steady union leadership serves as a stabilizing source of information and political education for labor union affiliated immigrant populations in the United States. One member stated:

> Stable leadership is always good. Charles has given it a sense of stability. The union used to change leadership like people change shoes. Since Charles has brought in a stabilizing force, work is getting done! Turnout for elections within the union is extremely low which indicates people are satisfied. Our union hasn't had a major issue to deal with in recent history, so people don't turn out to vote in *our* labor elections, but they do in national elections.

The lack of participation among SSEU Local 371 members in their own labor elections could possibly have attributed to what D. C. Nelson (1979) defined as political trust, such that respondents who exhibited high levels of political trust were less likely to vote and participate because they had faith in their elected officials to represent them.[11] Because of the convert and overt racism that continues to plague native-born and foreign-born blacks despite economic gains, subsequent distrust persists among black groups (Nunnally 2012). Therefore, the lack of participation in local labor elections presents an interesting quandary. If blacks do not participate because of systemic racial discrimination and political marginalization, as Nunnally suggests, reasons for their lack of participation in local labor elections present the opposite justification. In interviews, several members expressed their complete confidence in President Ensley as a leader who delivered "results." These results, members explained, were largely related to the bargaining agreements and political dealings with city hall and the mayor of New York City. As I probed deeper in the interviews, one member stated, "It doesn't matter if the mayor is a Democrat or a Republican, Charles [Ensley] can work with them to get us results." What appears to be a considerable level of faith in the labor leadership helps explain, on the one hand, the increased levels of black political participation in national elections because of union mobilization and leadership. On the other hand, we find decreased political participation in internal labor elections because of elevated levels of political trust, something rarely seen among blacks when expressing their political interests.

Cregan (2005) has argued that workers are more likely to join a union if a group ethos emerges in the workplace. There are constant reminders of the philosophy of Local 371: fighting for social and political justice, battling against injustices throughout the city that affect not only the labor members but the populations they serve, and understanding that collective action results in reactions and change. These three primary factors have also affected overall union voting rates for the past several election cycles, as one member stated:

> Being in the union has sobered me and has helped me to listen more. We're being so fragmented if we don't agree on everything; we must agree on one or two things if we are to succeed. (1) We need to look at big box corporations as criminals and not the immigrants or people of color. They are the victims of these corporations who want to exploit them. (2) We need to go back to the good old-fashioned boycotting. Send a message. We are the biggest consumers, and [if] we don't send a message, we are in trouble. If we want to fix it, we must come to a consensus.

The importance of members linking their individual struggles to the larger needs of their various groups—racial, ethnic, union, neighborhood, or economic—provides a foundation for our understanding of Local 371's success in larger group mobilization. Some of the activities, instigated by the union leadership to assist in member engagement, involve canvassing for candidates, attending political events, and providing forums for candidate and political issue education for members. How individuals' social environment aids in strengthening their political participation is largely a factor of group mobilization (Leighley 2001). Mobilization by union leadership, as well as the interest of the rank-and-file membership, has largely led to the above-average participation rates of Local 371 members. The intersection of distinct ethnic identity and overarching racial categorization has significant effects on one's attitudes and behaviors once in the United States. National ethnic identity directly affects the ways in which black immigrants view race. There exists both a duality and multifaceted integration of national origin and black racial identification for black immigrants once they are in America. Therefore, this analysis further complicates the existing literature that emphasizes the model Caribbean immigrant striving for the American Dream while enduring racism, prejudice, and institutional discrimination (Foner 2001; Waters 1999a; Kasinitz 1992). It extends the analyses of Afro-Caribbean and African immigrants simultaneously benefiting from white perceptions of the distinctions between foreign-born blacks and their black American counterparts (Kasinitz 1992; Rogers 2006), while these newer black ethnic groups simultaneously benefit from the previous civil rights struggles of black Americans. By comparing Afro-Caribbean and African immigrants with black Americans controlling for occupational status and class,[12] I am able to more accurately measure and interpret the attitudes and opinions of both native and foreign-born blacks.

Voter participation is largely related to socioeconomic factors such as education, income, and also race. Research has shown that occupation, political climate, and culture can have significant independent effects on individuals' political activities, both in traditional and nontraditional forms (Brady, Verba, and Schlozman 1995; Verba et al. 1993; D. C. Nelson 1979). People express themselves through varying forms of political participation based on their desire to solve a particular problem or set of problems. D. C. Nelson's (1979) work on ethnicity and socioeconomic status observed that social scientists have been unwilling to conceive ethnicity as an enduring element of social division. He also observed that ethnicity and subsequent social class status have been derived from social characteristics such as race, religion, and nationality. Further, several scholars have argued that ethnicity is an essential source of political participation (Junn et al. 2011; Junn and Haynie 2008; Bashi 2007; D. C. Nelson 1979; Greeley 1972).

Questions about political participation extend beyond race and ethnicity. Participation of individuals and groups must be supported by institutional mechanisms as Fuchs, Minnite, and Shapiro (2001) argued: Urban communities with lower socioeconomic statuses and communities that are disproportionately inhabited by people of color and immigrants lack social capital.[13] This scarcity of social capital explains the weakness and often times dearth of social networks[14] existing within an urban or inner-city population (McAdam, McCarthy, and Zald 1996; Berry, Portney, and Thomson 1993; W. J. Wilson 1987). Moreover, social institutions capable of facilitating and promoting social capital and networks are in decline in these areas, and "the bridges required for systemic political change in America's poor urban communities require political organizations that emphasize the value of traditional forms of political engagement, especially voting" (Fuchs, Minnite, and Shapiro 2001: 294). Therefore, for many members of SSEU Local 371, their voluntary membership in an organization that promotes social capital through electoral participation further engages members in political activity (Coleman 1988; Fuchs, Minnite, and Shapiro 2001).

Black immigrants—those who maintain their cultural identity as separate from their black American identity, whether self-imposed or imposed by external groups—have straddled two camps: that of their home country, and that of their new identity as blacks in America. The political organization of newly arrived and also first-generation black immigrants shows that time away from a home country decreases one's likelihood of participating in the activities of one's country of ancestry. Immigrants experience several barriers to incorporation and political participation, due to disruption in past home country participation patterns, broken social networks, and possible losses of social and economic status once in the United States (Jones-Correa 1998b). Therefore, organizing immigrants, within a group, presents additional obstacles for political participation (Lee 2011; Lee, Ramakrishnan, and Ramirez 2006).

The significance of joining a union and the subsequent increases in social and political capital mobilizes individuals to participate. However, the political distrust of blacks toward the government still exists, even within the mobilizing institution of a union. In survey data, blacks were more likely than whites to express greater political distrust. This distrust, scholars contended, translated into a political efficacy that encouraged unconventional tactics and modes of participation (Tate 1993, 1991; Gurin and Epps 1975), depending on race, class, and region (Shingles 1981). Therefore, blacks' sense of political efficacy and trust translated into increased political involvement and activity in various forms (Tate 2004; Gay 2002; Shingles 1981; Muller 1977; Gamson 1968). High levels of participation for blacks with low levels of trust in the government were also affected by personal efficacy (Shingles 1981; Guterbock 1980). Dawson (1994) argued that blacks' political participation and group interests hinged largely on the belief that their lives were, to some degree, determined by what happened to the group as a whole.[15] For blacks, if distrust, political efficacy, participation, and interest are largely determined by past ancestral experiences in the United States and shared group oppression (Verba and Nie 1972), then to what extent will the participatory tendencies of black immigrant groups be affected?

It is very likely that the social climate set forth by SSEU Local 371 leadership, the unique level of various forms of political participation, and its continued ties with the civil rights and social justice movements have all affected the participation rates of this particular group of respondents. The unique characteristics of SSEU Local 371 members make national comparisons a necessary component in explaining the behaviors of black ethnic populations in an urban labor context. Both the SSEU Local 371 black ethnic members and blacks on the national level have been consistently aligned with the Democratic Party for the past five decades. Their sustained Democratic Party loyalty raises important questions pertaining to the relationships of their demographic profile, their political partisanship, efficacy, and ultimate participation.

Black Voting, Presidential Elections, and Union Identification

The extent to which union membership shapes the participation levels of black ethnic members can be seen in their participation levels in local and national elections. The 2005–6 Social Services Employees Union Local 371 Survey reveals that 95 percent of black American union members, 85 percent of Afro-Caribbeans, and 78 percent of African respondents voted in the 2004 national election, compared to 82 percent of black union member and 75 percent of nonunion black respondents in the 2004 NES. According to the 2004 US Census Current Population Study, overall black participation peaked at 60 percent for the 2004 national election, compared to 44 percent of the New York State blacks who voted in 2004. The significant numbers of black members who voted from this particular New York City labor union suggest the effects labor membership and union leadership have on voter participation. The 2004 Current Population Survey (CPS) found that nationally 64 percent of whites voted in the 2004 presidential election, compared to 60 percent of blacks and 47 percent of Latinos. Table 3.1 reports voting by race on the national and state level.

At the state level, the percentage of New York voters in the 2004 presidential election was below the national average. The voting percentages of citizens in New York State are also substantially less than the percentage of Local 371 members. In addition, increased rates of political participation for all groups are evident in the 2008 presidential election. Black, white, and Latino groups all voted at greater rates in the 2008 presidential election. However, blacks had the greatest percent increase in voting. As many scholars have documented, the excitement of contributing to the historic election of the first black president was a motivating factor for many in America, especially blacks (Lee 2011; Bonilla-Silva 2010). As table 3.2 shows, the voting rate for black members of Local 371 was well above the 2004 NES and the 2004 Current Population Survey national averages for black respondents, by 11 and 26 percentage points, respectively.

Table 3.1 **2004 and 2008 Presidential Voting on National and State Level (in percentages)**

	All Groups	Blacks	Whites	Latinos
2004 National	65	60	64	47
2004 State Level	53	44	58	31
2008 National	64	65	66	50

Sources: Current Population Survey 2004; [1] Pew Research Center 2009[1] The 2004 Current Population Survey does not disaggregate black ethnic populations for voting in the 2004 national election.

Table 3.2 **2004 Presidential Voting for Black Respondents (in percentages)**

	Local 371 Survey	2004 NES	2004 CPS National Level	2004 CPS New York State
%	86	75	60	44
N	248	164	14,016,000	1,042,000

Sources: 2005–6 SSEU Local 371 Survey; 2004 NES (Cumulative File); CPS-2004.

The differences in percentages between SSEU Local 371 members and the NES national sample of black voters in the 2004 presidential election suggest the significance of union membership. The significance of labor membership on the national level is also evident when, among the 2004 NES respondents who self-reported as union members, turnout in the 2004 presidential election was 78 percent. For *black* union members in the 2004 NES, their 2004 presidential election turnout was 82 percent, compared to the 86 percent for black union members from Local 371 (see chart 3.1).

Although voter turnout has declined steadily since the 1960s, NES voting turnout has not (Burden 2000; Gronke 1992). The gaps between NES self-reporting and voting-eligible population estimates are highest during national election years (Martinez 2003). It is necessary to note that, for the 2004 NES, there were only 172 black respondents total, 28 of whom were union

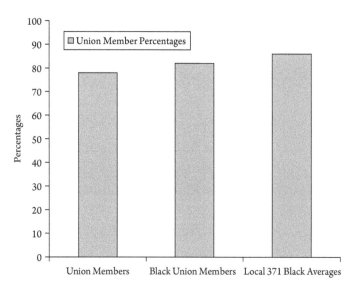

Chart 3.1 2004 NES Union and Local 371 Member Percentages: Voting in 2004 Presidential Election

Source: NES Cumulative File 1948–2004; 2005–6 SSEU Local 371 Survey

members. Twenty-three (or 82 percent) of the 28 black union members voted in the 2004 presidential election, as compared to 82 (or 56 percent) of the 144 black respondents who voted in the 2004 presidential election, were not union members. Several scholars have analyzed the overreporting of voting in the NES (Abramson et al. 1992; McDonald 2003). They argue that citizens most likely feel pressure to vote and thus misrepresent their propensity to vote, even when they fail to participate in elections. Overreporting is most common in districts with large concentrations of African American and Latino voters (Bernstein, Chadha, and Montjoy 2001). Also, the NES asks respondents to self-report voting.

It is important to remember that even though blacks face racialized obstacles such as feelings of political, social, and racial distrust in the political realm, they still find ways to engage in political discourse and political activities (Pinderhughes 1997b; McAdam, McCarthy, and Zald 1996). However, the extent to which a group participates is dependent on the availability of resources derived from economic and social institutions (Brady, Verba, and Schlozman 1995; Verba et al. 1993). For SSEU Local 371 members, the union serves as a multidimensional organization that encompasses economic, social, and political resources. Black union members' participation in the mayoral election of 2001 was slightly lower than their participation in the presidential election of 2004 (see table 3.3) (Browning, Marshall, and Tabb 2003).[16] However, the rates of Local 371 participation in local election are significantly higher than the average voting rates of New York City residents in local elections. The decreased level of local political participation in local elections could be attributed to a few factors. First, New York City local elections are held in "off" years. The original impetus behind the "off year" decision was to increase political participation and attention to local-level candidates and

Table 3.3 **Ethnic Voting in the 2001 Mayoral and 2004 Presidential Elections (in percentages)**

	Black Amers	Afro-Caribs Mbrs	Africans	Whites	Latinos	2004 NES Black Union
% who voted in election						
2001	90	70	56	73	85	–
2004	95	85	78	93	93	82
N	132	47	91	41	53	28

Sources: 2005–6 SSEU Local 371 Survey; NES 2004.

issue by asking voters to focus on an election without the interference of national-level campaigns, candidates, commercials, and overarching national issues. However, the odd-year elections, in addition to the local-level achievements of candidates of color in various citywide positions, has also contributed to the decreased level of participation in New York local elections, when compared to participation in presidential election years (Browning, Marshall, and Tabb 1984).

The high percentage of Local 371 respondent voting is particularly noteworthy due to the activism of Local 371 with respect to the local city government.[17] Scholars note that turnout for local and lesser elections are usually bolstered if those elections are held in the same years as national elections. The increases in voting in national elections are evident among all SSEU Local 371 members,when comparing the 2001 local mayoral election to the 2004 national presidential election. Black Americans' national-level voting has not reached the same levels as that of Local 371 members, particularly black Americans and Afro-Caribbean members. It is important to note the effects of union membership on the contribution to local-level politics. Although unions serve as invaluable organizing agents for national presidential elections, often delivering money, manpower, campaign resources, and votes to particular candidates, the significance of unions on local-level elections is of great import to mayors and city council members alike (Delaney, Masters, and Schwochau 1988).

White and Latino members, as well, exhibit increases in voting from the 2001 local election to the 2004 presidential election. White Local 371 voting increased by twenty points, while for Latino members it increased by eight. Seventy-three percent of white members reported voting in the 2001 mayoral election, and 93 in the 2004 national election, compared to 85 percent of Latinos in 2001 and 93 in 2004. Ultimately, all Local 371 respondents, regardless of race or ethnicity, exhibited an increased electoral participation level when comparing percentages of voters in the 2001 mayoral election versus the 2004 presidential election. It is useful to compare black ethnic increases in voting from 2001 to 2004, and also presidential voting among other blacks at the national level. The 1984–2004 NES data reveals that black (and white) voting gradually increased over that period (see figure 3.1). In 1984, 65 percent of blacks reported voting, compared to 75 percent in 2004. Similarly, observing the NES 2004, 76 percent of whites reported that they had voted in 1984, compared to 81 percent in 2004. For both groups, fewer percentages of respondents stated they had voted in off-year elections.[18]

Consistently, the voting rates of black respondents in Local 371 were higher than those of their white counterparts, whereas, according to the

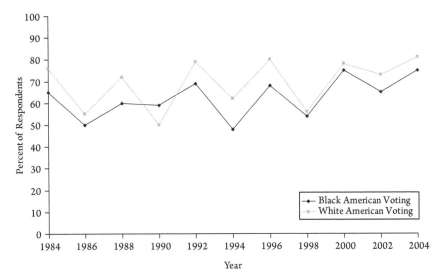

Figure 3.1 NES 1984–2004 White and Black American Voting in Presidential Elections
Source: NES Cumulative File 1948–2004

1984–2004 NES data (see table 3.4), the percentage of whites voting in national elections was greater than that of black Americans. Theories of political participation expect blacks to participate at lower rates than whites in the aggregate (Tate 1991), and this holds in the 2004 NES data: 81 percent of white survey respondents reported that they voted in the 2004 presidential election compared to 75 percent of blacks. This contrasts with black Local 371 members, who participated more than their white counterparts, particularly in the 2001 local election.[19] The increased local-level participation by black Local 371 members could be attributed to the tangible results of local New York City elections. Local 371 member contracts are negotiated with the New York City mayor subsequent elected and appointed members of the mayor's choosing. Therefore, Local 371 member interest in local New

Table 3.4 **NES 1984–2004 Black Voting (percentages who voted)**

	1984	1986	1988	1990	1992	1994	1996	1998	2000	2002	2004
Black	65	50	60	59	69	48	68	54	75	65	75
White	76	55	72	50	79	62	80	56	78	73	81
Black N	221	327	218	259	289	202	179	153	161	125	164
White N	1,208	919	987	738	1,353	863	935	529	925	777	617

Source: NES Cumulative File 1948–2004.

Table 3.5 **Black Local 371 Member Voting and Eligibility in 2004 Election (in percentages)**

	Black Americans	Afro-Caribbeans	Africans	Whites	Latinos
Yes	95	85	78	93	93
No	2	2	8	7	6
Not Eligible	3	13	14	0	2
N	134	46	91	41	54

Source: 2005–6 SSEU Local 371 Survey.

York City politics has very real potential benefits or punishments depending on city-elected leaders.

The divide among blacks in Local 371 who were not eligible to vote in the 2004 election should also be noted. Table 3.5 reports that 13 percent of Afro-Caribbean and 14 percent of African union members reported that they were not eligible to vote, compared to 3 percent of blacks in the union. Respondents who indicated that they chose not to vote in the 2004 presidential election were classified differently from respondents who were not eligible to vote and thus did not participate in the 2001 or 2004 elections. By contrast, all white respondents indicated that they were eligible to vote, and only 2 percent of Latinos stated they were ineligible (see appendix 3B for citizenship percentages).

Labor Education, Membership, and Theories of Participation

In my interviews, President Ensley stated that education regarding the political process, candidate backgrounds, and policy stances have been a significant part of labor leadership, complimenting the institutional educational background the members already possess. He explained that the union does not support parties; rather, it supports individual candidates, and in doing so, it aims to provide the best electoral representation for the union:

> In our union, it's not the party, it's the individual candidates political persuasion that's important to us. We don't support candidates just because they're the presumed winners; we support people who are best for the union. We support candidates who have supported our issues, who cares if they're the presumed winner.

The union leadership indicated that it is their aim to provide political education to its members in hopes of creating a more politically efficacious body of workers. One member stated:

> The membership is changing and our way of organizing must reflect the new immigrant management. We must be more holistic and learn to communicate in different ways. We must balance our communication styles. Rigidity and the same rule of thumb won't work anymore, we must listen to the rapidly changing membership. I must be "multilingual" no matter what the issue is. The change in language is understanding how to communicate with new populations and as social workers we do a bad job of taking care of one another. The job must get done and the easiest way to get the job done is to understand what works.

Research has indicated that individuals with a sense of efficacy, civic duty, and those who possess a general interest in politics are more likely to participate in the political process. In addition, education levels are major determinants of political participation (Verba and Nie 1972). Local 371's combination of high levels of formal education combined with an institutional framework of political education have created an exceptionally participatory group of members.

Verba and Nie (1972) found that blacks with similar socioeconomic statuses as whites participated at higher rates than whites. The blacks in the current study are not "resource poor"—that is, they do not lack political skills, information bases, or significant levels of education. The political resources of this unique population contribute to the basic motivations that are essential for political participation. However, as Verba and Nie (1972) also observed, "resource rich" black populations were still less inclined than their white colleagues to trust the government and political leaders. They found that overall these groups felt more alienated. This ties in directly to Dawson's (1994) theories surrounding blacks with increased education and occupational success and their increased attachment to lower-income blacks, despite their middle- and upper-class attachments. The differences between black and white participation rates were attributed to a level of race consciousness present among blacks of higher socioeconomic statuses. Blacks who were of a higher socioeconomic status were also more conscious of their race and how it affected one's political choices (Verba and Nie 1972).

The constant reminders of the civil rights struggles and the triumphs of black leaders within larger labor struggles should not be understated. The permanence of a black labor president for over twenty years in Local 371 has most significantly contributed to a more race-conscious union population. One union member stated that their labor struggle has been constantly linked to larger national struggles. It is this mentality that enables workers to link their social service occupations with other and larger choices, thereby linking labor, race, social injustices, and overall participation. One member explained,

> A union is a lifestyle choice. One must make decisions if they are to be a part of labor. I have made decisions not to go to Starbucks or Walmart, because anything that affects workers [affects me].

President Ensley believed that even though race and ethnicity should not make a substantial difference in labor leadership, sometimes they did. He observed:

> It's human nature. In a real sense of a true union model it wouldn't make a difference. You'd elect the best leadership regardless of gender, race, et cetera. 1199 is predominantly black but they elected a Latino and that's a good thing because they find him an effective leader. A successful model is based on talent, but ethnicity and race do play a role.[20]

Scholars have expounded on Verba and Nie's theory and added that groups who feel their members lack relative resources when compared to other groups are more likely to be politically active (Miller et al. 1981).[21] Blacks living in the United States have experienced the negative effects of race baiting, pandering, and tactics used to frighten one racial group into allying with another, for fear of the third "taking over" (Bobo and Hutchings 1996; Olzak 1992). However, it is unclear to what extent neat racial categories such as "black" actually encompass likeminded individuals or merely individuals who look alike. The press has been unsure how the interactions of newly emerging ethnic groups will translate into cooperation or possible coalitions among these groups. For example, one columnist from the *New York Times* wrote:

> The demographic shifts, which gained strength in the 1960's after changes in federal immigration law led to increased migration from Africa and Latin America, have been accompanied in some places by fears that newcomers might eclipse native-born [blacks]. And they have touched off delicate musings about ethnic labels, identity and the often unspoken differences among people who share the same skin color. (Swarns 2004)

Thus, interethnic distrust threatens to disrupt varying forms of political participation. For some, perceptions of interethnic resource competition may either promote unified political activities in the form of partisan politics and participation, or result in the suppression of political participation, in the form of political apathy.

Partisan Politics and Ethnic Distinctions

During in-depth interviews with members of Local 371, some members contextualized the unusually high levels of black union member turnout in elections. They believed that, in addition to the leadership that supports and promotes rank-and-file participation and the significantly high education levels of its union members, factors that contributed to the high black union member turnout in the 2004 presidential election included the political climate and circumstances surrounding the election of 2004, on the heels of the contested and highly partisan presidential election of 2000. The efforts of Democratic institutions to target labor organizations for assistance in the election of Democratic nominee John Kerry in 2004 contributed to the high turnout of black union members, who disproportionately identified as Democrats.

There is a long-standing history of black populations overwhelmingly supporting the Democratic Party. In the NES 1984–2004 data, union members were more likely than nonunion members to identify with the Democratic Party (see table 3.6). The additional effect of union membership on black

Table 3.6 **1984–2004 NES Union and Nonunion Party Identification (in percentages)**

	Blacks		Whites		Latinos	
	Union	Nonunion	Union	Nonunion	Union	Nonunion
Strong Democrat	47	41	20	13	25	21
Weak Democrat	24	23	20	16	29	26
Independent Democrat	16	16	15	12	20	13
Independent	7	9	9	11	11	13
Independent Republican	3	4	13	14	4	11
Weak Republican	0	3	14	18	4	10
Strong Republican	2	2	9	16	7	5
Don't Know	1	2	0	1	0	1
N	233	1,723	2,678	11,674	179	954

Source: NES Cumulative File 1948–2004.

Democratic Party identification is a significant finding in that it strengthens an already solidified race-party identification.

Combining strong and weak Democratic identification at the national level, table 3.6 shows that 71 percent of black union members identify with the Democratic Party, compared to 64 percent of black nonunion members.[22] Among whites and Latinos, union members identified with the Democratic Party more than nonunion members did: 40 percent of white union members, compared to 29 percent of nonunion affiliates, identified as either strong or weak Democrats. Similarly, 54 percent of Latino union members identified as strong or weak Democrats, compared to 47 percent of nonmembers. Although the percentage differences in party identification are not drastic, the consistent evidence of increased Democratic Party identification among union members is still impressive.

For the black Local 371 members who reported that they had voted in the 2004 election, combining those who identified as either strong, weak, or independent Democrats, the percentage of Democrats ranged from 88 percent for black Americans to 79 percent for Afro-Caribbeans, 83 percent for Africans, and 82 percent for blacks in the 2004 NES. The 2005 and 2006 New Americans Exit Poll asked with which party survey respondents were registered. Eighty-seven percent of black respondents were registered Democrats in 2005 and 88 percent in 2006 (see table 3.7a).[23]

Further, observing the 2004 NES, only 32 percent of blacks identified as strong Democrats. The responses from blacks in the national sample show Democratic Party strength levels at 13 to 22 percentage points less than for SSEU Local 371 members (see table 3.7b).

There is significant correlation of union membership on increased levels of partisanship. However, the increased levels of partisanship do not presuppose that black voters are completely satisfied with the Democratic Party. One member went on to say, "Go with the devil you know." Similar sentiments were expressed throughout several interviews with Local 371 members. In the survey, SSEU Local 371 members were asked how they felt toward the Democratic Party. The question was worded as follows:

> Feeling Thermometers. These questions seek to measure how you feel toward a particular group. When you see the name of a group, I would like you to rate it with a feeling thermometer. Ratings between 50–100 degrees mean that you feel favorably or warm toward the group. Similarly, ratings between 0–50 represent that you do not feel favorably toward the group and you do not care too much for the group. If you do not feel particularly warm or cold toward a group, you can rate them at 50. If you come to a group you do not know much about, you may

Table 3.7a **Condensed Table of Party Identification for Voters (in percentages)**

	Blacks	Afro-Car	Africans	2004 NES Blacks	2005 NAEP Blacks	2006 NAEP Blacks	2006 NAEP Carib
Democrat	88	79	83	82	87	88	87
Independent/ Other	3	11	7	11	2	2	3
Republican	3	0	4	7	5	5	5
Don't Know/ No Party	6	11	6	0	6	5	5
N	125	38	70	186	381	379	106

$p < 0.01$.

Sources: 2005–6 SSEU Local 371 Survey; 2004 National Election Study; 2005 and 2006 New American Exit Polls.

Table 3.7b **Party Identification (in percentages)**

	Blacks	Afro-Car	Africans	2004 NES Blacks	2005 NAEP Blacks
Strong Democrat	52	45	54	32	Democrat 87
Weak Democrat	10	16	9	30	
Independent-Democrat	26	18	20	20	
Independent	3	11	7	11	Other 2
Independent-Republican	2	0	1	5	
Weak Republican	1	0	1	1	
Strong Republican	0	0	1	1	Republican 5
Don't Know	6	10	6	0	No Party 6
N	125	38	70	186	381

$p < 0.01$.

Sources: 2005–6 SSEU Local 371 Survey; 2004 National Election Study; 2005 New American Exit Poll.

refuse to answer. Please write your feeling thermometer score on the line next to the word listed below.

The responses were coded into a seven-point scale.[24] When comparing means of black Local 371 members, African union members were most likely to report warm feelings toward the Democratic Party at 79.6, compared to 73.3 for black Americans, and 68.1 for Afro-Caribbean members (see table 3.8). The means for Local 371 blacks were overall less than the reported mean of 83.06 for black NES 2004 respondents. This finding presents an interesting puzzle in that Local 371 members had greater levels of voting in national elections when compared to national-level black voting responses. However, Local 371 positive feelings toward the Democratic Party were considerably less than national-level black responses. The means reported for all black respondents' feelings of warmth toward the Democratic Party in both Local 371 and NES respondent data were considerably greater than the reported means for feelings of warmth toward the Republican Party. The mean identification with the Republican Party for NES black respondents was 54.14. In comparison, the reported means for black union members were 27.3 for black Americans, 26.1 for Afro-Caribbeans, and 42.2 for African respondents.

The means for black ethnic party thermometers indicate that African respondents have the most warm feelings toward both the Democratic and Republican Parties. The overwhelming warmth for the Democratic Party may suggest a combination of the strength of African immigrant positive association with an organized small-*d* democratic body, as well as an affinity to the party due to past civil rights struggles linking black populations with the Democratic Party. African immigrants were also the group most inclined to demonstrate the warmest feelings toward the Republican Party. Compared to the cool feelings exhibited by black American and Afro-Caribbean populations, the warmth exhibited by the African union members possibly suggests African immigrants' warm feelings toward a dual-party system. A more detailed explanation for African respondent levels of warmth toward parties could be attributed to African members who indicated that they hailed from a weak political state. The warmer feelings toward the Republican Party could be indicative of warm feelings toward a democratic two-party system. One African member of the union said, "Being from a dictatorship helps you appreciate democracy and political parties." The vast majority of African survey respondents indicated they hailed from a country with weak or very weak political stability (see appendix 3C). No African respondents indicated that their home country was "very stable"; they were more likely to indicate that they had migrated from a home country with relatively weak political stability. Some factors that contributed to African respondents' beliefs that they

Table 3.8 **Democrat and Republican Thermometers**

Democrats

	Blacks	Afro-Car	Africans	2004 NES Blacks
Cool Feelings	1	5	1	1
2	3	2	0	2
3	3	2	0	3
4	31	26	16	8
5	8	21	13	40
6	15	16	28	25
Warm Feelings	39	28	42	22
N	119	43	79	175
p < 0.05				p < 0.05
Means (standard errors in parentheses)	73.3 (2.21)	68.1 (3.92)	79.6 (2.25)	83.06 (.462)

Republicans

	Blacks	Afro-Car	Africans	2004 NES Blacks
Cool Feelings	42	44	19	25
2	13	9	14	6
3	5	14	6	14
4	31	28	41	25
5	4	5	11	24
6	4	0	4	3
Warm Feelings	0	0	5	2
N	121	43	79	173
p < 0.10				p < 0.01
Means (standard errors in parentheses)	27.3 (2.30)	26.1 (3.57)	42.2 (2.84)	54.14 (.740)

Sources: 2005–6 SSEU Local 371 Survey; 2004 National Election Study. The overall means (standard errors in parentheses) for each Party Thermometer were Democratic Party 71.99 (1.29) and Republican Party 32.17 (1.39) for black respondents.

hailed from a country with weak political stability were likely linked to the sociopolitical events following independence struggles. Several other African nations experienced civil wars after they received independence from British, Belgian, Portuguese, and French governments. Experiencing dictatorships, dire economic conditions, military decrees, and limited advanced educational opportunities following independence surely contributed to Africans' reports of weak political stability. Many African nations have had weak party and fragile democratic systems, which have often led to dictatorial regimes (Ogbaa 2003).[25]

Although many Local 371 members identified as strong Democrats, many also expressed their indifference to the Democratic Party. One vented:

> Political parties still play a role, that is, identification as a Democrat or Republican. We are still dissatisfied with the Democrats, but the first-generation immigrants are a lot more Republicanesque, and the Republican message is honing true to them, even though Republicans don't want them in the party.

Black immigrant union members also find themselves in a conundrum. Because of their new racial classification of "black" American, they identify with the Democratic Party on certain social justice issues. One member explained that it seemed like the Democrats were more willing to "work with diverse groups of people." In many ways, black immigrants behave similarly, politically, to their black American counterparts. Given the relatively small number of black immigrants compared to Latino groups, they find themselves most often aligning with the Democratic Party. Although no formal outreach to these groups by either party has visibly occurred, the substantial effects of "blackness" on their ethnic identity and the very fact of their membership within the union suggests alliances with the Democratic Party as the Republican Party has continued to grow increasingly more hostile toward labor.

These SSEU Local 371 members, then, still attach themselves to the Democratic Party either because of their race, because there is no viable alternative or "third" party, or because the Democratic Party is the party that purportedly most supports the labor movement and civil rights struggles. Many members interviewed, however, expressed not an overwhelming attachment to the Democratic Party, but an understanding that the political parties and labor are complex bedfellows. One member stated his frustration:

> We vote Democratically, but the AFL-CIO and AFSCME support Republicans depending on the election. Members are told to go and

vote Democratic (i.e., let's take back the Senate), but the pamphlet says support the Republican for this particular election, even if the candidate is saying he supports kicking immigrants out of the country.

Another member stated:

Members are now confused and this is keeping members from voting at all. Saying one thing and doing another, not being consistent, therefore, we can't get things done on the city or national level and therefore not supporting one team gets us nothing.

President Ensley previously stated that SSEU Local 371 supports the best candidate for the union, not solely the presumed winner. He did not say whether or not he, as the Local 371 leader, would support a Republican candidate. Even though SSEU national labor leaders court both parties, it is most commonly known, understood, and accepted that the Democratic Party and the labor party are somewhat synonymous. The flirtations of national labor leaders with the Republican Party presents a quandary for many union members who feel the Democratic Party does not fully serve their needs. However, by trying to straddle both parties, they feel as though they are ending up empty-handed. One member said, "The Democrats are more for us than the Republicans, and we keep giving them votes. But when do we start to see the promises the Democrats make to us?"

While some members feared that national labor leaders awkwardly attempt to straddle both parties, others feel the Democratic Party has made an effort to mobilize its "black base" with greater intensity than in the past. Some respondents indicated that the national leadership of labor organizations have become so entrenched within the Democratic Party that their efforts to increase member turnout and participation have come at a cost to rank-and-file members, as leaders seek to strengthen their own personal relationships with the Democratic Party. One member stated:

Political parties carry far too much weight. The global labor movement leaders are concerned with positions within the political parties more so than their rank-and-file members. Labor leaders get involved in campaigns at the expense of the workers. It appears that leaders are more concerned with influencing politics and now we're in a worse position. The focus is all wrong. We're no longer talking about a national labor president delivering for the people he represents. It's the party's respect he wants.

Essentially, union membership and party affiliation have had a significant impact on black union participation in national elections. As empowerment by blacks has increased, so has political involvement (Bobo and Gilliam 1990). It is clear that union leadership and extremely high levels of education have contributed to a viable and politically active body of union members. However, for this highly educated group, it appears that it is their union membership and not always their national union leadership that has contributed to their high level of electoral participation.

A focus on union membership and leadership as a mobilizing force that contributes to increased group political participation is evident in the organizational structure of Local 371 and the leadership of President Ensley. The social activist foundation of the union has mobilized members to participate in national-level politics as well as local-level elections at rates greater than nonunion groups, including nonunion black groups. The benefits of union membership and the stability of labor leadership and the subsequent political contributions to the polity are worth exploring further with different types of unions and various leadership styles throughout the United States. This research was conducted before the 2008 election and the presence of Barack Obama on the national ballot. However, the national data shows increases in black political participation from the presidential election of 2004 to 2008. One can largely conjecture that the participation of Local 371 members in the 2008 election was even greater than national averages. Although black ethnic Local 371 members illustrated similar participatory and partisanship tendencies, in the following chapter, I explore the interethnic relationship of black Local 371 members in the workplace.

CHAPTER 4

"You win some, you lose some"

HARD WORK AND THE BLACK PURSUIT OF
THE AMERICAN DREAM

There is no surer way of understanding the Negro or of being misun-
derstood by him than by ignoring manifest differences of condition and
power.
—W. E. B. Du Bois (1899)

In chapter 3, the significance of Local 371 membership on cohesive partisanship and subsequent participation were evident. The significance of union membership assisted in the creation of a relatively racially homogeneous interaction
with the political process. When compared to national data, the significance of
race and also union membership were made clear. Black groups strongly identify
with the Democratic Party at greater rates than whites both within the union and
within the national data.

In order to further highlight the similarities and differences within the black
population, this chapter offers a detailed account of the feelings and perceptions
of foreign-born and native-born black union members using the SSEU Local
371 survey. I argue that black intraracial differences, even if they are only subtle
nuances, elicit attitudes and opinions that greatly influence the US political system. I include a qualitative analysis of the genesis of many of these perceptions
and feelings of black groups living and working in New York City and how these
opinions affect black perceptions of the American Dream.

In this chapter, I analyze opinions pertaining to intraracial attitudes and perceptions of other black ethnic groups using SSEU data.[1] I focus on specific intraracial attitudes and opinions of native-born and foreign-born black populations
with respect to issues regarding intragroup solidarity and notions of elevated

minority status. Specifically, I ask three primary questions in this chapter: [2] (1) To what extent do negotiations with the American Dream divide black ethnics? (2) What perceptions do blacks have of each other once in the United States? (3) What are the implications for partnerships and future leadership?

I find that although Afro-Caribbean populations will ethnically distinguish themselves at times, they are also the group most ardently supportive of a black racial identity, and they articulate most forcefully the inequities persistent in the United States. These views differ from African populations who express positive opinions pertaining to the possibility for success in America and the least favorable attitudes toward other black ethnic groups. While black Americans expressed favorable attitudes toward other black ethnic groups, they reported a certain levels of threat pertaining to job security.

Exploring black ethnicity contributes to the understanding of black intraracial opinions and attitudes by separately investigating the significance of ethnicity.[3] Previous scholars have argued that the generational cycle for West Indians, and increased assimilation into black culture and society, at times, restricts opportunities for social success and incorporation. They observe that West Indians attempt to circumvent this perceived downward spiral into black American culture by clinging to their ethnic identities (Portes and Rumbaut 2001). They have further argued that the longer period of time West Indians remain in the United States, tensions with African Americans arise, which further complicate the formation of and negotiations with their racial and ethnic identities (Portes and Rumbaut 2001). As a result, I would expect that (1) newer arrived immigrants will express the most favorable attitudes and opinions toward the US government; (2) black ethnic groups will feel that nonblack groups residing in the United States are treated better than they are; and (3) all groups will feel most favorable to their own group and will also feel their group works the hardest.

My findings indicate that Afro-Caribbeans are the least optimistic about the possibilities for success once in the United States, unlike African respondents who are relatively optimistic about the prospects of hard work equaling success. Although each black ethnic group most closely identifies with their own specific ethnic group, there is also a significant level of racial group understanding of the inequities in treatment of black groups in the United States. The survey results reveal that black Americans view coalition possibilities in a more skeptical manner than their ethnic counterparts, while Afro-Caribbean and African respondents are more open to the possibilities of joining forces. African respondents are likely to view the United States as a land of opportunity, whereas Afro-Caribbean respondents more often view the United States as "closed" for *all* black ethnic groups. Black American opinions sometimes mimic the opinions of Afro-Caribbean respondents about the inability for blacks to succeed in America. However, black Americans are also the most skeptical in forming

partnerships with Afro-Caribbean and African groups. Because of these varying black ethnic responses, a complex blend of ethnicity, length of time in the
United States, and acculturation processes influence the differences between
black Americans, Afro-Caribbeans, and Africans.

Afro-Caribbean and African perceptions toward black American populations
create dual understandings of racial identification with phenotypically black
populations, on the one hand, and ethnic distinctions between people of African
descent, on the other. How black ethnic opinions are articulated, manifested,
and displayed as a result of particular groups' investment in the American Dream
has contributed to certain strains and interethnic difference. In addition, black
union member perceptions of themselves and other black ethnics and their position within the American democratic system contribute to varying negotiations
with possibilities for advancement and success.

Political identities and paths to incorporation have directly affected political
differences between blacks and whites in the United States. The objective of this
chapter is to offer an empirical analysis that expounds on previous qualitative
studies. The qualitative work of Kasinitz, Waters, Foner, and Rogers addresses
relationships between native-born black Americans and West Indian populations in a labor force, assimilation, residential, and political contexts, respectively. However, I explore how black populations view themselves, perceive their
black ethnic counterparts, and weigh the possibilities of intraracial group formation and partnerships. One's culture is both an independent and a dependent
variable, and one's attitude toward democratic liberties is strongly influenced by
one's position in the political system (de la Garza and Yetim 2003; Seligson and
Booth 1979). Therefore, by observing the intraracial attitudes of black ethnic
populations at a moment when black immigration, particularly African migration, is rising and significantly changing the landscape of black America, black
politics, and negotiations of race and political integrations, this work enables us
to view democracy in the "developmental process" for black groups in New York
City (de la Garza and Yetim 2003; Diamond and Plattner 1994).

Reuel Rogers's (2006) groundbreaking book *Afro-Caribbean Immigrants
and the Politics of Incorporation* identified the politics, identity, and residential
negotiations between Afro-Caribbean and black American groups living in
New York City, as well as the socioeconomic, home country, and ethnic status determinants that directly affect black racial and ethnic relations. Rogers
found that the existence of transnational ties for Afro-Caribbean populations
serve as emotional attachments for immigrants and influence their political
thinking, behavior, and views of themselves. The political and cultural attitudes and racial and ethnic group attachments inform how these immigrants
adapt and assimilate into the US polity. Rogers's analysis and approach provides a theoretical basis for intraracial distinctions among black American,

Afro-Caribbean, and African union member political beliefs, intraracial attitudes, and policy preferences.[4]

The arrival of new black populations has affected native-born black American interethnic perceptions and attitudes toward black immigrants. This increased migration of blacks from Africa and the Caribbean has had significant effects on native-born blacks' views of themselves, feelings toward other phenotypically similar immigrants, and questions surrounding their political future, relevance, and access to power. As the data in this chapter show, native-born black American opinions vacillate between feelings of solidarity with black immigrant populations and feelings of threat from foreign-born black populations who appear as competitors for jobs, resources, and overall political advancement in American democracy. Although Africans and Afro-Caribbeans express feelings of solidarity with black Americans, in congruence with previous scholarship, they also distinguish themselves as immigrants, and at times they subscribe to notions of an elevated minority status.

To reiterate, the concept of elevated minority black immigrant groups is that they are viewed, largely by nonblack groups, as elevated or "better" than native-born blacks. However, black immigrants are still not thought to possess the education levels, economic possibilities, and aspirations of other nonblack immigrant groups in the United States. This recognition of black immigrant groups as Americans with the mandatory modifier "black" not only distinguishes the black immigrant experience from all other immigrant groups, it also creates a combination of shared racial identity, ethnic maintenance, and occasional tensions regarding shared resources and racialized competition among black ethnic groups.

Black identity has intrigued scholars since the turn of the twentieth century—whether concerning native-born black Americans emerging as citizens in the South and rural areas, the migration patterns of native-born black Americans to budding urban centers in the North, or the complexities of integration and Jim Crow for black American and Afro-Caribbean workers during World War II (Baptiste 2003; Black and Black 1987). More recently, scholars have documented the interplay of native-born black American and Afro-Caribbean efforts to obtain equity in the job market, housing and neighborhoods, and even public office. Rogers (2006) has provided an excellent framework outlining the tenuous role of race and racism for native-born black American and Afro-Caribbean immigrants. And Sowell (1994) and James (1999) use the rise of black leadership to briefly illuminate the tangential rise of Caribbean leadership on the local and national level. They argue that the high rates of literacy, education, and organizing abilities assisted Caribbean leaders in achieving their radical political agendas in the United States.

Currently, the rise of African immigrants with varying migration narratives is further complicating the black leadership narrative. As African groups attain US education and move more solidly into the black middle and upper classes (Rimer and Arenson 2004), while other African groups work to establish themselves in any available US sector possible, the interplay of race and racism, coupled with diverse class statuses, will contribute to a complex blend of intraracial identity and solidarity at times, and interethnic and/or black interclass tensions at others.

Racial and Ethnic Distinctions: Shared Identity or Cultural Discord?

Ethnic difference occurs in a few ways. When people are hired and we have orientation, you notice the Africans all sit together, the black Americans, the Caribbeans, and now the North Africans sit together.
—Local 371 Member

In attempts to clarify and more accurately define ethnicity, researchers have indicated that there are subtle distinctions—real, perceived, and created—among black ethnic populations. What determines the extent of intraracial unified identity in some instances and interethnic conflict in others? Changes in attitudes and interethnic perceptions among blacks encompass (1) negotiations with white populations both positively and negatively, (2) intraracial interactions, (3) portrayals and perceptions of black Americans, and (4) individual and group expectations of life chances once in the United States.

My expectations can be grouped under two headings: (1) shared black identity and (2) historical and cultural distinction. The two central assumptions of intraracial black identity are that first, particular issues will elicit a distinct and significant overarching shared black identity. Also, black ethnic respondents will view their life chances in the United States as inextricably linked to those of other blacks. The second assumption rests on the consideration of historical and cultural distinctions of blacks. There are intraracial distinctions, and, depending on the issue, black populations will not always view other black ethnic groups as sharing the same linked fate.[5] Some scholars have contended that deep-seated differences exist largely among native-born black American and Afro-Caribbean immigrants.[6] Rogers (2006) stated that the different groups share common interests that could serve as a basis for coalition building. He argues, however, that interethnic conflicts surrounding descriptive representation deflect from a larger shared common interest. Rogers's evaluation involved analyzing the intragroup attitudes of blacks and the issues pertaining to public policies and immigration effects that directly concern black populations in the United States.

The most poignant difference between native-born and foreign-born black populations and the issue that threatens to disrupt larger black coalition formation stems largely from differing negotiations with the American Dream.

Hochschild (1995) argued in *Facing Up to the American Dream: Race, Class, and the Soul of the Nation* that, as immigrants, foreign-born groups demonstrate an acceptance, willingness, and eagerness to fulfill and experience the American Dream. This quest for attainment is further explained by what she has stated as a balance between "what the polity must do because individuals cannot and, on the other hand, what individuals must do because the polity cannot" (Hochschild 1995: xiv). As discussed in greater detail throughout this chapter, the Afro-Caribbeans surveyed in this study express great overall disillusionment with the capacity of the polity and therefore with the prospects for attaining the American Dream.

Hochschild (1995: xvii) has defined the American Dream as a goal that extends beyond the attainment of wealth and riches—as "the promise that all Americans have a reasonable chance to achieve success as they define it—material or otherwise—through their own efforts, and to attain virtue and fulfillment through success." Although Hochschild's analysis of the American Dream appears to lend itself primarily to an understanding of a binary evaluation of race and class between black and white populations due to continued racism against black peoples in the United States, many of Hochschild's theories regarding the pursuit of the American Dream apply to ethnic populations. She argued that "well off African Americans are intertwined with other blacks, both because they choose to be and because they cannot escape" (Hochschild 1995: 124). Similarly, Dawson's (1994) theory of linked fate also posits that class is a unifying factor for blacks in America. Therefore, in viewing the American Dream as an extended form of linked fate, my understanding of the American Dream presents an intertwined understanding of race, ethnicity, and class in its pursuit and attainment.

Comparing the intraracial attitudes of blacks residing in the United States presents an interesting puzzle. Dawson (1994) has argued that much of the formation of social identity rests on the process of comparing in-group and out-group members. At first glance, native-born black Americans, as nonimmigrants,[7] would presumably be considered the in-group and thus possess a stronger group identity.[8] However, since black immigrants to the United States have been largely viewed and analyzed by scholars as somehow "different" from their black American counterpart, that is—better-educated, harder-working, and more successful as wage earners—black *immigrant* status may lend itself to a more in-group status when compared to native-born black Americans. Views of black immigrant elevated minority statuses have been promoted by scholars, whites, other racial and ethnic groups, black immigrants, and even native-born blacks themselves. The question of whether the concept of black immigrant elevated minority status and its long-term benefits in the American polity is fact or fiction still presents a peculiar placement for foreign-born blacks as possible members of the group most closely aligned with the dominant social in-group.

Two crucial components are necessary in evaluating intraracial black identity and attitudes. For group identity to affect blacks living in the United States, the assumption of a larger linked fate must be present in the minds of native-born black Americans and black immigrants—that is, what happens to the entire group affects the members' own individual lives (Dawson 1994).[9] Evidence of the construction of this linked identity could be articulated through the instances and evaluations of violence, historical and present-day, toward blacks in the United States and throughout the globe. One may argue that widespread populations of blacks, as a result of the international slave trade, have created a sense, possibly a false sense, of an overwhelming African or "pan-black" diaspora.[10] However, there are several factors that link blacks living in America, thereby creating a set of shared characteristics, histories, circumstances, or cultural norms that bind and connect them.[11] It appears that Africans residing in America have largely sought to find a sort of strength in numbers by identifying and finding common ground with other Africans living away from their native homelands, Africans who are not necessarily from their particular country, ethnic group, or region.[12] Penn (2008: 6) has argued that "ethnic groupings are fixed, but identities are not." This type of strength and sometimes safety in numbers has created a diasporic growth of African peoples living abroad in the United States.

The second crucial component involves the recognition of the cultural, social, and political diversity among black Americans and African and Caribbean immigrants. Increased migration has created a significant heterogeneous population that is often defined as a monolithic group, due to phenotypic characteristics and complexions (i.e., skin color), even though substantial ethnic differences are exhibited. The underlying motivation of this study is to examine the content of the composition and attitudes of blacks in America.

I initially theorized that the most recently arrived immigrants would be the most accepting of the American Dream and populations who had resided in the United States the longest would be the least accepting—that black Americans who had resided in the United States the longest would feel the most disillusioned with the prospects for full incorporation, equality, and success. With this initial hypothesis, I placed black ethnic respondents on a continuum, with African respondents as the most eager to accept the notion of this dream, Afro-Caribbeans as second most likely to accept it, and black Americans as least likely.

Don't Accept Dream				*Accept American Dream*
Black Americans	-----	Afro-Caribbeans	-----	Africans

However, both the quantitative and qualitative data reveal that Afro-Caribbeans' positive attitudes toward the American Dream have been mostly abandoned. The continuum of black ethnic feelings toward the attainment of the American Dream for this group of highly educated, skilled, and relatively financially secure union members places black Americans between their ethnic counterparts:

	Don't Accept Dream			*Accept American Dream*	
Afro-Caribbeans	-----	Black Americans	-----	Africans	

Afro-Caribbeans expressed the greatest levels of disillusionment with the American polity, with prospects for advancement in the land of opportunity, and with its treatment of all black populations. Overall, they are the least optimistic when compared to other black ethnic groups. In contrast, African respondents express the greatest levels of trust in the American system in fulfilling its promises, so long as groups work hard and strive for success. African respondents express this belief in the American Dream while also believing that black populations are treated differently and sometimes unfairly once in America. Native-born black Americans say the American polity falls short yet does not fail in fulfilling its promise of the American Dream. They are perceived as, and also perceive themselves as, the least hardworking. Black Americans are also the most skeptical toward black immigrants.

The remainder of this chapter will dissect black interethnic feelings. If increased time in the United States ultimately leads to increased frustration and distrust and/or disbelief in the American Dream, then why are black Americans more optimistic than their Afro-Caribbean counterparts? What at first glance appears to be a contradiction can be explained by a few factors: generational effects, length of time in the United States, initial expectations, and exit options. The significant effect of raising children and/or being raised by immigrant parents in the United States (Portes and Rumbaut 2001), time in the United States and subsequent interactions with white and nonwhite populations, experiencing the sometimes negative effects of having black skin in the United States, and the inability to return to one's country of origin all contribute to a black ethnic experience unlike any other. Because of the negative effects of race and racism once in the United States, Afro-Caribbean groups are currently the least invested in the promises of the American Dream.

"Where are you *from* from?": Generational Effects and Disillusions with the Dream

The demographics of the black ethnic sample population show noteworthy generational effects.[13] The black American respondents are overwhelmingly native-born and raised in the United States—86 percent and 92 percent, respectively. The African respondents are overwhelmingly what sociologists would classify as first-generation, not born and not raised in the United States—2 percent and 36 percent, respectively. And last, the Afro-Caribbean population presents the most unique demographics of the black groups, often referred to as the second generation, individuals who were raised in the United States, but whose parents were not born in the United States. However, Afro-Caribbeans can also be defined as the 1.5 generation (Portes and Rumbaut 2001)—that is, as people who immigrated to a new country during their formative years. The label "1.5 generation" refers to the characteristics brought from their home country as well as their assimilation and socialization in the new country: their identity is a hybrid of their home culture and new traditions.

As table 4.1 shows, while only 26 percent of Afro-Caribbean respondents were born in the United States, 77 percent were raised there, thus creating a sample population largely born abroad, but raised in the United States during their formative years. The 1.5-generation Afro-Caribbeans are significant for several reasons, since I theorized that with increased time spent in the United States, blacks would

Table 4.1

Born in US	Whites	Blacks	Afro-Car	Africans	Latinos
Born in US	80	86	26	2	61
Not born in US	20	14	74	98	39
N	41	130	47	90	44
Grew up in US					
In US	80	92	77	36	90
Outside US	20	8	23	63	10
Don't know	0	0	0	1	0
N	41	125	47	90	48
Length of time in NYC					
0–5 years	2	2	2	5	0
6–10 years	2	2	0	11	2
11–15 years	15	2	2	14	4
15 years and over	63	92	91	64	90
Do not reside in NYC	17	2	4	5	4
N	41	132	46	91	51

p < 0.01
Source: 2005–6 SSEU Local 371 Survey.

become more acculturated to this country and, more specifically, the nuances and relevance of American racism. My initial hypothesis was that black Americans would be the least accepting of the American Dream. However, the Afro-Caribbean 1.5 generation's lack of investment in the American Dream raises two necessary theoretical possibilities: (1) the data reflect dual racial and ethnic statuses and segmented assimilation generation effects, or (2) other black immigrant groups feel the limitations of their American Dream pursuit due to skin color and (what may be a presumed) shared racial identity with black Americans. Regarding the first possibility, segmented assimilation, in which success rates and outcomes vary substantially across and even within minority groups (Rumbaut and Portes 2001), contribute to some groups' desire to maintain ethnic status for advancement within white society and thereby experience what they perceive as the benefits of being not a "black" American, but a black immigrant or black ethnic.

For black immigrant groups in the United States, they often feel both a part of their ethnic group as well as de facto members of the larger racial group known as "blacks." First, 1.5-generation Afro-Caribbeans appear to suffer from a dual minority status, which is best described as distinguishable yet indistinguishable black ethnics; some sociologists regard Afro-Caribbeans as the "invisible immigrant" (Waters 1999a). Insofar as their formative years have been spent in the United States, they have experienced the racial barriers present for black American groups, a group they often find themselves associated with in societal, educational, and residential contexts. Being raised in the United States, therefore, decreases some of the optimism most often felt by newly arrived and first-generation immigrants. Second, the frustration Afro-Caribbean populations express can be attributed to a more complex form of what sociologists define as segmented assimilation and the subsequent inequities they experience, as compared to their fellow nonblack immigrant counterparts (Rumbaut and Portes 2001). It is not that Afro-Caribbeans view associating with black Americans as an automatic downward assimilation; in fact, Afro-Caribbean populations express deep-seated racial attachments to black populations, both black American and African. What has occurred for Afro-Caribbeans is the all-too-common effect of segmented assimilation, whereby Afro-Caribbeans recognize the inconsistencies of their immigrant and black statuses. On the one hand, Afro-Caribbean populations are purported to be elevated minorities and, in certain circumstances, are treated as such by particular individuals, both white and nonwhite. However, in their daily existence, Afro-Caribbeans have felt the very real effects of racism, something their elevated minority status is unable to shield from them. The valorized status of immigrant has been negated by the barriers and disadvantages experienced on very tangible levels.

Ethnic relations in this analysis are complicated by generational effects, that is, where one is born and also how one is raised. Diverse attitudes of black groups are informed not just by their membership within a particular racial or ethnic group, but also by their assimilation and integration process, both socially and culturally. Differing black ethnic attitudes toward questions surrounding achievement of the American Dream can also be attributed to the fact that most African immigrants in the study, and nationally, have spent less time in the United States, thus further complicating the narrative of intraracial relationships of blacks in the United States. This particular surveyed population consists of respondents who can be categorized generally as consisting of predominantly first-generation Africans, second-generation or 1.5-generation Afro-Caribbeans, and native-born black Americans who have resided in the United States for several generations.[14] One Afro-Caribbean union member expressed her frustration thus:

> Even when working at the union, I identify most closely with the immigrants [because of my parents' immigrant status], but I am still stuck in the middle. I am not considered American, but I was *not* born in a developing nation. It is still us versus them. People don't understand the work it takes to overcome anti-immigrant sentiment. It's hurtful because you are never seen as American but people won't see me as Haitian either. This is the difference of second generations.

The tenuous relationship between native-born black Americans and black immigrants is especially poignant between black Americans and second-generation immigrants. Scholars have observed the dichotomies for black immigrant children who are seen by mainstream America as "black" (Portes and Rumbaut 2001; Waters 1999a, 1999b, 1994). Some scholars have argued that second-generation Afro-Caribbeans may choose to define themselves as "ethnics" depending on their familial social class, education, and affiliations with ethnic social enclaves, thereby potentially decreasing the negative effects of US racism toward black Americans (Portes and Rumbaut 2001). Other scholars have contended that second-generation black immigrant groups whose lives are more linked to black American populations may lead more racialized lives and are thus affected by racist limits (Cordero-Guzman, Smith, and Grosfoguel 2001). Portes and Stepick (1993) have argued that black immigrant parents have viewed the racial dichotomy as one of two choices: assimilation into the mainstream middle class or adoption into the racial underclass. Because of these competing forces, black immigrant parents have desperately tried to aid their children in succeeding on the ethnic path of upward mobility, so as not to "Americanize" into a minority model of a downward oppositional culture that is black America.

Cordero-Guzman, Smith, and Grosfoguel (2001: 15) saw this dichotomy as the struggle of immigrants who:

> Choose and are forced to define themselves in juxtaposition to negative images of African Americans, usually with the result that the juxtaposition affirms explanations of differential progress positing different work ethics among immigrants and African Americans. The second generation has a more complex relationship to the immigrant analogy, with some in the second generation accepting it and seeing themselves as different from native minorities, and others seeing their futures as more similar to those of same natives.

If Afro-Caribbean populations follow similar paths to incorporation as black Americans, while Afro-Caribbean populations remain in the United States over more generations, their extreme disillusionment may adapt into a version of the "democratic wish" (Morone 1998):[15] that is, Afro-Caribbean populations will exhibit opinions more aligned with black American attitudes, recognizing the inequities in American democracy, but also recognizing the opportunities for economic and social advancement. The key differences between black American and Afro-Caribbean populations is what Rogers (2006) defines as the significance of home ties to black ethnic political and cultural development for Afro-Caribbeans, even while residing in the United States. With a direct home country and distinct familial and cultural ties and history, black immigrant populations who do not feel the American Dream has lived up to its promise still have the option to return "home." In many ways, this exit option or "out" presents differing strategies for black ethnic immigrants who may not feel the need to redefine the American Dream as a mere wish. The realistic option for the twenty-first-century black immigrant rests in the option to either re-create their own version of the dream in their home country or remain in the United States.

Actual attainment of the American Dream for African populations may differ from that of black Americans and Afro-Caribbeans. Some of the factors that contribute to these distinctions are perceptions of how African populations are viewed by white Americans, the extent to which they wish to achieve particular goals, and the place from which they are migrating. Thus, if African immigrants arrive in the United States from war-torn countries, filled with interethnic strife, they may not perceive race and racism in the same distinct and troubling ways as African immigrants formally educated abroad or in the United States. Success for some may come in the form of basic life choices, whereas for other African immigrants, success would entail full incorporation and opportunities. In addition, particular African immigrants do not have the option of returning to their home country. Therefore, a level of satisfaction or willingness to make America work on their behalf may dictate one's perceptions of attainment and incorporation. However, the African immigrant and refugee status distinctions may have very tangible effects on African perceptions of the American Dream and subsequent demands or general acceptance of what the polity must and should provide. This is not to say that the past is erased. One member stated the tensions that arise among union members and individuals assigned to assist them with grievances:

> Sometimes people will call with grievances and ask for the African grievance representative. And the reverse occurs as well. Sometimes people will call and say they do not want us to send out the African grievance representative. African members will try to explain to me and tell me about past problems between tribes and villages, but I say it has no place within the union.

As more black ethnic groups continue to migrate to the United States, especially from Africa, what will happen to black ethnic perceptions of the American Dream? As the now steady influx of diverse groups of African migrants enter the United States and begin the process of assimilation and incorporation into the political, economic, and US social sectors, how will their relationships evolve with other black ethnics? Without a simple exit option narrative, both politically and geographically, will African groups seek to maintain an immigrant identity even when multiple generations have lived in the United States? These questions leave fertile ground for scholars who are interested in what could be the most unique and complex black ethnic group of all. To date, there are fifty-seven African countries, with extreme interethnic, geographic, political, and economic diversity. As African immigration increases, their interactions with one another and with different ethnic groups and generations of black American and Afro-Caribbeans will contribute to an even more nuanced definition of elevated minority status for all groups involved.

Measuring the American Dream: Perceptions and Treatment

Attitudinal similarities and differences between black Americans, Afro-Caribbeans, and Africans can be measured by how each group conceptualizes life chances in the United States: (1) how they feel they and others are treated, (2) what factors affect possibilities for success, (3) what political alliances are necessary, and (4) how they perceive other black ethnic groups. In order to measure attitudes pertaining to the work ethic of ethnic groups, the survey included several questions surrounding the treatment of racial and ethnic groups by the government, feelings of overall group attachment, and the possibility of black immigrant incorporation into black America. Four primary research questions ask whether significant differences exist between black American, Afro-Caribbean, and African populations on racial and ethnic dimensions. Specifically:

1) To what extent do issues divide black ethnic populations?
2) What perceptions do blacks have of each other once in the United States?
3) Are there implications for participation, partnerships, and future leadership for black ethnics?
4) What do black ethnic relationships mean for larger questions of collective action and representation?

The responses to these questions are examined in order to assess the strength of alliances and any possible tensions between native-born and immigrant black populations. Will the dual racial and ethnic identity for black ethnic groups foster a sense of coalition building? Essentially, it is not a question of whether race will trump ethnicity; rather, it is a question of the effect of ethnic identity, coupled with a shared identity, that contributes to an ability and desire to build substantive coalitions to advance larger racial needs and issues.

White Treatment in America and Subsequent African American Spending

So much of how ethnic groups are perceived and how they subsequently view themselves is through the lens of white society and white public opinion. The economic and political inequities that persist in the United States continue to disproportionately affect populations of color. This is not to ignore the millions of white Americans who lack agency and representation due to class. However, it is appropriate for new black immigrants to view (and question) the economic and political structures that continue to benefit, particularly, middle- and upper-class white Americans. When asking Local 371 respondents about their feelings pertaining to how whites are treated in the United States, all native-born and foreign-born black populations agreed that whites were treated fairly in this country. Union members were asked the specific question "Do you think this country fairly treats whites?" Black ethnic groups overwhelmingly agreed with this question.

In table 4.2, black respondents expressed overwhelming agreement to the question of white treatment in the United States. White opinions are also presented to show the differing levels of strong agreement when compared to native-born and foreign-born black populations. At times, black immigrants have been faced with the reality that hard work in the United States does not

Table 4.2 **Do you think this country fairly treats whites? (in percentages)**

	Whites	Blacks	Afro-Car	Africans	Latinos
Strongly Agree	11	55	58	62	35
Agree	64	36	36	35	42
Disagree	22	6	4	3	21
Str Disagree	3	3	2	0	2
N	36	128	45	87	48

p < 0.01.
Source: 2005–6 SSEU Local 371 Survey.

ultimately translate into success or advancement of oneself or one's group. All too often, newly arrived blacks have found that the rules of the game and the playing field for white immigrants differ from their own experiences, solely due to phenotype and race. Therefore, the narrative of hard work equaling success for whites translates into what Cordero-Guzman, Smith, and Grosfoguel (2001) have articulated as a narrative absolving the larger society of ultimate responsibility for its continued racist practices. They state, "The problem … lies in the failure to consider the effects of racial segregation in housing, and devastating and persistent effects such segregation and differences in resources can have" (Cordero-Guzman, Smith, and Grosfoguel 2001: 5).[16]

Only 11 percent of white respondents strongly agreed, as opposed to the 55, 58, and 62 percent, respectively, of native-born black American, Afro-Caribbean, and African respondents.[17] When "strongly agree" and "agree" responses are combined, black respondents, overall, agreed that the country treats whites fairly, at 91 percent for native-born black Americans, 94 percent for Afro-Caribbean and 97 percent for African respondents. Although African respondents were among the most adamant in their assertion that whites were treated fairly, several black and Afro-Caribbean union members expressed difficulty working with African members and attributed it to African members propensities to "work with" and "respond to" white colleagues over black. One member said, "Often times when Africans are challenged by black Americans, they assume it's because they are African. But when they are challenged by a white person, they don't make that leap."

Although only 11 percent of white respondents strongly agreed that white populations were fairly treated in the United States, when combining strongly agreed and agreed responses, a total of 75 percent of white respondents indicated that they believe they were fairly treated in the United States. Thirty-five percent of Latino respondents strongly agreed that whites were treated fairly. Their responses are situated between black ethnic respondents and white responses. A total of 77 percent of Latino respondents strongly agreed and agreed that whites were fairly treated in the United States, a percent slightly higher than white respondents, but not nearly as declarative as black ethnic responses.

The overwhelming agreement of black respondents toward the question of fair white treatment in the United States indicates not only a shared understanding of race and in-group status in America, but raises the question whether this overwhelming imbalanced fair treatment contributed to a possible black ethnic need for institutional programs to assist blacks in obtaining equity. Black ethnic groups clearly expressed their attitudes of overwhelming fair treatment of whites in the United States, therefore, additional questions were asked to assess the respondents' inclination to support spending for affirmative action policies. Local 371 members were also asked whether or not other immigrant black groups should be beneficiaries of affirmative action policies. The two distinct affirmative action questions are meant to illicit racial as well as ethnic opinions. Affirmative action is a system instituted to level many aspects of the institutional playing fields, which excluded black Americans and so many other groups for generations due solely to one's lack of white, male, privileged status. Asking black ethnics their feelings toward affirmative action spending is meant to illicit racial feelings for a program largely defined (albeit many times incorrectly) as a means to assist black people in the United States. The second question regarding affirmative action spending for Afro-Caribbean and African immigrants is meant to dissect feelings of shared "economic" and opportunity resources based on ethnicity. This question was especially meant to measure the extent to which black Americans viewed Afro-Caribbean and African immigrants as deserving of affirmative action benefits and thereby begin the process of measuring racial unity when scarce resources are to be shared.

Two questions were asked: (1) Would you like to see spending for affirmative action policies increased, decreased, or stay the same? (2) Should African and Afro-Caribbean immigrants benefit from affirmative action policies? The majority of native-born and foreign-born black groups agreed to increases in affirmative action spending, unlike white and Latino respondents. Black respondents also agreed that Afro-Caribbean and African immigrants should be included in affirmative action benefits. However, when comparing black ethnic populations, black Americans were considerably less likely to strongly agree that African and Afro-Caribbean immigrants should benefit from affirmative action policies, when compared to other Afro-Caribbean and African respondents.

Table 4.3a shows that two-thirds of black respondents agreed that spending on affirmative action policies should be increased, roughly one-third of all black respondents felt spending for this policy should stay the same. Regarding spending on affirmative action policies, 29 percent of whites and 41 percent of Latinos

Table 4.3a **Spending on Affirmative Action Policies (in percentages)**

	Whites	Blacks	Afro-Car	Africans	Latinos
Increase	29	64	68	61	41
Stay Same	46	30	32	33	55
Decrease	24	6	0	6	4
N	41	128	47	89	54

p < 0.01.
Source: 2005–6 SSEU Local 371 Survey.

supported increases in spending, as compared to roughly two-thirds of all black ethnic respondents. It is important to note that only 4 percent of Latino and 6 percent of black American and African respondents sought decreases in funding for affirmative action policies, as compared to 24 percent of white respondents. Although the data indicate a difference between Latino and black ethnic opinions, the most significant distinctions are between black ethnic and white populations. Essentially, black and white opinions continue to serve as bookends for Latino opinions. Even as scholars continue to include Latino (and Asian American) groups into political analysis (Junn and Singh 2009; Lee, Ramakrishnan, and Ramirez 2006) and as Latinos solidify their place as the second-largest group in the United States, the black-white dichotomy still persists.

This black-white paradigm is evident when observing table 4.3b. Again, Latino respondent opinions are situated between white and black ethnic responses. White populations are the least likely to strongly agree and agree that African and

Table 4.3b **"African and Afro-Caribbean Immigrants should benefit from affirmative action policies" (in percentages)**

	Whites	Blacks	Afro-Car	Africans	Latinos
Strongly Agree	10	14	32	43	9
Agree	38	60	45	49	50
Disagree	30	13	4	2	22
Str Disagree	10	7	6	0	2
Don't Know	12	6	13	6	17
N	40	132	47	89	54

p < 0.01.
Source: 2005–6 SSEU Local 371 Survey.

Afro-Caribbean immigrant populations should benefit from affirmative action policies, at 48 percent. Latino populations are slightly more willing to strongly agree and agree that black ethnic populations should benefit from affirmative action policies, at 59 percent. However, both white and Latino respondents are less likely to support affirmative action policies than their black ethnic counterparts. The racial presence and cohesion among black populations for this particular policy issue is indicative of a larger black group understanding of the class inequities that persist for all phenotypically black groups in the United States.

When observing the data pertaining to African and Afro-Caribbean immigrants benefiting from affirmative action policies, native-born black American and Afro-Caribbean aggregations of strongly agree and agree responses indicate that 74 percent and 77 percent of black union members, respectively, believe that black ethnic immigrant groups should benefit from affirmative action policies. Africans overwhelmingly agreed to this question (92 percent). The awareness of the relevance of race, racism, and the distinctions made between blacks and other racial and ethnic groups in the United States most likely contributed to these shared responses.

When aggregating responses of strongly agree and agree, native-born black respondents clearly believe that foreign-born blacks should benefit from affirmative action policies. However, it is important to note the differences in "strongly agree" responses of native-born black American Local 371 members, as compared to Afro-Caribbean and African respondents. Observing strongly agree responses of black Americans indicates that only 14 percent of black Americans strongly agree that black immigrants should benefit from affirmative action policies. Afro-Caribbean and African respondents strongly agreed with the statement at rates of 32 and 43 percent, respectively. This particular racial solidarity, coupled with ethnic feelings of competition, present an ever-present duality for black groups as they negotiate racial needs and the protection of seemingly "ethnic" resources.

The overwhelming agreement that white populations are treated fairly in the United States contributed to black ethnic agreement for increased spending for affirmative action policies, and the inclusion of black immigrants as beneficiaries to those policies. However, the black ethnic similarities within the survey began to wane with subsequent questions.

Understanding the Possible Differences: Black Ethnic Treatment in the United States, Blame, and Perceptions of Hard Work

Although black ethnics may share similar fates once in the United States, due to their classification of black in America, these three groups express relatively diverse opinions pertaining to work ethics, treatment once in the US, and over-all intragroup attitudes. Afro-Caribbean respondents expressed the strongest opinions, stating that they themselves and other black ethnic groups were discriminated against. Afro-Caribbeans were also the least optimistic about success once in the United States if their prospects for success were based on hard work alone. They also expressed the most positive and favorable attitudes toward other black groups. African immigrants, however, expressed opinions that were overall the most optimistic regarding attainment of success, and expressed only modest favorable feelings toward other black groups. Black American respondents often expressed opinions somewhere between those of Afro-Caribbean and African immigrant respondents on issues pertaining to group perceptions, spending, and possibilities for success in America.

RACIAL TREATMENT AND BLAME

Specific intragroup feelings were measured using three distinct sets of questions that were asked of all black ethnic groups about all other black ethnic groups, including their own group. Survey participants were asked, "Do you think this country fairly treats black Americans? Afro-Caribbean immigrants? African immigrants?" Tables 4a–c show the distribution of responses to these questions.

In table 4.4a, deviations in opinion and possible group cohesiveness emerge when the questions pertaining to fair treatment of black ethnic groups were asked. Beginning with black American populations, it appears that African immigrants agree that native-born blacks are treated fairly, at 22 percent. This contrasts with black American agreement of only 8 percent. The differences are most stark when looking at the 21 percent of African respondents who strongly disagree with the statement that black Americans are treated fairly. Forty-one

Table 4.4a **Do you think this country fairly treats black Americans? (in percentages)**

	Whites	Blacks	Afro-Car	Africans	Latinos
Strongly Agree	5	0	7	0	2
Agree	41	8	7	22	13
Disagree	29	49	44	56	60
Str Disagree	15	41	42	21	19
Don't Know	10	2	0	2	6
N	41	133	45	91	53

p < 0.01.
Source: 2005–6 SSEU Local 371 Survey.

and 42 percent of black American and Afro-Caribbean respondents strongly disagree with the statement. Although only 19 percent of Latino respondents strongly disagree that black Americans were treated fairly, 60 percent disagree with the statement, for a total of 79 percent of Latino respondents who disagree that black Americans were treated fairly in the United States. White respondents, at 46 percent, when integrating strongly agree and agree responses, were the most likely to agree that black Americans were treated fairly.

In table 4.4b, when observing the question as it pertains to Afro-Caribbean treatment in the United States, again, African respondents were the most likely of the black ethnics to agree that Afro-Caribbean populations were treated fairly in the United States. Roughly one-quarter of African respondents agreed that there was unfavorable treatment of black American and Afro-Caribbean groups, once in the United States. Although the figures are not astronomical, they do suggest initial clues in unraveling the nuanced distinctions that contribute to the intraracial opinions of native-born and foreign-born black populations, as well as the nuanced differences between not only ethnic groups, but differing generations of black ethnics in the United States. Of the three black ethnic groups, African respondents overwhelmingly have spent the least amount of time in the United States and have arrived from home countries that do not afford as many of the liberties as the United States offers. Their respective home country backgrounds are what are most likely driving the more favorable and positive attitude toward black treatment in the United States.[18] In interviews with African Local 371 members, there was an overwhelming articulation by African members to "make it work" in the United States. Their stronger desire to assimilate more easily into mainstream US society than their black ethnic predecessors was evident in African union member interviews, even though these members did not believe black groups were treated as fairly as whites in the United States.

Table 4.4b **Do you think this country fairly treats Afro-Caribbean immigrants? (in percentages)**

	Whites	Blacks	Afro-Car	Africans	Latinos
Strongly Agree	2	0	4	0	2
Agree	39	15	7	28	15
Disagree	37	55	43	53	60
Str Disagree	10	26	46	14	17
Don't Know	12	4	0	4	6
N	41	132	46	90	53

$p < 0.01$.
Source: 2005–6 SSEU Local 371 Survey

In table 4.4c, when observing the question pertaining to the treatment of African populations, again African members were most likely to agree that they were treated fairly in the United States, but only at 18 percent, not 22 and 28 percent, as for black American and Afro-Caribbean populations, respectively. Overwhelmingly, Afro-Caribbean respondents were the least likely to believe that any black group was treated fairly in the United States. This unique population was largely born outside of the United States (77 percent), yet 91 percent of Afro-Caribbeans have resided in New York City for fifteen years or more. The peculiar placement as non-native blacks who have resided in New York City for significant periods of time has possibly contributed to increased hostile perceptions and feelings toward acceptance in the United States, in that Afro-Caribbeans have experienced segmented assimilation, problems with full integration when comparing themselves to other nonblack immigrants, and an inability to assimilate fully due to their racialized phenotype.

Overall, African immigrants are most likely to believe the country treats them well when compared to other black ethnic groups. For example, when Local 371 members were asked if they felt the country treated native-born black Americans, Afro-Caribbeans, and Africans fairly, native-born blacks disagreed with the statement at rates of 90, 91, and 82 percent, respectively. Similarly, when Afro-Caribbean immigrants were asked if they thought black Americans, Afro-Caribbeans, and Africans were treated fairly, respondents disagreed with the statement at rates of 86, 89, and 92 percent, respectively. African respondents did disagree with the statement that the three black groups were treated fairly, but at rates of 77, 67, and 77 percent, respectively. Although African immigrants were more likely than black American and Afro-Caribbean respondents to agree that black Americans and Afro-Caribbeans are treated fairly in this country, the majority still feel that blacks are not treated fairly in America.

Table 4.4c **Do you think this country fairly treats African immigrants? (in percentages)**

	Whites	*Blacks*	*Afro-Car*	*Africans*	*Latinos*
Strongly Agree	2	1	4	0	2
Agree	39	12	4	18	15
Disagree	37	52	46	51	57
Str Disagree	10	30	46	28	19
Don't Know	12	5	0	3	7
N	41	131	46	90	53

$p < 0.05$.
Source: 2005–6 SSEU Local 371 Survey.

Interestingly, Latino responses indicate that a majority of respondents believe black American, Afro-Caribbean, and African populations are not treated fairly in the United States. However, Latinos did not express opinions indicating that they strongly believed black ethnic populations were not treated fairly. Their opinions were relatively consistent when observing their attitudes toward all three black populations, which suggests a possible uniform view of black groups by Latino populations. Similarly, white populations expressed nearly identical attitudes for all three black groups. Their responses indicate a relative uniform opinion that 44 to 47 percent of whites agree or strongly agree that black groups are treated well in the United States. White responses for Afro-Caribbean and African populations' treatment were identical.

What is noteworthy when observing white attitudes are the proportion who indicated that they "don't know" whether the country treats blacks populations fairly. Their "don't know" responses could represent the segregation of blacks residentially, even within a shared occupation. The "don't know" responses could also represent whites' inability to negotiate the feelings they have regarding black populations that they actually know versus black populations that are often represented in the media. The differing intraracial perceptions of black respondents provide an indication of identification with the plight of native-born black Americans and blacks in America, while also presenting subtle differences and interpretations of treatment once in the United States.

If the majority of black respondents do not feel that the United States treats them or other black groups fairly, then how do these populations feel about doing well in life in the United States? With this particular union, the perception is that African members "listen to the winners." That is, they are perceived as working harder to establish relationships with white coworkers who they believe hold the secrets to success. One union member believed that:

> Racist culture has said "You're special" to the Caribbeans [and Africans], and the same slavery mentality of promoting one over the other is still present. Whites will promote an African male who is beneath a black American female and the hate is misdirected. The psychology of power and the message of "You're different" [continues].

The perception of Afro-Caribbeans as the successful, good, kind, immigrant and the reality of the disillusionment that Afro-Caribbeans feel about this status should be noted. Dodoo (1997) argued that the myth of the successful Caribbean immigrant is just that: a myth. Afro-Caribbean responses clearly show their disillusionment felt once in the United States and their attachment to a larger black group identity.

Here we begin to see the roots of Afro-Caribbean disillusion with the American Dream. As the group that has been in the United States longer than first-generation and newly arrived African immigrants, but not as long as many ninth-generation black American groups, Afro-Caribbeans expressed discontent with being told they are special and different on one hand because of their ethnicity, yet consistently discriminated against because of their race. Unlike their black American counterparts who essentially believe in the "You win some, you lose some" philosophy of being black in America—in that, as one member explained, they may have an opportunity to become a doctor, or they may spend decades in the prison industrial complex for possessing a small amount of marijuana—Afro-Caribbeans continue to express their lack of faith in the promise of the American Dream.

Local 371 members were asked to respond to this statement relating to black ethnic group perceptions of doing well in life: "If racial/ethnic minorities do not do well in life, they have no one to blame but themselves." Native-born black American and Afro-Caribbean respondents largely agreed that the country did not treat black groups fairly and that others can be blamed for a lack of success once in the United States.

In table 4.5, African immigrants responded at 47 percent agreement that one was to blame if racial and ethnic minorities did not do well in life. When aggregating strongly agree and agree responses, native-born blacks agreed at 32 percent that no one is to blame if racial and ethnic minorities do not do well in life, compared to Afro-Caribbean respondents at 17 percent. Afro-Caribbean opinions about life chances in the United States present an emerging picture of a group of individuals largely seen as special, different, or "good" throughout the social science literature. However, the opinions that Afro-Caribbean union

Table 4.5 "If racial/ethnic minorities do not do well in life, they have no one to blame but themselves" (in percentages)

	Blacks	Afro-Car	Africans
Strongly Agree	11	11	17
Agree	21	6	30
Disagree	43	60	35
Str Disagree	23	23	16
Don't Know	2	0	2
N	134	47	88

$p < 0.05$.
Source: 2005–6 SSEU Local 371 Survey.

members exhibit are those of a population who do not feel that their treatment or even their potential for success is in their hands. One particular Haitian union member explained a tenuous position within black and Afro-Caribbean social circles when he was in school. He stated:

> My parents never suggested we identify as Haitian. We slid in with the Spanish folks because my family also spoke Spanish. My parents had to learn seven languages to come out of school. French was my first language because it was in the home. I felt isolated for a while.

Again, Afro-Caribbeans were least likely to believe that the government treats black ethnic groups fairly, and if racial and ethnic minorities do not do well in life, they have no one to blame. Black American union member responses were again situated between Afro-Caribbean realities and African respondent optimism. African respondents were the most optimistic about doing well in life. One member explained: "I was told that because of my color I would have to study harder and work harder to get married. My grandfather was happy I didn't come out any darker because I would have a harder time in life."

It is apparent that generational distinctions contribute to elements of black ethnic effects. However, since Africans are currently the fastest-growing black ethnic group and do not have the same exit options as Afro-Caribbeans, their desire to subscribe to the American Dream could, on the one hand, position African ethnic groups as the most optimistic black ethnic group that continues to invest in the American Dream, despite racial limitations, or could, on the other hand, drive African groups to feelings of disillusion, similar to current Afro-Caribbean attitudes.

EVALUATING ELEVATED MINORITY STATUS ON THE INDIVIDUAL LEVEL: THE LAND OF OPPORTUNITY, HARD WORK, AND STOLEN JOBS

Every hour sees the black man elbowed out of employment by some newly arrived emigrant, whose hunger and whose color are thought to give him a better title to the place.
—Frederick Douglass (1853)

First, the stopping of the importing of cheap white labor on any terms has been the economic salvation of American black labor.
—W. E. B. Du Bois (1929)

Local 371 of the SSEU is a union group where members provide social services to racially and ethnically diverse populations throughout New York City. Because of the relatively uniform aspects of Local 371 member occupations and interactions with the populations they serve, one might assume relatively shared opinions among Local 371 members. In order to better understand the opinions of black ethnic Local 371 members, explicit questions pertaining to the work ethic of each individual black ethnic group was included in the survey. As stated previously, there are definite intraracial distinctions articulated by black ethnic members, and the extent to which the various groups believe the polity provides an equitable set of life circumstances is called into question. The results indicate distinct black ethnic opinions pertaining to specific black group work ethic. When evaluating the data, African immigrants are perceived, by native-born black Americans, Afro-Caribbean immigrants, and African immigrants, as the hardest-working of black ethnic groups.[19] The question relating to black ethnic group work ethic was phrased this way:

> Imagine a 7-point scale on which the characteristics of the people in a group can be rated. A score of 1 means you think almost all of the people in the group tend to be LAZY. A score of 7 means you think almost all of the people in the group tend to be HARDWORKING. A score of 4 means that you think most people in the group are not closer to one end or the other, and of course, you may choose any number in between.

African immigrants overall scored the highest percentage from each black ethnic group.

Perhaps what is most interesting about table 4.6 is not the fact that African immigrants are perceived as the hardest-working. As the newest arrived immigrants, they are likely perceived and perceive themselves as the most fastidious pursuers of economic opportunities (Kasinitz 1992). One would likely assume that when observing the assessment each group gives themselves, one could expect a particular ethnic group to rate oneself the highest overall. This is not the case. African respondents do rate themselves as the hardest-working at a rate of 75 percent. However, Afro-Caribbean and native-born black Americans do not rate their respective groups as hardest-working; instead, they perceive African immigrants as such. Only 16 percent of African respondents rate black Americans as hardworking, compared to 63 percent who rate Afro-Caribbeans hardworking. When asked the same questions, Afro-Caribbean respondents rate African populations as hardest-working. Seventy-eight percent of Afro-Caribbeans rate themselves as hardworking, yet 85 percent of Afro-Caribbeans rate Africans as hardworking.

Perhaps most surprising are the percentages native-born black respondents gave themselves and other foreign-born blacks. When asked the questions regarding work ethic, 63 percent of black Americans rated Africans as the hardest-working. The second-hardest-working groups according to 57 percent

Table 4.6 **(Condensed Table) Perceived Work Approaches of Native-Born Black Americans and Afro-Caribbean and African Immigrants (in percentages)**

	Black American	*Afro-Carib*	*African*
Native-Born Black Americans			
Very Hardworking	21	17	7
Extremely Hardworking	19	15	9
Afro-Caribbean Immigrants			
Very Hardworking	31	40	25
Extremely Hardworking	27	38	38
African Immigrants			
Very Hardworking	30	49	28
Extremely Hardworking	33	36	47
N	135	47	92

All chi-squared values were significant at the p < 0.10 level.
Source: 2005–6 SSEU Local 371 Survey.

of black Americans, are Afro-Caribbean populations. Although black Americans gave themselves the lowest rating, with only 39 percent of black Americans expressing opinions that they themselves are hardworking, their percentages were still higher than the Afro-Caribbean and African respondent perceptions of black American work ethics, at 32 and 16 percent, respectively. One member stated: "Jamaicans told my father that 'black Americans are lazy.' He told the Jamaican that we [Caribbeans] are from a country ruled by blacks and were freed earlier. Essentially, Caribbeans and black Americans are from different inequalities."

So how are we to interpret these results? Obviously, African immigrants are viewed by all three member groups as hardest-working, with Afro-Caribbeans situated as hardworking, and black Americans perceived as the least hardworking of all three groups. So black Americans and Afro-Caribbeans rate Africans as a harder-working group; but what is possibly the most significant result is the extent to which black Americans themselves indicated that they, as a group, are not hardworking. If Dawson is indeed correct and one's fate is linked to the success of one's fellow group members, then what exactly are the quantitative results indicating? A concrete answer, or even an explanation, did not emerge throughout the interviews with Local 371. The closest explanation came from a member who stated that she could feel as though *she* were successful and hardworking, but she indicated that the question asked about the *group*. Another member echoed that sentiment and stated, "Black Americans would be better off as a group if more blacks worked harder like Caribbeans." There appears to be a recognition among black Americans as well as Afro-Caribbean and African union members that there are "regular" hardworking black Americans. However, as a group, black Americans fell short of a black ethnic belief in their overall group work ethic.

Although Africans were considered the hardest-working among black ethnic Local 371 members, the reputation of the hardworking Caribbean persists within the literature (Rogers 2006; Dodoo 1997; Conover 1988). Newly arrived black immigrants are considered to be the model black ethnic for black Americans to aspire. One union member stated:

> There were so many stereotypes of being Haitian and liking to work. It saddens me that it is still this way. Even in [black Americans] voting themselves as lazy, they are not lazy. You don't know how beaten down you are. In Haiti there is a rich history that is repeated, known, and they see themselves as renegades. It is different here.

The link between hard work and attaining the American Dream are inextricably linked. If a particular group is consistently treated as the out-group and presented as the comparison group (as in the case of new immigrants quickly being inculcated in the black versus nonblack division), there is likely a disproportionate ability to fail at attaining one's goals. Often, these individuals are blamed and, ergo, blame themselves for their inability to succeed. A stigma and cycle of failure, real or perceived (in this case, among highly educated and employed members of Local 371), is then carried by the individual as a member of the denigrated or nonvirtuous group (Hochschild 2005).

When further dissecting black linked fate with feelings toward fellow diverse racial group members, it is necessary to fully understand the tripart relationship for black ethnics in the United States—that is, negotiating the life of being a black individual, belonging to a particular ethnic group, and having membership (whether one has asked or not) in a larger racial group. African respondents have indicated their acceptance of a shared racial identity, but they do not view themselves as a failed group, nor do they feel like anyone is to blame if they do not succeed. In addition, when observing African immigrant respondent attitudes toward work ethics once in the United States, African immigrants present an interesting portrait of optimism in the belief that hard work is the fundamental crux of American success. Again, there are stark distinctions between African immigrants compared to native-born black American and Afro-Caribbean immigrant respondents. One black American union member described African union members by saying, "African men are quick to go to management positions; they are very ambitious." Another member believed the "confusion" between African and black American union members is directly linked to the job the social service providers accomplish each day. She stated:

> African members have the job of removing homes from people and cultural judgments are made against black Americans especially. Before, Caribbeans would never call the authorities to report on other Caribbeans, similarly with Asians and all other immigrant groups, no one ever called it into the system because of illegal statuses. Because people are mainstreaming now, the immigrant population is having trouble raising kids just like any other group and are now interacting with the system.

The levels of African member optimism, when compared to native-born black American and Afro-Caribbean immigrant respondents, is one of overwhelming agreement to the question relating to black ethnic group perceptions of success based on hard work. We asked those surveyed to respond to the statement "America is a land of opportunity in which you only need to work hard to succeed." African immigrants were the most likely to strongly agree with the statement, at 46 percent, while native-born black Americans and Afro-Caribbean immigrants only strongly agreed, at 14 and 9 percent, respectively (see table 4.7).

When aggregating strongly agree and agree responses of black ethnics, African immigrants overwhelmingly believe hard work equals success. Eighty-one percent of African respondents agreed with the statement, compared to only 30 percent of Afro-Caribbeans and 49 percent of native-born black Americans who agreed with the statement.[20]

Table 4.7 **"America is a land of opportunity in which you only need to work hard to succeed" (in percentages)**

	Blacks	*Afro-Car*	*Africans*
Strongly Agree	14	9	46
Agree	35	21	35
Disagree	32	47	16
Str Disagree	19	21	3
Don't Know	0	2	0
N	132	47	90

p < 0.01.
Source: 2005–6 SSEU Local 371 Survey.

Perceptions of work ethic between black ethnic groups stem from larger perceptions of in-group/out-group complexities, notions of elevated minority statuses for immigrant populations, and overall historical notions of black Americans as an inferior group (Brewer 1979). The responses of African immigrants to the question of hard work as the foundation of success present a significantly larger percentage of African immigrants who believe in the merits of hard work alone. One union member believes the optimism expressed by African, and not Afro-Caribbean, members is a generational effect. He stated:

> The Caribbeans in the union are more second-generation and are already in the working and middle class in the United States. These populations are different from the Nigerian member who was an accountant in his homeland and is working at the union until he can go and practice accounting in the United States.

The different exit options for Afro-Caribbean and African respondents, as well as segmented assimilation effects, largely contributed to the opposing views on possibilities for success based on hard work alone. And again, black Americans find themselves situated between the two ethnic groups, as the most established of the black ethnic groups in the United States, knowing that some opportunities for success are plausible and others remain dreams only.

African immigrants again present contrasting attitudes to those native-born black Americans and Afro-Caribbean immigrants when asked to respond to the statement "If *black Americans* tried harder, they could be as successful as certain immigrant groups." Eighty-one percent of African immigrants agreed or strongly agreed, compared to 44 percent of native-born black American and 59 percent of Afro-Caribbean respondents (see table 4.8). Although black American respondents were less likely than African and Afro-Caribbean immigrants to agree, the numbers of native-born black Americans in agreement was still considerably high. Again, the black American negotiation between individual-level beliefs and larger ethnic group perceptions present a picture of an ethnic group that subscribes to its own version of the elevated minority for Afro-Caribbeans and Africans in the United States.

In reviewing tables 4.6 and 4.7, African respondents show considerably less favorable views of black American work ethics, and their ability to succeed in the United States, which directly correspond with African respondent attitudes when analyzing table 4.8. So what exactly do the black American responses mean when analyzing how this particular group views its placement within the US labor force, its ability to succeed, in comparison to other black ethnic and immigration groups? When aggregating black responses, black American

Table 4.8 **"If black Americans tried harder, they could be as successful as certain immigrant groups" (in percentages)**

	Blacks	Afro-Car	Africans
Strongly Agree	11	13	33
Agree	33	46	48
Disagree	32	26	15
Str Disagree	21	15	3
Don't Know	3	0	1
N	132	46	89

p < 0.01.
Source: 2005–6 SSEU Local 371 Survey.

subscription to an elevated minority when viewing Afro-Caribbean and African groups in the United States is evident. Black Americans consistently viewed other black ethnic groups as possessing the ability to work harder and serve as the model for black Americans as a group to aspire. Although black Americans acknowledge the limits of the American Dream, they have also internalized their ability and inability to succeed fully in the United States.

The influx of foreign-born individuals joining union organizations through-out the country over the past few decades has challenged traditionally racial-ized sectors of the labor market. The increasing numbers of racial and ethnic newcomers have contributed to black American populations articulating shared racial slights and inequities with other black ethnic groups. However, the same black American groups have also expressed increased feelings of threat. As resources become scarce, groups often shift their understanding and perception of success from the absolute to the relative, and ultimately to the competitive (Hochschild 1995); one member stated, "I don't know how to explain it, but there is an idea that Caribbeans take jobs. The first and second generations are viewed as if they are taking something. There is a perception that something is being taken." Another member argued:

> Black Americans do feel threatened by the influxes of immigrants. They will complain, "The Africans are getting everything…. The white peo-ple hate us and like them [the African members]." If there is an African supervisor, black Americans and even Caribbeans will complain he is looking out for Africans. This may or may not be true.

When respondents were asked to respond to the statement "Immigrants take jobs away from people who were born in America," definitive ethnic dissention

Table 4.9 **"Immigrants take jobs away from people who were born in America"**
(in percentages)

	Blacks	Afro-Car	Africans
Strongly Agree	14	4	1
Agree	21	6	3
Disagree	52	43	39
Strongly Disagree	11	47	56
Don't Know	2	0	0
N	134	47	89

p < 0.01.
Source: 2005–6 SSEU Local 371 Survey.

was evident. When aggregating "agree" and "strongly agree" responses, 35 percent of black American respondents agreed that immigrants take away jobs. Only 10 percent of Afro-Caribbean respondents and 4 percent of African respondents agreed that immigrants take jobs from native-born Americans. Although 35 percent of black Americans is not an incredibly large percent of respondents in agreement, it is still worthy of note that one-third of black American respondents surveyed feel occupational threat (see table 4.9).

One reason why black American opinion regarding immigrants taking jobs was not as high as possibly expected could be a union effect. There has been a level of individual job security within the union. Therefore, the black American opinions regarding immigrants taking jobs could illustrate a previously analyzed effect pertaining to the perception of how one behaves, as opposed to real experience of exposure with the group and subsequent issues at hand, in this case, that of immigrants taking jobs from black Americans.

Conclusion

This chapter shows that black ethnics exhibit poignant opinions toward one another that demonstrate the significant ethnic particularities present in union respondents. The responses indicate varying attitudes pertaining to modes of success and achievement efforts once in the United States, as evidenced in the distinctive attitudes among black ethnic populations. A significant black racial identity is present among native-born and foreign-born populations, when presented with interracial questions regarding whites. Ethnic differences are also present in the ways in which black ethnic populations view their treatment in the United States, who is to blame if success is not attained, the merits of hard work and their correlations with success, and the intersection of immigrants and job availability. The results indicate unity in an interracial context, that is, blacks in contrast to nonblack populations. However, what does not seem as easily negotiable is coalition building in an intraracial context. That is, among black ethnic groups what seems to be a much more successful strategy would be to continue to frame debates with the racially dichotomous black-white paradigm.

How might we then understand elements of black cohesion and also the specific areas of disunity? In analyzing the Local 371 survey data, the answers to these questions lie in ethnic and demographic factors, such as birth and length of time in the United States, which directly affect native-born and foreign-born groups. Compared to native-born black American and Afro-Caribbean immigrants, African immigrants have the most distinctive demographic and socioeconomic variables pertaining to birth in the United States, and length of time in New York City. Almost all African immigrant respondents were born outside of the United States and have spent the least amount of time in New York City.

All three of the black ethnic groups are largely united in opinion when it comes to treatment once in the United States, but they differ in relative warmth toward one another and, which tools are necessary to succeed in the United States, and whether it is hard work, lack of blame, or overall increased efforts that prevent success and incorporation. Overall, none of the black ethnic groups feel they are treated fairly in the United States, although at different degrees. And all black ethnic groups feel African and Afro-Caribbean groups are abundantly more hardworking.

These analyses indicated that Africans are viewed as the most elevated of the black ethnic elevated minorities. They view themselves, and are viewed by other black groups, as the hardest-working. Afro-Caribbeans express constant frustrations with making their own fate and fulfilling the American Dream, versus having their fate handed to them because of their phenotype. Black Americans express a sense of frustration that differs from Caribbean groups in the recognition of individual limits of particular black American groups' members. Therefore, black Americans feel it is individual members of the group that decrease chances of success, but Afro-Caribbean respondents feel it is the institutional limits that prevent incorporation and maximum success and fulfillment of the American Dream.

Black ethnics are united on a racial group level, but differ when questions ask direct ethnic questions. Some Americans realize that even if they do everything they can, they still fail. Some come to understand that their efforts and their talent alone are not enough to guarantee success in America (Hochschild 1995). This line of analysis would explain positive black American attitudes toward black immigrants because they know the effects of race and the barriers that exist for individuals with black skin, and the psychology and prejudice behind the wall that blocks absolute success and vehicles toward advancement.

Black Americans have difficulty "persuading" other black ethnics, due to the fact that their black ethnic counterparts, for the most part, believe that, although black Americans have not been treated well by the country, they still believe overall that black Americans are lazy. African respondents, the newest immigrants, most especially believe that black Americans have no one to blame for their lack of success and that if they tried harder they could attain success.

Overall black ethnic and generational effects contributed to lower levels of racial group unity, thus signaling the import of discerning attitudes of newly arrived black populations in order to better understand future generation's opinions toward larger racial group identification. If future generations of African populations behave similarly to Afro-Caribbeans, then the prospect for a substantial and sustaining group identity are possible.

I found that distinct ethnic opinions emerge regarding the possibilities of fulfilling the American Dream. Afro-Caribbeans expressed unusually high levels of dissatisfaction with the incorporation and acculturation process in America. These results call into question the future of black political participation, the effects of length of time in the United States for black immigrants, and the possibilities for black ethnics' attainment of the American Dream as individuals, as separate ethnic groups, or as a single racial population. This chapter showed that black ethnics exhibit poignant opinions toward one another that demonstrate the significant ethnic particularities present in union respondents. Because of these differing opinions, is it possible for black ethnics to ever become political partners, allies, or leaders? The responses indicate that although varying attitudes pertaining to modes of success and achievement efforts once in the United States present distinctive attitudes of black ethnic populations, a significant overreaching black racial identity is present among native-born and foreign-born populations. Ethnic differences are present in the ways in which black groups view their treatment in the United States who is to blame if success is not attained, the merits of hard work and their correlations with success, and the intersection of immigrants and job availability. The results indicate the possibility of coalition building on an interracial level, that is, blacks in contrast to nonblack populations. However, what does not seem as easily negotiable is coalition building in an intraracial context.

CHAPTER 5

Union Leadership and Policy Choices

TRENDS IN NEUTRAL AND RACIAL GOVERNMENT POLICIES

Previous research on black public opinion suggests that race remains salient in black American's political consciousness and that black groups possess distinct race-based opinions toward government policies (Price 2009; Tate 1993). This chapter suggests two alternative theories surrounding black opinions. First, blacks view the policy issues covered in the survey data not as monolithic, but as distinct types of issues: (1) national spending and (2) spending that is racial or race-based. I find that Local 371 respondents who racially categorize themselves as black separate issues into policy areas that either (1) affect the entire polity or (2) affect their racial group more significantly. Second, certain factors contribute to the impact of ethnic identity and how it in turn influences policy attitudes. Attitudinal distinctions that occur are a result of intraracial attitudes and opinions that black ethnic populations exhibit toward one another. Local 371 black members exhibit differing understandings as to the possibility of obtaining the American Dream, even though a shared racial identity exists. Although Local 371 members participate at higher rates than the national population (Greer 2008), African Local 371 members, the newest arrived group, participated the least (V. S. Johnson 2008). I argue in this chapter that scholars must conceptualize black public opinion in a multifaceted and ethnic way because of the steady influx of African immigrants to the United States in the past three decades. African group immigration has been among the highest levels of new group immigration (Capps, McCabe, and Fix 2011), and the different types of immigrants (educated, refugees, asylum seekers, economic migrants) and the diverse geographic locales present a new understanding of the black population in the United States. Thus I posit that one's ethnicity affects attitudes toward some but not necessarily all government spending issues. The extent to which this occurs is linked to the level of union education provided to the entire member population by Local 371 leadership.

Government spending is an issue that often evokes feelings of entitlement, inequity, neglect, and competition for resources. More recently in mayoral, gubernatorial, and presidential debates and discourse, the fight for government programs and spending has divided communities and constituencies along race, age, class, educational, and even geographic lines. Attitudes toward government spending also evoke feelings of intragroup conflict, competition, and continued struggles for secure placement and advancement in US economic spheres. More generally, attitudes toward spending on particular issues illuminate the needs, wants, and priorities of groups in the United States.

Scholars argue that there are two dimensions that encompass black American belief systems: economic policy and racial group status (Dawson 1994; Pinderhughes 1997a). The interests of black ethnics have an economic component that is both governmental and racialized, whereby individuals view spending as an economic decision that weighs their needs as citizens in the polity and their needs as black citizens as well. The complexity faced by black ethnics is a series of situations whereby they are consistently faced with the duality of race and ethnicity when it pertains to policy decisions. And although ethnicity does factor in specific policy choices at times, there is an overwhelming prevalence and cognizance of race in native-born and foreign-born blacks' decision making. This chapter explores further the significance of race and ethnicity on union members' policy choices, in the cases of black ethnic attitudes toward government spending and policy issues.

The policy issues in this chapter are divided into the two components: "public" and "racial" spending issues. "Public" spending issues include spending on (1) public education, (2) health care, (3) Social Security, (4) defense, and (5) the environment. "Racial" issues include spending on (1) aid to immigrants, (2) welfare programs, and (3) aid to Africa. By public government spending issues, I refer to policies that do not have a specific or explicit racial agenda. These particular policies are in some ways "neutral" in how individuals initially perceive the issue. However, it is important to note that these seemingly public nonracialized policies may have latent racial nonexplicit effects. The distribution of high-quality public education, health care, and Social Security funding in particular do have covert and sometimes overt racial effects. Because the initial political intent of these particular issues was not to elicit a racialized perception, as aid to immigrants or aid to Africa might have been the particular government spending issues were classified as public spending issues. In this context, a racial policy is defined as a policy that has direct racial implications or has origins that, either real or perceived, disproportionately affect populations of color in the United States. The specific policy questions pertaining to aid to immigrants and aid to Africa have specific and direct connotations that relate to and affect populations of color—more specifically, black groups—in the United States. Because African immigrants are currently migrating to the United States at greater rates that Afro-Caribbean immigrants, all three ethnic group perceptions of aid to immigrants and Africa have real racial implications. Similarly, welfare spending has consistently been framed as a racialized policy, even before Reagan's infamous "welfare queens" speech, which forever framed black women and families as the primary dependents (and also undeserving recipients) of this particular government program. In this particular instance, a "neutral" public government program initially instituted to temporarily assist the poor has become a racialized program in the eyes of white and nonwhite individuals and groups.

This chapter evaluates SSEU Local 371 labor union member attitudes toward domestic and international policy issues and finds that black ethnic respondents share similar opinions with their fellow colleagues toward public government spending issues. It also shows that ethnicity is salient when racial or ethnically related spending issues are presented. Scholars contend that opinions of groups and subgroups are subject to change depending on perceived benefits (Sanders 1988; Jacoby 1994). Especially noteworthy are the distinctions in black ethnic attitudes toward aid to immigrants and aid to Africa. For spending on Africa, Local 371 black American members reported attitudes that placed them firmly between nonblack and black ethnic members. In addition, black Americans were the least willing of all black ethnic groups to support increased spending on aid to immigrants.

Little is known about the nature of black foreign-born opinions regarding government spending. However, evidence from the Local 371 survey show that differences in these opinions do exist among black ethnics. To the extent that the respondents feel the issue directly affects their racial and/or ethnic groups' standing or placement in society, distinct opinions come to the fore. I find that ethnicity for Local 371 black respondents' contributes to distinctions between "public" or national spending issues and "racialized" spending—for policies or programs with racial and/or ethnic repercussions. Second, I find that union membership affects black respondent attitudes toward particular national spending issues but does not affect opinions toward issues that were not discussed, educationally promoted, or strategized about by Local 371 leadership.

The education of union members regarding such issues as public education, health care, and Social Security indicates the highly cohesive issue awareness exhibited by Local 371 members. For public spending areas where issue education neither occurred for rank-and-file members nor was promoted by union elites, no conclusive union member attitudinal patterns emerged. However, union education and formal discussions did not ensue for the more racial spending issues and therefore did not affect attitudes in the same politically relevant ways. In addition, black union members exhibited stronger ethnic attitudes when answering racialized spending questions—representing the balance between racial and ethnic group attachments, union memberships, and education on specific spending issues. These individuals are not blank slates, and their processing of political information is affected by their political knowledge (Lock, Shapiro, and Jacobs 1999) and the changing prioritization of group affiliation and identity.

For the three government spending issues utilized in the union survey (i.e., public education, health care, and Social Security), the findings showed that institutionalized political education has helped create a politically sophisticated and cohesive population. According to President Charles Ensley, there were several mechanisms through which the union could educate its members on issues such as health care benefits and debates surrounding policies funded by the union. According to Ensley:

> We have a union newspaper, the *Unionist*. We have a growing Political Action Committee. We also have union meetings, monthly delegate meetings. We also hired ten workers, union organizers, who visit locations on a daily basis to visit workers and have meetings or one on one contact. Also, we leaflet locations regarding [these] specific issues. Those are some of the ways we disseminate information throughout the union and educate our members.

Scholars have spent significant amounts of energy comparing white versus black opinions as they relate to government spending (de la Garza and DeSipio 1998; Dawson 1994). Attitudes toward economic and racialized policy choices have led to a complex belief system for blacks.[1] Scholars continue to acknowledge black political "constraints" imposed by white politics (Price and Hampton 2010; Tate 2004). The presence and interaction with white politics creates a multidimensional political space for blacks. Black Americans have historically supported "liberal" economic policies that contribute to the overall betterment of the group. Policies such as increased spending for medicare/Medicaid, Social Security, and even welfare spending have traditionally been supported at greater levels by blacks than by whites. This increased support by blacks is largely an extension of a shared identity and linked fate blacks feel toward the group (Dawson 1994). Therefore, economic dimensions coupled with the presence of a racialized politics create a unique niche for black American political discourse. What distinctions, then, exist within the black ethnic labor community surrounding government spending on public and racial government spending issues? And to what degree do black ethnic groups further complicate the multidimensional space for economic, racial, and now ethnic issues as well?

Data and Brief Findings

To answer the questions surrounding public and racialized government spending, I use data from the 2005–6 SSEU Local 371 Survey, the 2006 Cumulative General Social Survey (GSS), and the 2004 NES.[2] I initially hypothesized that black union members would share the same opinions toward public government spending issues because of union issue education by union leadership. I also hypothesized that black ethnics would exhibit specific ethnic distinctions when presented with racialized government spending issues. Although I hypothesized that black ethnic distinctions would persist for racialized spending issues, I also hypothesized that black ethnic responses would be more cohesive when compared to white and Latino attitudes toward racialized government spending issues. Several interesting findings emerge from the Local 371 data. First, black respondents view the issues asked about as two distinct sets: racial verses neutral government spending issues. Second, I find that Local 371 black ethnic opinions toward neutral government public spending issues are relatively identical. Third, I find that Local 371 black ethnics exhibit distinct opinions regarding issues not promoted by the union. For issues not consistently discussed by Local 371 leadership, black Americans and Afro-Caribbeans responded the most similarly regarding the environment when compared to African members. The similar opinions of black American and Afro-Caribbean members raise important questions surrounding the effect that length of time in the United States has on black opinion formation and shared attitudes. Previous scholars have argued that increased length of time in the United States has contributed to increased Afro-Caribbean identification with black Americans and has possibly led to "downward assimilation" and association. Therefore, when observing differing African member attitudes regarding public government spending as compared to other black ethnics, it is necessary to note not just the ethnic effects, but the generational effects as well. Although, black American and African members showed the most similar responses regarding defense spending, for spending issues not promoted by the union, black American opinions were situated in between those of Afro-Caribbean and African members.

Last, I find that Local 371 black American attitudes toward government spending on policies such as aid to immigrants and aid to Africa differ drastically from their black ethnic counterparts' attitudes, in that black Americans were less supportive of increased aid. However, black American support for increased aid to Africa was substantially greater than white and Latino Local 371 members. When asked about increased spending for aid to Africa, a continent that represents a shared diasporic relationship, black Americans did support increased spending, but not at the levels of black ethnics. However, the most interesting finding was the overwhelming support for increased aid to Africa by Afro-Caribbean respondents. Black ethnic groups within Social Services Employees Union Local 371 exhibited substantially similar attitudes toward public government spending issues promoted by the union. There was even an element of racial cohesion regarding issues not promoted by the union leadership. However, black ethnics displayed compellingly distinct differences in opinion toward aid to immigrants. Foreign-born blacks felt a greater necessity to support aid for immigrants than black Americans did. The results indicate that ethnicity does affect policy attitudes. The results also show a complex overlapping of union, black racial, and specific ethnic identities when analyzing government spending issues.

Observing racial and ethnic group attitudes surrounding increased spending for public education, health care, and Social Security, white union member opinions were the least congruent with other racial and ethnic groups. This could be attributed to what Price and Zaller (1993) explained as "learning gaps", in that for certain populations there was a disconnect between exposure and reception. Even with increased education efforts by union leaders surrounding these policy areas, however, whites exhibited the most distinct opinions when compared to other Local 371 members.

My hypotheses about black attitudes pertaining to racial government spending were further tested using 2006 GSS and 2004 NES to measure blacks' attitudes.[3] To measure attitudes toward government spending using national samples of black populations, the standard GSS questions were utilized. These questions ask whether the government spends too much or too little on public education, health care, Social Security, welfare programs, environment, and defense. Specific government spending questions pertaining to aid to newly arrived immigrants, and aid to Africa were not asked in the national surveys used.[4]

The 2006 GSS respondents exhibited less supportive attitudes toward government spending issues. For the three issues—public education, health care, and Social Security—where the union leaders incorporated issue education into the dissemination of information to its members, Local 371 members supported spending for these policy issues at much more substantial rates than groups in the national data. For government spending issues that were not promoted by the union leadership, there were no consistent findings when compared with the national survey data. On the national level, respondents supported increases in defense spending at greater rates than Local 371 members but did not support increases in spending on the environment at the level of Local 371 members. The 2004 NES and 2006 GSS data were used to provide national comparisons to "racial" spending issues. Comparing national and union data, Local 371 members were more supportive of increased spending on welfare policy matters, which is not surprising, since the Local 371 members are employees of a social welfare union. However, Local 371 respondents had differing levels of support for aid to immigrants and immigration when compared to national 2004 NES samples.

Government Spending on Nonracialized Issues and Cohesive Member Attitudes

Government spending for nonracial issues forces individuals to think about singular and group needs and wants (Gilens 1999). Often we think of nonracialized issues as not having racial implications; however, we know nonracial policies do have implicit racial implications because they are tied to how individuals view the government. And because spending issues are linked to attitudes and perceptions of the government, these spending policies are inextricably linked to race, the American Dream, that is, the potential of the polity to provide an equitable good. A portion of Goren's (2003) definition of attitudes toward government spending has provided a framework pertaining to these issues. He stated that group attitudes are based on "how positively or negatively people evaluate federal spending on programs that provide material benefit" (Goren 2003: 202–3). Although Goren was most interested in social welfare spending (Jacoby 1994) and how attitudes toward federal spending on such issues are structured in one's memory, his conceptual framework was useful for this study's analysis. Goren suggested that attitudes toward government spending are unidimensionally and coherently structured in the long-term memory. He further argued that the politically educated are "exposed more frequently to public discourse and are more likely to retain the implications of what they encounter" (Goren 2003: 204). Because of that, Local 371 members' attitudes toward education, health care, and Social Security spending are noticeably different from the national data. These issues areas are consistently reinforced throughout the union, which has contributed to cohesive opinions on these particular issues. The three specific issues President Ensley spoke about most emphatically were public education, health care, and Social Security. When analyzing black union member responses, all racial and ethnic groups exhibited overwhelming attitudinal cohesion when responding to questions concerning three issue areas. And all groups believed money for these social programs should be increased.

PUBLIC EDUCATION SPENDING

Believing that public education is a good that the polity provides its citizens may be naive. We know all public education is not equal. However, it is often the combination of the segregation of people of color and class constraints that contribute to the unequal allocation of public education resources and funding. Perhaps we must begin to view public education in the same light that Local 371 members do—that is, to view public education spending as a civil right.

The questions in the SSEU Local 371 survey asked, "Should spending for X be increased, stay the same, or decrease?" When respondents were asked about government spending for public education, 95 percent or more of all respondents, except for white respondents (who were ten points less supportive), expressed a desire to increase funding for public education spending (see table 5.1a).[5] Union respondents support for public education can be related to their feelings of what the polity can and should provide. Public education is a common good that, in theory, can be shared by all members of society. Turnball and Turnball (1998), for example, found that public education and equitable educational opportunities are a resource that democratic nations provide all citizens.

Table 5.1a **Local 371: Public Education Spending (in percentages)**

	Whites	*Blacks*	*Afro-Car*	*Africans*	*Latinos*
Increase	85	98	100	95	96
Stay Same	12	2	0	4	4
Decrease	2	0	0	1	0
N	41	129	46	91	54

p < 0.10.
Source: 2005–6 SSEU Local 371 Survey.

President Ensley and the Local 371 membership consistently framed increases in public education spending as a necessity that should be provided by the local, state, and national governments. When extending the view of public education spending to national data, the GSS data spending question was "Do you think the national government spends too little, the right amount, or too much on X?" Nationally, GSS respondents did support spending increases for public education, but not at the same overwhelming levels as Local 371 members. In both the national and the Local 371 data, black respondents were more likely to express a desire to increase spending for public education (see table 5.1b). The national data reported that 77 percent of black Americans and 73 percent of foreign-born blacks supported increased public education spending.

It is evident that the influence of union leadership on the discourse surrounding public education contributed to overwhelming union support for public education. President Ensley often articulated the social justice mission of the union using education as the primary vehicle to move the union forward. Access to public education was articulated by the president and the executive leadership

Table 5.1b **GSS: Public Education Spending (in percentages)**

	Native-Born Blacks	Foreign-Born Blacks	Whites	Others
Too Little	77	73	69	77
Stay Same	21	26	25	21
Too Much	2	1	6	2
N	1,853	126	11,039	380

P < 0.01.
Source: 2006 General Social Survey.

as the primary means for advancement—that is, the continuous education of its members.

In other words, increases in public education across the board can uplift all sectors of a community, both rich and poor (Fernandez and Rogerson 1996). According to President Ensley, overall increased spending in education is perceived as a mutual benefit for the well-being of all in a community, be it a union, neighborhood, city, or the nation as a whole.

HEALTH CARE SPENDING

The most obvious question for many Local 371 members pertained to their opinions regarding increases in health care spending. As a union whose primary mission is to assist populations who rely on social services provided by employees whose job has been contextualized as a civil rights mission, the question pertaining to health care illustrates racial cohesion between members who view health care as an extension of mutual benefits for all members of society.

When union members were asked about spending for health care, 96 percent or more of all respondents, except for whites, indicated that increased spending was desired. The formalized political education regarding policy issues by the Local 371 leadership has contributed to the cohesion of black respondents and the support for increases in health care spending. White member responses differed from black ethnic and Latino members by 15 and 17 percentage points, respectively, which suggested a level of "immunity" to institutionalized union education regarding issues discussed by Local 371 leadership. However, it is important to note that 81 percent of white members did support an increase in government spending for health care (see table 5.2a). It is also of interest to note Latino respondent cohesion with black ethnics. These shared opinions raise interesting questions surrounding how issue framing by leadership leads to collective attitudes on spending issues (T. E. Nelson and Kinder 1996; Page and Shapiro 1992). Latino member responses also raise important questions

Table 5.2a **Local 371: Healthcare Spending (in percentages)**

	Whites	Blacks	Afro-Car	Africans	Latinos
Increase	81	96	96	98	98
Stay Same	17	4	4	1	2
Decrease	2	0	0	1	0
N	41	129	47	90	54

p < 0.01.
Source: 2005–6 SSEU Local 371 Survey.

surrounding extended racial coalition building between black and Latino groups within the union for nonracial issues.

Union members may conceptualize health care spending as a predictor of attitudes regarding the general responsibility of the polity. Linking these responses to member attitudes regarding the American Dream and the role and responsibility of the polity illustrates union membership attitudes regarding the responsibility of the national government and how the role of the government affects one's life chances are discussed in greater detail. Increases in health care spending are often "value judgments about non-quantifiable issues involving quality of care" (Mashaw and Marmor 1994: 455). In this instance, the distinct racial solidarity surrounding this issue suggests some group interest effects. What data and elite level interviews cannot account for are the distinctions in white member opinion. White respondents still show significant support for increases in health care spending, just not at the same levels as black ethnic and Latino respondents.

Almost 100 percent of black respondents agreed to increases in health care spending. President Ensley explained:

> Part of the union's rhetoric and one of the benefits of union membership is health insurance. This is a college-educated group that understands this and have seen benefits eroded over the years, for prescription drugs and increased copays, to keep up with rampaging increases in costs. They're reacting to reality that their share is going up, and it's a real concern.

Because of the real effects of health care benefits affecting union members, the overwhelming support for increased spending on health care is not surprising. Observing national data, native-born and foreign-born blacks were the most eager to support increased health care spending compared to other racial groups (see table 5.2b). When comparing union responses to national data,

Table 5.2b **GSS: Healthcare Spending (in percentages)**

	Native-Born Blacks	Foreign-Born Blacks	Whites	Others
Too Little	80	78	68	73
Stay Same	17	21	26	22
Too Much	3	1	6	4
N	1841	126	10977	380

p < 0.01.
Source: 2006 General Social Survey.

national levels of support for health care spending were still less than union member responses, thereby suggesting the effect of issue framing by the union leadership.

The GSS national data indicate that there is a considerable percentage of respondents who believe the government spends too little on health care, however, no overwhelming agreement was attained regarding increased spending as compared to the Local 371 survey. No matter the context, white support for increased health care spending is less than the black population, both native-born and foreign-born. There are well-documented racial health disparities in access to food, cultural competency of care prodivers, and in the implementation of policy and program development, to name a few (Gordon-Larsen et al. 2006; Williams and Jackson 2005; Brach and Fraserirector 2000). The studies highlighting these disparities may help explain the union and national data. Racial and ethnic disparities extend to data pertaining to health procedures, surgeries, and overall utilization of the health care system. Well-documented analyses concluding that whites receive more adequate health care in the United States correlate with responses by blacks urging increased spending for health care (Baicker et al. 2004). Black ethnic support for increased health care spending is therefore not out of the ordinary.

SOCIAL SECURITY SPENDING

In addition to public education and health care spending, union member responses to Social Security spending revealed a level of racial and ethnic cohesion, which shows the effect of union member influences, especially when compared to the national data. Observing Social Security spending, Local 371 respondents indicated a desire to increase spending. However, the percentages of union members supporting increased Social Security spending did not reach the exuberant levels of those supporting increased public education and health care spending (see table 5.3a).[6]

Interestingly, the data indicate that African member respondents were the least likely to express a desire to increase funding for Social Security compared to other racial or ethnic groups. Eighty-two percent, however, is still a substantial percentage, and it is important to note that the vast majority of African respondents migrated from a nation with no formal (or informal) Social Security system.[7] The shared desire of union members for increased Social Security spending speaks to the larger union conversations pertaining to social welfare programs provided by the polity and the shared benefits for union members as well as members of the larger polity.

When comparing Local 371 responses to the national data, black respondents were more supportive of increased spending than whites were (see table 5.3b). National respondents were not as likely as Local 371 members of any race to support increased Social Security spending when comparing the reported data in tables 5.3a and 5.3b.

Often Social Security spending is associated symbolically with race, albeit in subtle ways (Winter 2006). The distribution of this universal government program has racialized political implications and direct effects on policy making. Importantly, it is not just native-born blacks' views of increased Social Security spending. Foreign-born blacks within the union as well as on the national level express a greater desire to increase spending for Social Security when compared

Table 5.3a **Local 371: Social Security Spending (in percentages)**

	Whites	Blacks	Afro-Car	Africans	Latinos
Increase	85	90	87	82	89
Stay Same	15	9	13	18	11
Decrease	0	1	0	0	0
N	41	128	47	91	53

Not statistically significant.
Source: 2005–6 SSEU Local 371 Survey.

Table 5.3b **GSS: Social Security Spending (in percentages)**

	Native-Born Blacks	Foreign-Born Blacks	Whites	Others
Too Little	75	66	53	67
Stay Same	22	30	40	27
Too Much	3	4	7	6
N	3,783	252	22,020	731

$p < 0.01$.
Source: 2006 General Social Survey.

to white respondents on both the union and national levels. This desire to increase government spending allows us to view more closely foreign-born black attitudes toward the role and responsibility of the government. It is apparent that union issue education contributes to increased levels of support for greater government spending. Overall, both tables present a racial picture where black groups, both native-born and foreign-born, support increased spending for Social Security at greater levels than whites.

Government Spending on Nonracial Issues and Differing Member Attitudes

The two remaining public government spending issues that were not formally discussed by President Ensley or the union leadership were defense spending and the environment. What is critical for interpreting and understanding these results is the importance of previous discussions by elites for union members. One member stated:

> Political education is on an ad hoc basis and comes out of pressing issues of our time. There is no formal instruction or setting for certain issues. We are involved in teaching members how to identify causes and move forward.

This lack of formal issue framing for particular issues can directly contribute to issue vacuums with the rank-and-file union membership. Given the diverse opinions of union members pertaining to issues which were not framed or articulated in detail by the Local 371 leadership, we are able to observe the extent to which union issue education contributes to cohesive and sometimes homogeneous issue opinions.

DEFENSE SPENDING

Not only do we observe differences between black and white groups; in addition, defense spending for Afro-Caribbean union members and foreign-born blacks on the national level raises important questions pertaining to the military industrial complex and the effect and support for increasing the US military on nonnative nonwhite populations. Increasingly, defense spending in developing nations failed to promote economic growth (Kusi 1994; Chowdhury 1991). Also, the socioeconomic structure and type of government in particular countries affects how defense spending is allotted (Mampilly 2011). This modest explanation makes Afro-Caribbean and foreign-born black attitudes against increased defense spending more salient. Individuals who migrate from nations with strong militaries, low GDP, and limited social services are warranted in their lack of support for increased defense spending. When observing responses for increases in defense spending, no more than 18 percent of any racial or ethnic group indicated that they would like to see increases in defense spending (see table 5.4a). The significance of Afro-Caribbean respondents' desire to decrease defense spending is consistent with several Afro-Caribbean interviewees: on the one hand, they appreciated the opportunities afforded them once in the United States; on the other, many felt the United States exercised too much power over individuals at home (pertaining to black groups) and abroad (pertaining to people of color around the globe). When asked specifically about the US government's military involvement in other countries, one Afro-Caribbean respondent simply stated, "It's not right." In contrast, one African member who migrated from Nigeria stated that he would not support increased defense spending if he still lived in Nigeria, but since moving to the United States, he saw the value of a strong defense as long as it did not oppress its citizens.

These opinions of large numbers of Local 371 members can be attributed to the fact that the union defines itself as a social justice labor organization. Although the rates at which members wanted to decrease defense spending vary, at least 40 percent of all groups expressed a desire to decrease spending, and black ethnic populations were the most likely to support decreases.

Although the union never declared an explicit antiwar position, President Ensley took an outspoken antiwar stance. President Ensley was very clear to union leadership and rank-and-file members that Local 371 is a union that represents a social justice mission that is antiwar. It is important to note that attitudinal distinctions exist among racial and ethnic groups toward decreased or stayed defense spending. In accord with previous findings throughout this study, Afro-Caribbean respondents were the least likely to support large-scale government initiatives. Several Afro-Caribbean union members relayed stories of their home country, either from vague knowledge as children or from stories

Table 5.4a **Local 371: Defense Spending (in percentages)**

	Whites	Blacks	Afro-Car	Africans	Latinos
Increase	15	10	9	18	17
Stay Same	44	33	21	30	40
Decrease	41	57	70	52	42
N	41	129	47	91	52

p < 0.10.
Source: 2005–6 SSEU Local 371 Survey.

they had heard passed down from their parents. One member explained, "My parents weren't progovernment because they were coming from a dictatorship. Labor means something different here than back home." Another member stated that the lack of support for extensive government programs and initiatives stems from a fear of government intervention. He said, "Many people did come here with nothing, they left violent governments to come here, and that's where the fear of government comes from."

A fear of government for many respondents directly relates to increased military involvement and therefore an increased role of government in their individual lives. Ironically, many respondents did not view social services programs and policies through the same lens of government involvement. Most black ethnic Local 371 members hail from countries with weak social service networks and strong military involvement and presence. For many Local 371 members, public education, health care, and Social Security were not government programs readily available in their home countries. Therefore, their belief in what the government should provide versus the draconian presence of the government contributes to their way of conceptualizing how the US government should allocate resources.

An interesting finding emerges from GSS national data. Foreign-born blacks were the group that believed the government spent too much on defense (see table 5.4b). Black respondents, native-born and foreign-born, were the least likely to support defense spending, when compared to white respondents on the national level. What this evidence suggests is a larger overall lack of black racial and ethnic support for increases in defense not just within a social justice union context, but on a national level as well. Although there was no explicit issue education against defense spending (and ergo the wars in Iraq and Afghanistan) by President Ensley or Local 371 leadership, the attitudes of Local 371 are similar to national black group attitudes. However, Afro-Caribbean union member attitudes suggest a specific ethnic motivation present.

Table 5.4b **GSS: Defense Spending (in percentages)**

	Native-Born Blacks	Foreign-Born Blacks	Whites	Others
Too Little	17	8	21	17
Stay Same	43	38	47	43
Too Much	40	53	32	40
N	1,749	118	10,865	360

p < 0.01.
Source: 2006 General Social Survey.

ENVIRONMENTAL SPENDING

Last, when respondents were asked about spending for the environment, there was some slight disunity among union respondents pertaining to increases in spending for the environment. Elliot et al. (1997) argue that individual-level and macro-level contexts contribute to feelings related to spending on the environment. They state that a myriad of factors, such as age, education, gender, ideology, and party affiliation, influence attitudes in nonsuccinct ways. Interviews with union members did not illicit any cohesive understanding of environmental policies and spending preferences. When interviewing union executives, they stated they did not explicitly link their work and mission to environmental issues. Therefore, environmental policies and concerns were not discussed as a unionwide conversation (see table 5.5a).[8]

Again, white union respondents were the least likely to support increases in environmental spending. When President Ensley was asked about his white members, he expressed unity with all union members. However, the possibility of a level of leadership immunity is plausible. President Ensley did describe the growing number of white labor members who are migrating from Eastern European countries. He did not know exactly how many new non-native-born white members the union had, but he did say that over the past twenty years he had noticed more white ethnic members assimilating into the union and integrating with other white members. If this is indeed the case, then the union, or unions in general, are homes for all newly migrated groups seeking to incorporate into the middle class (Warren 2005).

The national data shows that native-born and foreign-born blacks were again more inclined to report that the government spent too little on a spending issue (see table 5.5b).

In the Local 371 data and the national level data, attitudes for white respondents were almost identical. However, black responses indicated that foreign-born

Table 5.5a **Local 371: Environment Spending (in percentages)**

	Whites	Blacks	Afro-Car	Africans	Latinos
Increase	62	81	83	73	85
Stay Same	38	17	15	26	15
Decrease	0	2	2	1	0
N	39	128	47	90	52

p < 0.10.
Source: 2005–6 SSEU Local 371 Survey.

Table 5.5b **GSS: Environment Spending (in percentages)**

	Native-Born Blacks	Foreign-Born Blacks	Whites	Others
Too Little	68	70	63	69
Stay Same	26	26	29	26
Too Much	5	3	8	5
N	1,785	118	10,885	379

p < 0.05.
Source: 2006 General Social Survey.

and native-born blacks at the national level were less likely than Local 371 black members to indicate that the government should increase spending on the environment.

Black ethnic Local 371 members expressed relatively unified opinions regarding education, Social Security, and health care and have processed information that has been disseminated and explained by union leadership. Because of this, relative homogeneity has existed among black ethnic groups. A common union identity and political education was observed in attitudes toward public education, Social Security, and health care. However, for government spending issues that had not been fully explained or discussed by the union leadership, ethnic cohesion was present, but it was not overt. What was relatively consistent was the level of black ethnic cohesive opinions when compared to white responses on the Local 371 and national levels.

Government Spending on "Racial" Issues

Scholars contend that although standard political measures were of importance, such as political ideology, party identification, and other "core values," the most significant factor in one's attitude toward support for government spending were racial considerations (Goren 2003). Using social welfare spending framework set forth by Gilens (1999) that analyzed whites' perceptions of blacks, the welfare system, and the deserving poor, Gilens found that racial beliefs had significant effects on attitudes toward government spending. Most important here are that attitudes toward spending were partially driven by symbolic racism. This begged the question, when analyzing "racial" government spending issues, would black American respondents exhibit symbolic racism toward immigrant groups? Or would a perceived societal racism lead overwhelmingly to shared black ethnic opinions?

For blacks living in the United States, racial and ethnic status is salient and has contributed to a level of duality in decision making and opinion formation.

Tables 5.6a–8 report the overall attitudes of black ethnic, white, and Latino responses toward racialized government spending questions. In general, black American attitudes differed from African and Caribbean opinions on issues pertaining to immigrants. The one exception was aid to Africa. The shared racial responses of black ethnics toward aid to Africa did not extend to other racialized policy issues. Black American attitudes regarding increased spending to Africa were greater than Latino and white opinions. Although black American opinions pertaining to increased spending for aid to Africa did not reach the same rates of African and Afro-Caribbean responses, the presence of a linked fate and shared identity was evident in the survey responses and the interviews with Local 371 members.

Found within the data were (1) a level of cohesive attitude formation regarding public government spending issues, (2) a level of shared racial identification regarding issues that placed blacks in relative "opposition" to whites, as in aid to Africa and welfare spending, and (3) limited cohesion when individuals' specific ethnic identity was salient.

Reviewing the three "racial" government spending issues, distinct ethnic attitudes exist regarding government spending for aid to newly arrived immigrants, welfare, and aid to Africa. The spending issues that presented the greatest level of disunity among black Local 371 members involved aid to Africa and aid to legal immigrant populations. For the issues, black American respondents were the least supportive of aid to immigrants.

The lack of black American desire for increased government spending stemmed from black Americans view of immigrants, both black and nonblack immigrants, as threats to their political and tenuous economic "security." Black Americans' entrance into the middle class, political offices, and particular occupational, educational, and income brackets has largely been achieved within the past five decades, a relatively short period of time, which leaves the entrée of any other group as a threat to this newfound placement. Several Local 371 black Americans interviewees believed that an additional good for others translates into a subtraction of goods for themselves.

SPENDING ON IMMIGRANTS

Regarding attitudes toward aid to newly arrived immigrants, black Americans were the least likely, even less likely than white and Latino union respondents, to support increased spending. The SSEU Local 371 survey asked respondents, "Please indicate if you would like to see spending for it increased, decreased, or if you would leave it the same:...Aid to newly arrived immigrants." Only 14 percent of black American respondents, compared to 53 and 51 percent of

Table 5.6a **Local 371: Aid to Newly Arrived Immigrants Spending (in percentages)**

	Whites	Blacks	Afro-Car	Africans	Latinos
Increase	22	14	53	51	23
Stay Same	46	52	34	44	51
Decrease	32	34	13	4	26
N	41	128	47	90	53

$p < 0.01$.
Source: 2005–6 SSEU Local 371 Survey.

Afro-Caribbean and African respondents respectively, supported an increase in spending for aid to immigrants (see table 5.6a).

In interviews with black American union members, they suggested that their view of other immigrant populations as potential sources of economic drain lead to their limited support regarding spending for immigrants. The 14 percent of black Americans support for increased immigrant aid spending was less than the 22 percent of whites and the 23 percent of Latinos who supported increased spending on aid to immigrants. The complexity of racial solidarity and ethnic competition is evident among black ethnic groups. In this particular instance, black union members do not support increases in spending for minority groups despite the social justice framework provided by union elites. Several black American union members expressed the need to "take care of home" before additional money is spent on newcomers. Other black American members said that they saw American people struggling (financially) every day at their jobs— that is, the site visits and individuals who relied on social services. Because of this, they did not see how the system could withstand financial obligations to all newcomers. At times, the struggles and tensions within the union are racial as well as ethnically based. One member stated, "Old immigrants even fear new immigrants. They want to close borders because they feel threatened by those who may come and take what little they have."

Schiller et al. (1995) argue that "once we reframe the concept of immigration and examine the political factors which have shaped the image of the immigrant as the uprooted, a whole new approach to understanding immigration becomes possible." The 2004 NES questionnaire asked, "Should immigration be increased, decreased, or stay the same?"

The majority of black, white, and Latino respondents on the national level indicated that the rates of immigration should remain the same (see table 5.6b).[9]

Table 5.6b **NES: Should Immigration Increase, Decrease, or Stay Same? (in percentages)**

	Whites	*Blacks*	*Latinos*
Increase	26	33	36
Stay Same	69	58	47
Decrease	4	9	17
N	854	172	72

p < 0.01.
Source: 2004 National Election Study.

The overwhelming opinions of black, white, and Latino respondents to maintain the levels of immigration reflects what Schiller et al. (1995) argue regarding immigration. These groups in many ways are fine with the maintenance of the status quo: they do not want to take away aid money, but they do not support increases in funding either.

WELFARE SPENDING

When specific policy questions pertaining to immigrants were asked, black ethnic groups expressed ethnically distinct opinions. Local 371's black American respondents exhibited opinions more closely associated with those of Local 371's white members. However, observing national data, black Americans exhibited opinions more closely allied with Latinos. The attitudes of black ethnic opinions toward spending on welfare raise very important questions surrounding alliances, coalition building, and issue framing and formation across racial and ethnic groups. I defined spending on welfare as a racialized issue because discussions pertaining to welfare have often been conflated with class. Still, spending for welfare has become a racialized issue, even if it initially began as a purely government assistance issue.[10] In addition, Local 371 members work with populations who are largely welfare recipients (see appendix 5A for union thermometers toward people on welfare and poor people). The politics of race and the politics of the American welfare state have been intertwined since FDR and the New Deal, therefore almost all understandings and attitudes pertaining to any social services must be understood in a historical context of race and class (Davies and Derthick 1997).

   Group opinion on welfare spending was not as cohesive as the government spending issues that were heavily promoted by the union leadership. Fewer than half of all union members indicated that too little was spent on welfare programs. However, black American and Afro-Caribbean respondents were the most likely to support increases for welfare programs. In accord with earlier findings, it should not come as a surprise that African respondents were the least likely of black ethnics in the study to support welfare programs (see table 5.7a). African respondents indicated that they fundamentally believed that hard work equaled success in the United States; that people have no one to blame if they do not succeed; and that they can achieve a voice in the American system through voting. This belief in self-help is in concert with Africans attitudes toward welfare spending. One member explained:

> The African members come to the US better educated, and had they stayed in their respective home countries they would most likely be a part of the middle or upper class. They largely view this work as something to do until they can do the job in the profession in which they were trained in their home country.

However, other members think gender and culture play a role in member attitudes toward not just government involvement, but overall participation within the union. One member stated:

> African women do not take as active a role in the union as African men. The women will call and advocate for a particular person or change, but they will back up if called to do more. They very rarely go to the next level. I don't know if they do not want the responsibility or if they think it is not their place.

It is clear that other black members of the union are cognizant of the ethnic dynamics within the union. However, ethnicity and gender are clearly indicators of particular attitudes and behaviors for certain Local 371 members. In this particular instance, regarding welfare spending, white Local 371 member opinions more closely aligned to black American and Afro-Caribbean member attitudes. African and Latino Local 371 members were the least inclined to support increased welfare spending.

Table 5.7a **Local 371: Welfare Programs (in percentages)**

	Whites	Blacks	Afro-Car	Africans	Latinos
Increase	39	45	45	32	28
Stay same	34	40	40	43	52
Decrease	27	15	15	25	20
N	41	129	47	89	54

Not statistically significant; 2005–6 SSEU Local 371 Survey.

Race has long played a decisive role in social policy agendas and spending (Lieberman 2008; Quadagno 1994), and the effects of these debates can be seen in present-day attributes. FDR's extension of social welfare provisions to whites and the subsequent discrimination African Americans incurred was the price to pay for the New Deal policies. At the time white racism drove (and many would argue that even today it drives) many of the decisions made regarding social welfare policies. GSS data of black populations parallels Local 371 data in that black respondents, both native- and foreign-born, were more likely to support welfare as compared to nonblack groups (see table 5.7b). In this instance, social welfare policies have ceased being predominantly rich versus poor issues and have transformed into the transference of income and for select members of society (Quadagno 1994). Many overall exclusions of the original 1935 Social Security Act were founded primarily on racial exclusion (Lieberman 2008). Therefore, it is not surprising that blacks, both native-born and foreign-born, would argue that too little money is being spent.

Table 5.7b **GSS: Welfare Program Spending (in percentages)**

	Native-Born Blacks	Foreign-Born Blacks	Whites	Others
Too Little	40	41	17	27
Stay Same	31	27	33	39
Too Much	29	32	50	34
N	1,791	117	10,868	377

p < 0.01.
Source: 2006 General Social Survey.

Scholars argue that the distribution of policy preferences are citizens' attempts to satisfy two desires: (1) the desire for government and individuals to take responsibility for dealing with economic hardships (Shapiro et al. 1987), and (2) what Jacoby (1994) would call "ideological schizophrenia," where populations want both an increase in social spending and a decrease in the size of government. Local 371 members in particular continue to express a desire for increased government spending as well as a recognition of the limits of potential government involvement. However, this quandary has largely manifested itself in a racial cohesion among black Local 371 members across ethnic lines, and also as similar attitudes with national black populations.

AID TO AFRICA SPENDING

The question pertaining to aid to Africa is unique in that it is a specific and explicit racial question that is linked to financial interaction with the US government. If indeed a form of linked fate exists for black ethnic groups living in the United

States, then the responses to this specific questions should illicit a cohesive intraracial attitude toward increased spending for the continent by the US government. Reviewing attitudes toward government spending on aid to Africa, black American respondents were again the least likely of all blacks to express the need for increased aid to Africa (see table 5.8). They did, however, support increased aid to Africa at much greater rates than white and Latino Local 371 members.

Table 5.8 **Local 371: Aid to Africa Spending (in percentages)**

	Whites	Blacks	Afro-Car	Africans	Latinos
Increase	32	64	81	74	41
Stay same	39	26	15	19	44
Decrease	29	10	4	7	15
N	41	127	47	90	54

$p < 0.01$.
Source: 2005–6 SSEU Local 371 Survey.

It was initially posited that African respondents would be the most eager to support increases in spending for their continent, but Afro-Caribbean respondents were the most likely to state that increased spending was desirable. This response by Afro-Caribbean members was consistent with previous responses that indicated a larger sense (or the largest sense) of shared racial and ethnic unity. One Afro-Caribbean member said, "We're not going to divide up in a 'this versus that' type of black group. We want to embrace groups." When reviewing Afro-Caribbean responses, both quantitative and qualitative, they are the black ethnic group that is most enthusiastic in highlighting the potential for intraracial collaborations and coalition building. It is clear that Afro-Caribbeans are the most eager to express feelings of solidarity with other black ethnic groups in the hopes of forming some sort of interethnic solidarity. As chapter 4 indicated, Afro-Caribbeans are the group least likely to believe the United States provides resources and opportunities equally across races. It is this lack of faith in what the United States can equitably provide that seems to be driving the elevated levels of black racial solidarity.

The level of black Americans who supported an increase in spending for aid to Africa still indicated a certain level of diasporic understanding among some black American respondents. When asking Local 371 members why African members may not support increased spending for aid to Africa, some interviewees indicated that it was past time for Africa to help herself. The interviewees expressed detailed knowledge surrounding the pros and cons of external international aid and the subsequent independence and debt that follows aid to Africa.[11]

Conclusion

Preferences concerning redistributive policies have been susceptible to incomplete to inaccurate information (Shapiro and Smith 1985), and this lack of complete information has had direct implications for policy making. The results in this chapter, overall, suggest that (1) a clearer understanding of racial versus ethnic spending preferences are necessary in local and national politics and policy making, and (2) these issues also have significant implications for elected officials allocating resources, adapting laws, and responding to the wishes of their constituencies.

Questions surrounding black ethnic attitudes toward racialized and nonracialized issues remain. Jacoby (1994) stated that citizen spending preferences were not equally distributed and did not represent the full needs of citizens. Within this discussion is an underlying assumption that somehow black attitudes are shaped by elite institutions. Moreover, the significance of the duality of race and ethnicity for union members is apparent as various politicized issues are discerned. While the data in this chapter does not fully examine the intricacies of intraracial relationships and interethnic perceptions, it does offer a glimpse of policy spending preferences of blacks using both racial and ethnic identities.

This chapter assesses black ethnic attitudes toward policy issues, an essential component in understanding the intricate relationship of race and ethnicity for black ethnic union members. Comparing Local 371 data with national-level data, I found that depending on the particular issue, Local 371 members react in the same ways as blacks in a national sample. The strength of the racial identity shared between union members and blacks nationally are threatened by issues that tap into ethnic group preferences and priorities. In this chapter I analyzed whether or not black American groups would reveal a level of symbolic racism toward immigrant groups pertaining to "racialized" government spending issues or would they have shared opinions when the perception of racism by other groups existed. I found that blacks used both their racial and ethnic identification when sorting through race-related spending issues. For issues where the interracial divide was most commonly understood, as in welfare spending or aid to Africa, black Americans expressed relatively similar attitudes to black ethnic populations, as compared to whites. However, when the policy issue called for black Americans to identify ethnically—that is, when the question was asked surrounding spending for aid to immigrants—black Americans exhibited less willingness for increased government spending; and it was these specific issues that the Afro-Caribbean and African respondents supported both quantitatively and in member interviews.

Conclusion

Much has changed in the past fifty years. The entry of black ethnic opinions into the discourse of American politics, and more specifically black politics, has increased greatly within the past few decades, even if documentation of this change within the political science literature has been relatively sparse. The rise of black immigrant visibility on the local and even national levels presents the duality of melding their immigrant status with their American status, thus creating what appears to be a unifying effect on an interracial level. However, distinct ethnic attitudes, needs, and desires emerge on an intraracial level, depending on the issue presented. The question for future scholars, activists, and members of the polity is "How exactly can blacks achieve not just linked fate, but actual coalition building?" How can blacks use their shared racial identity and distinct ethnicities to create long-lasting policy that decreases competition for scarce and/ or seemingly scarce resources?

How do blacks in America negotiate the American Dream, and how do they see traditional forms of politics as avenues for the fulfillment of those dreams when the boundaries of race are drawn and largely predetermined before voluntary black immigrants arrive in the United States? The shared phenotype for blacks living in the United States has created not only an amalgam of shared resources, but also competition and a creation of multiple overlapping and even sometimes mutually exclusive communities. The decision to maintain both one's race and ethnicity once in the United States rests, to a certain extent, on how people view their prospects for upward mobility, integration, and ultimately assimilation.

Sociologists and economists have analyzed the ethnic differences among black populations in America in order to discern the significance of race, place, and prosperity for newly arrived black populations. This book examines the opinion differences and similarities that exist among black ethnic populations in order to demonstrate the significance of race and a specific ethnic identity on ones political beliefs and behaviors. Furthermore, this research explains how increased migration of black immigrants affects electoral group policy choices and ethnic identification when the definition and the actual makeup of the black population have changed so significantly since the 1960s. This book provides empirical evidence for what has largely existed as a theoretical and largely qualitative discussion among sociologists,[1] showing how blacks in America conceptualize intraracial interactions and competitions, and the extent to which their shared racial categorization determines how they behave politically, how the government should allocate resources, and what they believe their prospects for success may be. The ultimate goal of this book has been to assess whether native-born and foreign-born populations can forge a significant black coalition that amalgamates the linked fate of racial identity and the maintenance of distinct ethnic identities. The answer is yes, under certain conditions.

For blacks in the United States, at times their racial attachment is their primary identification, such as when events or circumstances affect black people largely due to the color of their skin. And at other times, ethnic attachments take precedence. The shared phenotype of black ethnic populations in the United States, of both native-born and foreign-born groups, contributes to a shared racial identity when assessing their treatment in the United States. However, the shared black phenotype has its limits. As the data show, when specific questions are asked which push respondents to define themselves ethnically, very clear ethnic attachments are evident. The relevance of ethnic identity is directly linked to the strength of one's identity in evaluating other black ethnic groups and contributes to how they negotiate future possibilities for success and advancement in the American polity.

Black ethnic groups in America have been negotiating multiple identities, that of being immigrants, phenotypically black, and American. The permanent "black" modifier is what distinguishes black immigrants from other nonblack immigrant populations, thus the significance of race for phenotypically black populations living in the United States is solidified not necessarily in place of, but rather in addition to, their ethnic identification. Many black immigrants have not given much thought to being "black" before migrating to the United States However, on arrival, they have been confronted with the reality of being black in America, of their treatment in the United States compared to white populations, and of becoming "American with a modifier." Full inclusion in the American polity for black immigrants is not the same as previous assimilations of white ethnics. Nor is it the same as the integration of Latino and Asian immigrants. If black ethnics are to be fully included in American society, scholars argue, they will not attempt to shed their immigrant status and identities in order to become "American." This contrasts with preexisting theories pertaining to the histories of white ethnic populations. Previously, "white" ethnic groups attempted to rid themselves of their immigrant status in order to more easily assimilate and integrate into American society. Instead, in today's America, many black immigrants work to maintain their ethnic identities.

The rationale behind the maintenance of an immigrant or ethnic identity stems from black immigrant populations' inability to assimilate into the American polity without the permanent modifier "black." Black immigrants seek to maintain their ethnic identity so as to distinguish themselves from black American populations. In addition, black ethnics do recognize their linked fate with other phenotypically black populations once in the United States. So the combination of lack of full assimilation for black immigrants, a permanent black modifier attached to their newly minted American status and a sense of linked fate with other phenotypically black peoples has led to a sense of shared identity, on the one hand, and a sense of an elevated minority status, on the other—that is, perceived by whites, nonwhites, and even black Americans as slightly "better" than native-born blacks, but not quite viewed as having the same potential and assimilation prospects as other nonblack immigrant and racial groups. The ways in which the black American, Afro-Caribbean, and Africans negotiate their racial and ethnic identities presents a wealth of questions for the study and future of black politics.

The dominant group, that is to say certain facets of white America, distinguishes black foreign-born populations from native-born blacks at times, yet amalgamates foreign- and native-born populations at other times. Subsequently, a tenuous "in-group of the out-group" status for non-native-born blacks has been created. Because of the racial identification placed upon newly arrived blacks by the dominant group, new black populations are racially classified with black Americans, given a modifier to their American status, and situated in the "out-group." However, because of the elevated minority status bestowed upon non-native-born blacks, their position as a member of the "out-group" with preferential status from the "in-group" creates a dual status for foreign-blacks and therefore further solidifies foreign-born blacks as elevated minorities. The multifaceted identity for many new immigrants has influenced their decision to keep ties with their home country; and for many African and Afro-Caribbean immigrants, the United States is seen as a destination in which to live, but not to die (Rogers 2006). Several African SSEU Local 371 members interviewed indicated that the United States is a destination to fulfill economic goals, but that they fully plan to return to their home countries. Whether or not they will in fact return to their home countries is still unclear. However, the intention to return is stated in abundance.

This project is timely and beneficial to scholars, politicians, and policy makers for several reasons. First, the increasing numbers of blacks in the population has risen from 26.5 million in 1980 to roughly 38.9 million in 2010 (US Census 2010), remaining 12 to 13 percent of the United States population for roughly thirty years. However, the composition of black ethnic groups within that percentage has changed considerably over the past thirty years. Second, this project addresses the geographic, national origin, and ethnic diversity of the black population. According to the 2010 census, Afro-Caribbean and African persons now comprise roughly 10 percent of the black US population.[2] And Africans are among the fastest-growing immigrant groups in the United States, surpassing Afro-Caribbean rates of migration to the United States (Capps, McCabe, and Fix 2011). Historically, when scholars and politicians referred to "African American" or "black American" populations, they were directly or indirectly referring to individuals who were descendants of US slavery. Today, however, the increased diversity of black populations is visible in electoral districts, candidates running for office, emerging policy debates that focus on pressing international issues, and growing differences in views toward domestic policies and programs that have historically assisted black American populations. There is now a significant growth in populations of Haitians in Miami, Jamaicans in New York City, and Ethiopian and Nigerian populations in Washington, DC, to name just a few of the urban centers. Diverse African and Afro-Caribbean groups have also begun to migrate to budding suburban and smaller urban centers such as Pittsburgh, St. Louis, and Madison.

Post–Civil Rights and Real-World Politics: Is a Black Ethnic Coalition Possible?

Black ethnics are also making their presence known in the political arena. Increased activism and mobilization of black immigrant groups has contributed to increased numbers of black ethnic elected officials on the local and now national levels. In New York, Florida, and Illinois, there are electoral districts now represented by Jamaican and Haitian individuals. This growth in black ethnic diversity demonstrates the effects of majority-minority districts as well as the increases in viable black ethnic candidates who are able to amass significant voting base populations (Epstein and O'Halloran 1999).

Because the number of black immigrants in the United States continues to grow, analyses of black ethnic populations have evolved from purely social and cultural interests into political discourse and debate. Let us consider the role of Yvette Clarke, the Brooklyn, New York, congresswoman of Jamaican descent who was elected in a Caribbean and black American district in 2006. Her election to New York's Eleventh District in the US Congress left her city council seat empty and multiple candidates vying for her former position. During the election season there were candidates of Caribbean descent, and a large portion of preliminary candidates were of Haitian descent or Haitian immigrants. Haitian immigrants have been a large presence in the district for years, but due to in-fighting, they could never seem to elect a Haitian candidate due to the numerous Haitian individuals competing for the same seat. For this open election, Haitian leaders united to support one candidate instead of having ten Haitian candidates fracture the vote. National newspapers included articles pertaining to the ethnic diversity of candidates running for city council in New York City and to the power negotiations between black American, old black immigrant, and newly arrived black immigrant populations. Therefore, in 2006, a district in Brooklyn, New York, found itself thinking about the rise of Haitian immigrant candidates in traditionally black American and Jamaican neighborhoods and districts, the prospect of a biracial white and Kenyan presidential candidate who views himself as African American, and the diverse needs and desires of black immigrants in districts represented by traditional black American candidates. This one district illustrated the necessity of an evolved understanding of black politics. In addition, districts in other parts of New York; Washington, DC; Miami; Atlanta; and even Boston were grappling with these same new questions.

Increased numbers of African and Afro-Caribbean candidates have been running and winning electoral offices throughout the country. This growing phenomenon begs the question "Will black immigrant populations emulate black American patterns of political advancement?" As Afro-Caribbean and African candidates make political strides, intraracial tensions are illuminated due to some black American political figures viewing black immigrants as "cousins," but clearly not immediate members of the family. Several black American political leaders from the civil rights movement are now respected elected officials in various levels of government and have called into question black ethnic candidates' racial "authenticity" and attachments to the black race. They argue that these populations have not paid their dues or properly formed the necessary foundations for an evolved political understanding of the black political experience (Harris 2012; Tesler and Sears 2010). For example, as Barack Obama became the first African American president of the United States, his ability to build racial and ethnic coalitions and his overall understandings of the black political experience were evident. He has been able to form descriptive and substantive coalitions having utilized more than the traditional post–civil rights formulas. Black diversity now extends beyond class and region and thus calls the theories of black political leadership, participation and incorporation into question (Dawson 2001).

The steady and current influx of black immigrants in the latter part of the twentieth century and now into the twenty-first has created a new set of questions pertaining to what it means to be "African American," what the future of black political participation will look like, and what similarities and distinctions now exist among the various groups comprising the American black diaspora. Politicians, social critics, and scholars of immigration have become more interested in and aware of the opinions, attitudes, and concerns of individuals migrating from the Caribbean and Africa. Scholars have begun to dissect many questions surrounding black immigrant populations, including these three: How incorporated are black ethnics into American society? What distinguishes them from black American populations? And will these "new blacks" participate in the electoral process in the same or similar ways as black Americans? There are still a multitude of questions for social scientists to unfold: For the purposes of future coalition building, is it beneficial to make ethnic distinctions among black immigrants, or will traditional racial classifications suffice? Will this growth in the black immigrant population and the globalization of America provide for a politically unifying moment for blacks in America?—that is, a unifying moment that extends beyond similar voting patterns and addresses racialized policy issues that affect groups as "blacks" as well as their specific ethnic communities? How does the migration of Afro-Caribbean and African groups to the United States parallel black American migration to Africa and the Caribbean? Because of the emergence of "new" blacks to the United States, the ways in which foreign-born blacks view native-born blacks and also their newfound black American status and, similarly, the ways native-born black Americans view their newly arrived black immigrant counterparts are indicative of a much larger puzzle.

So, yes, coalitions are possible. However, they will take unique forms depending on the geographic locale, the number of black intracial groups involved, the political stakes, and external racial interactions. Scholars have contended that the formation of coalitions among minority groups is possible if two groups are of the same status and class (Giles 1985). When there is an imbalance in size or power, the larger group often prevails. Therefore, less-well-positioned groups are less eager to form coalitions (Deutsch 1985; Meier and Stewart 1991; Sonenshein 1986; C. L. Warren, Stack, and Corbett 1986; Browning, Marshall, and Tabb 1984), and the smaller, seemingly less powerful group may attempt to form coalitions with whites. The smaller group may also become attractive to white populations, thus laying the foundation for "interminority" competition (Segura and Rodrigues 2006) for white support. Group size, intraracial perceptions, and interracial opinions contribute to a complex negotiation of racial and ethnic identity for all black groups involved on local and national levels.[3]

What the Local 371 Results Indicate

While the national origin and ethnic diversity of blacks in America continues to increase, ethnic diversity does not automatically translate into diversity of attitudes and opinions of groups classified as black in the United States. By exploring black attitudes and opinions pertaining to intra and interracial identity, participation, and perceptions of government incorporation, through a systematic evaluation of race, ethnicity, and identity for blacks at this moment in American history, this research (1) determines the participation rates of union members within Local 371 as compared to national data, (2) identifies the intraracial perceptions native-born and foreign-born blacks have of one another, (3) evaluates how policy preferences differ among foreign-born and native-born populations who are members of a highly socially and politically active labor union, and (4) observes whether perceptions of incorporation, inclusions, and success lead to increased linked fate, belief in the American Dream, and ultimately the possibility for coalition building among black populations living in the United States. By focusing on a unique black labor population in New York, I provide a more nuanced conception of black attitudes and political participation. These attitudes and behaviors are critical to our appreciation of race and immigration politics and to our understanding of participation, policy making, representation, and, ultimately, coalition politics.

Overall, Afro-Caribbeans expressed the greatest level of pessimism toward the American polity, equal life chances, and opportunities for black groups, which begs the question of whether or not, with time, this population will begin to adopt black American interpretations of the possibilities for success in America, where there is a recognition of the racial inequities that persist, yet a willingness to remain within the system and utilize political, partisan, and participatory resources in order to bring about change. There were several institutional mechanisms within the union, which contributed to the high levels of participation and Democratic partisanship. They have had the benefit of consistent leadership that has promoted varying forms of political participation. When compared to national populations, including black immigrant populations, Local 371 members were highly participatory. These results are congruent with previous theories which posited that immigrant populations need institutions to assist in incorporating them into the American polity and essentially serve as catalysts for political capital.

Local 371 union members were also educated regarding political issues by union leaders. Issue education within the union worked. If issue education worked for union members—native-born, foreign-born, highly educated professionals—what could be the effects of issue education in a more professionally diverse setting? The policy areas where labor leaders utilized the internal union political structures to introduce, inform, and educate its members about public education, Social Security, and health care yielded consistent and uniform attitudes of Local 371 members. However, for policy areas in which there was limited education by union leaders or for issues defined as "racialized" spending, in which members needed to negotiate racial and spending attitudes, member opinions, especially black ethnic attitudes, were divided, with black Americans exhibiting opinions different from those of Afro-Caribbean and African members. In short, the combination of race, ethnicity, occupation, and the significance of issue education raise substantive questions for future analyses of racial and ethnic politics.

Social scientists define group identification as having two components: a self-awareness component, which is one's membership in the group, and a psychological component, which is the sense of attachment to the group. They argue that it is inaccurate to assume that identification with a group yields a sense of psychological attachment (Miller et al. 1981; Conover 1984).

The Local 371 survey data, in conjunction with national data, point to racial identification that has led to distinctive patterns of perception and evaluation, which in turn have translated into a sense of group solidarity and shared interests (Carmines and Stimson 1982; Conover 1984) and an organization of thoughts and ideas around "visible social groupings" (Converse 1972), however racially motivated they may be.

The Future of Black Ethnic Politics

For some, the election of President Obama, the gains of blacks in the United States over the past twenty to thirty years, and what many continue to define as a "postracial" America have shifted the focus away from the institutional mechanisms of racism that continue to affect native-born and foreign-born black populations and have tended to focus on the overall gains of blacks in the United States. Although black ethnic groups in the United States have made significant gains, there are still several areas of research that can be explored further by scholars of race, ethnicity, immigration, identity, electoral politics, political sociology, urban politics, and related facets of comparative politics, to name a few.

A more clearly defined and continued nuanced interpretation and understanding of black intraracial attitudes and opinions have the potential to shape and structure the debates surrounding black politics, racial and ethnic politics, immigration politics, and the overall understanding of groups in the electorate. Intraracial group attitudes directly affect the ways in which black politics are viewed henceforth. For scholars of electoral politics, observing the differences among black groups who participate in the electorate, how they view government policies, interpret the potential for full incorporation, and express opinions about black ethnics living in the United States all have direct implications for the future of black politics. In the area of urban politics, several scholars have written about the changing face of American cities, the increase of urbanization, and the migration patterns of blacks from the South to urban centers such as New York City, Chicago, Detroit, and

Washington, DC (Shaw 2009; Thompson 2005; Katznelson 1981). The increase in black urbanization has spawned what some have coined as "white flight," that is, white city residents moving in droves to the suburbs.[4] However, with the arrival of new black groups to suburban areas has gradually increased and now reflects a new set of population characteristics (Jackson, Gerber, and Cain 1994).[5] Recent studies have argued that blacks are now less residentially segregated, but largely due to migration to suburban communities (Glaeser and Vigdor 2012). Therefore, the question of whether black immigrants will follow the same or even similar residential assimilation in and out of cities in the future is fertile ground for scholars of racial, ethnic, and urban politics.

This book was largely motivated by the dearth of literature within the field of political science, which has historically analyzed black populations as a ethnically homogeneous and one-dimensional population of study. Appreciating political behaviors of emerging populations, such as Afro-Caribbean and African groups, is critical to broadening our understanding of race in New York City and throughout the United States. By examining the opinions of union members through an institutional framework, the role of labor unions in shaping opinions and actions is evident, as is the role of labor unions as immigrants' entree into a more secure class and income status.

It is my hope that I have shed light onto the evolution of foreign-born black political behavior. Black ethnic populations have distinct political histories, and this project has ascertained their intragroup perceptions, policy stances, and perceptions of the American Dream. More specifically, the ways in which black groups view the work ethics and feelings toward other black ethnics, how these groups have the greatest levels of cohesive opinions when policies are presented as a "black versus white" and not a black ethnic frame, and how their ethnic identity and generational status affect their belief in the fulfillment of the American Dream. The aim was to treat black populations as heterogeneous political actors and to highlight the historical and cultural diversity flourishing within the US electoral system. Within union organizations, ethnically diverse black political actors are unique populations of study, and this book has examined the richness of a particular New York City labor community and has described the dynamic attitudes and participation tendencies of these and other black populations within the American political system.

Appendix 2A

AFRICAN IMMIGRANTS TO THE UNITED STATES, 1980 TO 2008–9

	# of Immigrants (thousands)				African Immigrants as % of Total			
African Immigrants	1980	1990	2000	2008–9	1980	1990	2000	2008–9
Nigeria	24	56	133	201	37	30	23	19
Ethiopia	5	34	66	143	9	18	12	13
Ghana	8	20	65	110	12	11	11	10
Kenya	2	6	29	68	3	4	5	6
Somalia	0	1	35	67	0	1	6	6
Liberia	3	10	39	64	5	6	7	6
Sudan	0	3	13	34	1	2	2	3
Sierra Leone	2	6	20	34	3	3	3	3
Cameroon	1	3	12	30	2	2	2	3
Cape Verde	2	4	10	22	3	2	2	2
All Other Countries	11	28	151	318	19	15	27	30

Source: MPI data analysis of 1980, 1990, and 2000 US Census; 2008–9 ACS.

Appendix 2B

LOCAL 371 RESPONDENT DEMOGRAPHICS (IN PERCENTAGES)

	Whites	Blacks	Afro-Car	Africans	Latinos
Male	61	30	30	73	38
Female	39	70	70	27	62
N	41	135	47	92	53
Education					
Less Than High School	0	2	0	0	2
High School/ GED	2	3	2	0	2
Some College	12	16	6	0	14
College Degree	54	50	53	43	67
Graduate/Profess. Degree	32	29	38	57	16
N	41	132	47	92	51
Income					
Less than $25,000	0	1	0	1	0
$25,000–$49,999	25	45	43	30	44
$50,000–$74,999	45	33	32	32	28
$75,000–$94,999	20	9	6	24	18
$95,000 and above	10	12	19	13	10
N	40	130	47	92	50

	Whites	Blacks	Afro-Car	Africans	Latinos
Age			.		
18–29	5	2	11	1	14
30–29	10	17	34	13	10
40–49	24	41	40	36	39
50–59	44	33	8	42	33
60–65	10	6	6	7	4
65 and over	7	1	0	1	0
N	41	131	47	90	51
Class					
Lower Class	0	2	0	2	2
Working Class	17	38	42	38	52
Lower Middle Class	12	15	9	6	8
Middle Class	46	26	22	34	27
Upper Middle Class	12	11	11	10	6
Upper Class	10	6	9	4	4
Don't Know	2	2	7	6	2
N	41	132	45	90	52

Source: 2005–6 SSEU Local 371 Survey. In percentages.

Appendix 2C

SSEU LOCAL 371 PARTICIPATION SURVEY

Your participation in this survey is very important to better understanding opinions of people in New York City. All responses reported in this survey are CONFIDENTIAL. Please return the completed survey in the attached, stamped envelope.

Here are some questions about issues and political representation.

Please indicate whether or not you strongly agree, agree, disagree, strongly disagree, or don't know to the following questions.

	Strongly Agree	Agree	Disagree	Strongly Disagree	Don't Know
It is not really a problem if some people have more of a chance in life than others.	1	2	3	4	5
I am proud to be an American.	1	2	3	4	5
America is a land of opportunity in which you only need to work hard to succeed.	1	2	3	4	5
I can trust the government to make decisions in my best interest.	1	2	3	4	5
People like me don't have a say in what the government does.	1	2	3	4	5

	Strongly Agree	*Agree*	*Disagree*	*Strongly Disagree*	*Don't Know*
People are best represented by leaders of their own **racial** background.	1	2	3	4	5
People are best represented by leaders of their own **ethnic** background.	1	2	3	4	5
I feel the problems of black Americans and black immigrants are too different for them to be political "partners."	1	2	3	4	5

	Strongly Agree	*Agree*	*Disagree*	*Strongly Disagree*	*Don't Know*
English should be the official language of this country.	1	2	3	4	5
Immigrants make this country open to new ideas and cultures.	1	2	3	4	5
Immigrants take jobs away from people who were born in America.	1	2	3	4	5
If racial/ethnic minorities do not do well in life, they have no one to blame but themselves.	1	2	3	4	5
Because of the slavery of *black Americans*, it has made it easier for immigrants to stay out of the lower class.	1	2	3	4	5
If *black Americans* tried harder, they could be as successful as certain immigrant groups.	1	2	3	4	5

	Strongly Agree	Agree	Disagree	Strongly Disagree	Don't Know
African and Afro-Caribbean immigrants should benefit from affirmative action policies.	1	2	3	4	5
Voting is the only way someone like me will have a say.	1	2	3	4	5

Here are some more questions.

	Strongly Agree	Agree	Disagree	Strongly Disagree	Don't Know
Do you think this country fairly treats whites?	1	2	3	4	5
Black Americans?	1	2	3	4	5
Afro-Caribbean immigrants?	1	2	3	4	5
African immigrants?	1	2	3	4	5
Latinos/Hispanic immigrants?	1	2	3	4	5
Asian immigrants?	1	2	3	4	5

I have a few questions about political participation.
Please indicate whether you have, have not, or don't know to the following questions.
In the past 12 months …

	Yes	No	Don't Know
Have you talked to people about why they **should** vote in a campaign?	1	2	3
Have you talked to people about why they **should not** vote in a campaign?	1	2	3
Have you ever given or helped raise money for any of the candidates?	1	2	3
Have you contacted, written, or visited a public official to express your views on a particular issue?	1	2	3

	Yes	No	Don't Know
Have you participated in a demonstration, a march, or protest on a national or local issue?	1	2	3
Have you attended a meeting about an issue facing your community?	1	2	3
Have you participated in any group meetings, including place of worship, working to improve conditions of racial/ethnic minorities?	1	2	3

	Yes	No	Not Eligible	Not Registered	Don't Know
Did you vote in the 2004 presidential election?	1	2	3	4	5
Do you plan to vote in the 2005 mayoral election?	1	2	3	4	5
Did you vote in the 2001 mayoral election?	1	2	3	4	5

In any given week, on average, how often do you do the following?

	Almost Always	Most of the Time	Some of the Time	Almost Never	Don't Know
Read a national newspaper?	1	2	3	4	5
Watch the local news?	1	2	3	4	5

Please answer the next five questions if you have *migrated to the US*. If not, please proceed to the next set of questions.

Some people who were not born in the US continue to participate in the politics of their home countries while others do not.

	Very Stable	Stable	Weak	Very Weak	Don't Know
How would you rate the political stability of your home country?	1	2	3	4	5

Since you have migrated to the US ...

	Yes	No	Don't Know
Have you voted in an election for a candidate in your home country?	1	2	3
Have you contributed money to a candidate running for office or political party in your home country?	1	2	3
Have you gone to a rally or event in the US in which a candidate for office or a representative of a political party from your home country spoke?	1	2	3
Have representatives of your home country's government contacted you or encouraged you to become involved in your home country's political or cultural affairs?	1	2	3

I would like to ask you a few questions about various government programs. Please indicate if you would like to see spending for it increased, decreased, or if you would leave it the same.

	Increase	Stay Same	Decrease
Public education	1	2	3
Defense spending	1	2	3
Welfare programs	1	2	3
Health care	1	2	3
Aid to newly arrived immigrants	1	2	3
Aid to Africa	1	2	3
Affirmative action policies	1	2	3
Environment	1	2	3
Social Security	1	2	3
Patrolling borders against illegal immigrants	1	2	3

Imagine a 7-point scale on which the characteristics of the people in a group can be rated. A score of 1 means you think almost all of the people in the group tend to be LAZY. A score of 7 means you think almost all of the people tend to be HARDWORKING. A score of 4 means that you think most people in the group are not closer to one end or the other, and of course, you may choose any number in between.

1 – – – – 2 – – – – 3 – – – – 4 – – – – 5 – – – – 6 – – – – 7

Lazy   **Not close to either end**   **Hardworking**

Where would you rate whites in general on a scale of 1 to 7, where 1 indicates lazy, 7 means hardworking, and 4 indicates most whites are not closer to one end or the other?	Enter # _____ (1–7)
Where would you rate black Americans on a scale of 1–7?	Enter # _____ (1–7)
Where would you rate Afro-Caribbean immigrants on a scale of 1–7?	Enter # _____ (1–7)
Where would you rate African immigrants on a scale of 1–7?	Enter # _____ (1–7)
Where would you rate Latino/Hispanic immigrants on a scale of 1–7?	Enter # _____ (1–7)
Where would you rate Asian immigrants on a scale of 1–7?	Enter # _____ (1–7)

Feeling Thermometers. These questions seek to measure how you feel toward a particular group. When you see the name of a group, I would like you to rate it with a feeling thermometer. Ratings between 50–100 degrees mean that you feel favorably or warm toward the group. Similarly, ratings between 0–50 represent that you do not feel favorably toward the group and you do not care too much for the group. If you do not feel particularly warm or cold toward a group, you can rate them at 50. If you come to a group you do not know much about, you may refuse to answer. Please write your feeling thermometer score on the line next to the word listed below.

0 – – – – – – – – – – – – – – – – 50 – – – – – – – – – – – – – – – 100

Do not feel favorably   Neutral (not warm or cold)   Feel favorably

The Democratic Party:	Black Americans:	Whites/Caucasians:
The Republican Party:	Afro-Caribbean Immigrants:	Jews:
Liberals:	African Immigrants:	Illegal Aliens:
Conservatives:	Latino/Hispanic Immigrants:	Legal Immigrants:
People on Welfare:	Asian Immigrants:	Business:
Poor People:	Gays and Lesbians:	Labor Unions:

Lastly, I would like to know some background information about you.
What is your gender?

- Male
- Female

What is your ethnicity/race?

- White/Caucasian
- Black/African-American
- Black/Afro-Caribbean
- Black/African
- Asian
- Latino/Hispanic
- Biracial: _____
- Other: _____

If you indicated Black/Afro-Caribbean or Black/African please answer the following.

- Which country or countries are your relatives from? _____

Were you born in the US?

- Yes
- No
- Don't know

If you were not born in the US, how long have you lived in the US?

- 0–5 years
- 6–10 years
- 11–15 years
- 15 years and over
- Don't know

Are you a citizen of the United States?

- Yes
- No
- Don't know

Where did you mostly live while growing up, in the US or in another country?

- In the US
- Outside of the US
- Don't know

Were both of your parents born in the US?

- Yes
- No
- Don't know

If parent(s) not born in the US, in what country was your mother born?
_____

If parent(s) not born in the US, in what country was your father born?
_____

Were any of your grandparents born outside of the US?

- Yes
- No
- Don't know

Were you raised in a Spanish-speaking household?

- Yes
- No
- Don't know

What is your age?

- 18–29
- 30–39
- 40–49
- 50–59
- 60–65
- 65 and over

What is the highest level of education you have completed?

- Less than high school
- High school graduate/GED
- Some college
- College degree
- Graduate or professional degree

Which category best describes your household-level income?

- Less than $25,000
- $25,000 to $49,999
- $50,000 to $74,999
- $75,000 to $94,999
- $95,000 and above

In which borough do you currently reside?

- Bronx
- Brooklyn
- Manhattan
- Staten Island
- Queens
- Outside of the five boroughs

How long have you lived in New York City?

- 0–5 years
- 6–10 years
- 11–15 years
- 15 years and over
- Do not reside in New York City

What is your religious affiliation?

- Protestant
- Baptist
- Catholic
- Jewish
- Muslim
- Other: _____
- None

Are you married or are you widowed, divorced, separated, or have you never been married?

- Married and living with spouse
- Never married
- Divorced
- Separated
- Widowed
- Live with partner

If you had to make a choice of belonging to a particular class, which class do you think would best describe you?

- Lower class
- Working class
- Lower middle class
- Middle class
- Upper middle class

- Upper class
- Don't know

When it comes to politics, do you usually consider yourself a liberal or conservative?

- Liberal
- Moderate
- Conservative
- Other: _____
- Don't know

When it comes to politics, do you usually consider yourself a Democrat, a Republican, an Independent, or something else?

- Strong Democrat
- Weak Democrat
- Independent—Democrat
- Independent
- Independent—Republican
- Weak Republican
- Strong Republican
- Other: _____
- Don't know

Appendix 2D

LOCAL 371 EARLY V. LATE SURVEY RESPONDENTS (IN PERCENTAGES)

	All	Black Amer	Afro-Car	African	White	Latino
Early	58	58	49	52	71	59
Late	42	42	51	48	29	41
N	413	135	47	92	41	54

Those who identified as "Other" were not included in the analyses.
Source: 2005–6 SSEU Local 371 Survey

Appendix 3A

LABOR THERMOMETER

Local 371 Feelings Toward Labor (In Percentage)

	Whites	Blacks	Afro-Car	Africans	Latinos
Cool Feelings	5	2	7	2	2
2	3	2	0	4	2
3	0	2	2	0	0
4	29	14	12	17	30
5	8	7	19	16	11
6	13	16	16	21	15
Warm Feelings	42	57	44	40	40
N	38	118	43	81	47
Means	5.39	5.98	5.60	5.62	5.51
	(.286)	(.135)	(.262)	(.170)	(.225)

$p < 0.10$
Source: 2005–6 SSEU Local 371 Survey

Appendix 3B

LOCAL 371 RATES OF CITIZENSHIP

One hundred percent of Latinos indicated they were citizens of the United States, making their response the highest percent of racial group citizens. When comparing the numbers of Latinos who answered the question pertaining to vote eligibility, it is important to note that eight respondents, or 15 percent of Latino respondents, did not answer the citizenship question. Black American and white respondents indicated they were citizens at 99 and 98 percent, respectively.

The 13 percent of Afro-Caribbean respondents who stated they were not eligible to vote directly corresponds with the number of Afro-Caribbean respondents who identified as noncitizens when asked, "Are you a citizen of the US?" Although 18 percent of African respondents indicated that they were not citizens, roughly 13 percent indicated that they were not eligible to vote in the 2004 presidential election. The remaining 5 percent could be attributed to response error or conflated with responses from members who indicated they did not vote in the 2004 presidential election. Another logical explanation could be attributed to interpretations of the question.

Local 371 Rates of Citizenship (in percentages)

	Black Americans	Afro-Caribbeans	Africans	Whites	Latinos
% Who Are Citizens					
Yes	99	87	82	98	100
N	129	47	91	41	46

Source: 2005–6 SSEU Local 371 Survey.

Appendix 3C

POLITICAL STABILITY OF
HOME COUNTRY (IN PERCENTAGES)

	Afro-Car	*Africans*
Very Stable	10	0
Stable	35	22
Weak	32	43
Very Weak	23	35
N	31	81

p < 0.10.
Source: 2005–6 SSEU Local 371 Survey.

Appendix 4A

BLACK ETHNIC WORK ETHIC PERCEPTIONS AND FEELING THERMOMETERS

Black American Lazy vs. Hardworking

	Mean	Standard Deviation	Frequency	Median
Black Americans	*5.14	1.28	131	
Afro-Caribbeans	4.91	1.31	46	
Africans	3.89	1.66	88	
Total	4.68	1.53	265	4

Afro-Caribbean Lazy vs. Hardworking

	Mean	Standard Deviation	Frequency	Median
Black Americans	5.58	1.22	130	
Afro-Caribbeans	6.11	0.89	45	
Africans	5.75	1.28	87	
Total	5.73	1.2	262	6

African Lazy vs. Hardworking

	Mean	*Standard Deviation*	*Frequency*	*Median*
Black Americans	5.7	1.21	131	
Afro-Caribbeans	6.13	0.84	45	
Africans	6.09	1.16	88	
Total	5.9	1.15	264	6

Note: The highest black perception of their group as hardworking is still lower than all black ethnic groups' perceptions for Afro-Caribbean and African populations' work ethics.

Source: 2005–6 SSEU Local 371 Survey.

Where would you rate *black Americans* on a scale of 1–7? (in percentages)

	Blacks	*Afro-Car*	*Africans*
Extremely Lazy	1	0	8
2	1	4	15
3	5	4	17
4	30	35	26
5	24	24	18
6	20	17	7
Extremely Hardworking	19	15	9
N	131	46	88

$p < 0.01$.
Source: 2005–6 SSEU Local 371 Survey.

Where would you rate *Afro-Caribbean immigrants* on a scale of 1–7? (in percentages)

	Blacks	*Afro-Car*	*Africans*
Extremely Lazy	1	0	0
2	1	0	0
3	1	0	7
4	18	4	13
5	21	18	17
6	31	40	25
Extremely Hardworking	38	38	38
N	130	45	87

$p < 0.01$.
Source: 2005–6 SSEU Local 371 Survey

Where would you rate *African immigrants* on a scale of 1–7? (in percentages)

	Blacks	Afro-Car	Africans
Extremely Lazy	0	0	0
2	1	0	2
3	2	0	2
4	18	7	3
5	16	9	17
6	30	49	28
Extremely Hardworking	33	35	47
N	131	45	88

p < 0.01.
Source: 2005–6 SSEU Local 371 Survey.

Feeling Thermometer toward Black Americans

	Mean	Standard Deviation	Frequency	Median
Black Americans	81.4	25.1	119	
Afro-Caribbeans	80.4	19.4	43	
Africans	69.2	22.5	81	
Total	77.4	24.0	243	75

Feeling Thermometer toward Afro-Caribbeans

	Mean	Standard Deviation	Frequency	Median
Black Americans	68.7	24.2	115	
Afro-Caribbeans	88.9	15.5	43	
Africans	67.8	22.3	77	
Total	72.1	23.6	235	70

Feeling Thermometer toward Africans

	Mean	Standard Deviation	Frequency	Median
Black Americans	66.9	23.9	117	
Afro-Caribbeans	77.4	21.6	41	
Africans	78.6	22.5	80	
Total	72.6	23.6	238	70

p < 0.01.
Source: 2005–6 SSEU Local 371 Survey.

Appendix 5A

LOCAL 371 ATTITUDES TOWARD PEOPLE ON WELFARE AND THE POOR

Attitudes toward People on Welfare (in percentages)

	Whites	Blacks	Afro-Car	Africans	Latinos
Not Favorable at All	11	8	5	14	10
2	16	11	12	8	2
3	3	2	14	5	8
4	51	55	40	49	55
5	5	9	16	6	12
6	5	11	7	6	6
Extremely Favorable	8	5	7	12	6
N	37	121	43	78	49
Not statistically significant. Source: 2005–6 SSEU Local 371 Survey					
Means	46.6	49.8	50.6	49.0	50.6
	(4.00)	(1.98)	(3.17)	(2.91)	(3.18)

(Standard errors in parentheses)

Attitudes toward Poor People (in percentages)

	Whites	Blacks	Afro-Car	Africans	Latinos
Not Favorable at All	5	4	0	3	2
2	3	2	0	1	0
3	3	2	5	3	0
4	47	39	24	29	35
5	16	12	17	13	20
6	10	14	24	15	12
Extremely Favorable	16	27	31	36	31
N	38	120	42	75	49
Not statistically significant. Source: 2005–6 SSEU Local 371 Survey					
Means	60	66.2	74	72	70.9
	(3.74)	(2.32)	(3.16)	(2.80)	(3.15)

(Standard errors in parentheses)

NOTES

Introduction

1. I am defining "dominant group" as a combination of the real and perceived political, economic, and class power utilized by white populations in the United States. Much of the real and perceived power of the white dominant group stems from historical white privilege that has persisted to varying degrees into the twenty-first century.

2. The phrase "fail to get along" encompasses issues ranging from the lack of collective action on a large scale by blacks in America. It also includes many of the attitudes blacks express pertaining to other ethnic blacks when nonblack racial and ethnic groups are not present. These attitudes range from the perceptions of black immigrant groups feeling they are better or different from native-born black populations or that native-born black populations are not as hardworking as their black immigrant counterparts.

3. Reuel Rogers (2006) is the pioneer political scientist who has compared Afro-Caribbean political attitudes with those of black Americans; there are a few data sets who have included Afro-Caribbeans, but African group inclusion and comparisons are relatively nonexistent.

4. I find the term "postracial" inaccurate and completely false. This country has not moved beyond race. There have been negotiations with race, but the idea that four hundred years of racial subjugation (of almost all groups of people living in America) are erased in an election cycle is a completely absurd premise.

5. By "groupness," I mean the status of a collection of individuals classified and categorized in a similar way. Sometimes this classification takes place without the complete willingness of the "group's" members.

6. Residential segregation and exclusion do not automatically lead to group identification or cohesion. However, for blacks in the United States, the segregating effects do contribute to shared interactions and discriminatory practices, as well as intragroup distrust and competition for resources.

7. I prefer not to use the term "minority" due to the majority numbers of people of color around the globe.

Chapter 1

1. This label was applied to Jackson for his many protests pertaining to civil rights, equal rights, corporate divestment from South Africa, housing equity, etc.

2. Currently, African migrants to the United States are some of the fastest-growing immigrant groups (Capps, McCabe, and Fix 2011).

3. In many ways writing this book has consistently made me think of the 1988 comedic movie *Coming to America*, which tells the story of how a young African prince moves to the United

States and learns about American class, culture, and race relations through his interactions with the black community in Queens, NY. *Coming to America* shows the solidarity and levels of "foreignness" between native-born black Americans and immigrant blacks, but also the tensions that arise due to his "African" customs. As the main character visits the community barber shop, walks the inner-city streets, attends a black awareness rally, and attempts to mimic black American culture, the shared racial identity quickly evolves into acceptance within the community, yet the vast cultural differences create clear ethnic distinctions between the native and non-native-born blacks in the film. The articulation of a shared idea of race and the distinctness of ethnicity lead to much larger questions surrounding a duality faced by many blacks in America.

4. This is an extension of Wong's (2010: 3) concept of imagined boundaries.

5. Issues ranging from housing equity, occupational advancement, police brutality, and educational opportunities are just a very few of the factors that affect black chances in the United States.

6. It is not a coincidence that darker-skinned individuals throughout the globe—in Panama, Cuba, Brazil, Mexico, and South Africa, for example—are held in subordinate positions within the political, social, and economic spheres.

7. Throughout this book the terms "ethnic" and "ethnicity" are used interchangeably to refer to ones national origin. Black American populations are classified as an ethnic group so as to distinguish them from those whose ancestors, parents, or they themselves have migrated from a Caribbean or African nation.

8. Rogers's understanding of how past experiences shape the diverse lens through which black ethnic groups translate their experiences and extend these events into diverse levels of participation also applies to African ethnic groups. For example, African groups who have no "exit strategy"—that is, they have no intention to return to their home country for political, economic, and/or social reasons, will largely perceive the costs of participation, the quest for inclusion and assimilation, and the patience needed to deal with the persistent inequities within the American polity as minor impediments to their quest for full assimilation.

9. Often defined as white Americans of a particular class privilege.

10. The 2000 presidential election in Florida and the recent 2012 voter ID laws notwithstanding.

11. There is a host of literature that outlines how Jewish, Italian, Irish, and other white ethnic populations became "white." However, although their paths to incorporation may have begun with an identification with blacks during the early stages of assimilation, these immigrant groups were able to transcend ethnicity and identify racially, thus shedding light on the fluidity of ethnicity and the permanence of race. Whites are grouped into a homogeneous category. Sipress (1997: 181) comments: "The 'whitening' of Irish-Americans provides an example of a marginal social group that embraced a racial identity to advance its own interests." The "whitening" of the Irish race is discussed by Ignatiev (1995: 1), who notes that "whites" are "those who partake of the privileges of the white skin in this society. Its most wretched members share a status higher, in certain respects, than that of the most exalted persons excluded from it." Similar assimilation tactics were used by Italian and Jewish immigrants in the nineteenth and twentieth centuries as well (Fears 2003). These ethnic groups often used party politics and coalition building to bridge the cultural divide (Logan 2003). However, the political inclusion, participation, and ultimate assimilation of Irish, Italian, and Jewish immigrants has also been largely due to the color line in America. Whereas these immigrants were not considered white at some point in time, the color line shifted, and inclusion followed suit.

12. Multiracial coalitions primarily focus on the issues of racial and ethnic equality (Hochschild and Rogers 2000). However, this emphasis on equality in the face of diverse histories and negotiations with assimilation and incorporation, often leading to groups fragmenting into competitive factions. Thus, biracial and multiracial coalitions are thought to be unattainable due to past political disagreements, individual attitudes about other groups, and fears among

minority groups within the larger group (Tedin and Murray 1994). Intraracial distrust exists among black ethnic populations and has thus contributed to ethnic factions and decreased rates of collective actions (Okamoto 2003). However, possibilities for coalition building will still be greater among groups with a shared racial classification even if cross-racial migratory narratives may appear more similar. See also Hochschild, Weaver, and Burch 2012.

13. Betancur and Gills (2000) also argue that coalitional efforts are undermined when influential leaders advance only the interests of one group to the exclusion of others. This is most clearly demonstrated in Miami when observing the NAACP and the loss of significant numbers of members of Haitian descent. The defection of Haitian members from the NAACP as well as the National Urban League signaled a disconnect between the black American leadership and predominantly black American membership within the these two organizations, and a small but growing population who felt their needs and wants (i.e., increased attention to international issues, specifically issues affecting Haitians both in Haiti and in Florida) were not being addressed by the organization elite.

14. Whites' views of Asian populations as "model minorities" have had significant effects on cross-group coalition formation, thus decreasing and substantially limiting their ability to form partnerships with other groups of color.

15. Greater black ethnic homogeneity existed around nonracial issues, thus raising questions regarding the fundamental policy issues in which to introduce black ethnic populations into coalition politics. It also raises the question surrounding the union as an issue building and issue educating institution for groups.

16. Further work needs to occur to establish the extent to which class status over time will affect black ethnic groups in the same or similar ways as native-born black Americans (Dawson 2001).

17. Dawson defined the black utility heuristic thus: "As long as African Americans' life chances are powerfully shaped by race, it is efficient for individual African Americans to use their perceptions of the interests of African Americans as a group as a proxy for their own interests" (2001: 61).

18. That is, we cannot assume that the relationships and experiences of black immigrants will mimic black American interactions with whites, thereby creating parallel black immigrant and native-born experiences.

19. Okamoto (2003) argued that the construction of pan-ethnic boundaries and a pan-ethnic identity affect collective action efforts. Similarly, Padilla (1985) stated that differences in language, culture, and immigration histories also affect organizing capabilities and understandings of a common fate.

20. In-group status is often a social unit with boundaries that are collectively generated and maintained in order to mark the differences between insiders and outsiders.

21. That is, black immigrants who were granted access to more equitable educational and housing systems post the Hart-Cellar Act and also the Civil Rights Act of 1965. Essentially, the phrase "the benefits without the burden" refers to the feeling of some black Americans that they have laid the foundation for black immigrants to migrate to the United States and enjoy the fruits of previous black generation's political struggles and triumphs. Therefore, along the pathway to the pursuit of the American dream, several potholes exist for black ethnic coalition-building possibilities.

22. See Davis (1998) for a more extensive conversation regarding benefit and burden distribution.

23. Rogers contrasts the pluralist versus the minority group views that assist in our understanding of how immigrants in the twenty-first century adapt to US political practices. He outlines how the pluralist model's suggested egalitarian principles are in direct contrast with the minority group model's suggestion of limited inclusion for nonwhite populations due to sustained racial inequities. Implicit in the minority model view is that nonwhites will coalesce around common political causes and strategize to overcome their political predicaments. This model squarely places nonwhites on one side of the racial divide and whites on

the other, in contrast to the pluralist model, which portrays blacks as an anomaly, a group that for some reason has not been able to subscribe to the equity provided within a liberal democracy (Rogers 2006). Essentially, I argue that Afro-Caribbean and African groups are struggling with perceptions of a pluralist model, realities of a minority group model and a vacillating sense of shared political common causes in a similar but not identical racial predicament. So, as Gunnar Myrdal asked so many decades ago: How do we reconcile American egalitarian principles with continued repressive and inequitable racial practices? (1944)

24. Doing so would associate black ethnics with a segment of people largely viewed as psychologically damaged, due to roughly three centuries of American racial slavery (Sowell 1994).

25. This status has its own series of levels and can be extended more easily to Jamaican and English-speaking Caribbeans in the United States who find assimilation easier because of fewer language barriers. An even more complex elevated minority status is evident, for example, when comparing Jamaican immigrants to Haitian immigrants.

26. I am defining "race-based slavery on American soil" as the slave trade that involved the buying and selling of African slaves in the New World and lasted from the early 1600s to the mid-nineteenth century.

27. Some scholars have stated that a relative pan-ethnic identity is possible for black ethnic populations, due to black groups living in close proximity to one another (Padilla 1985). When thinking about the future possibilities of coalition building among black ethnic populations, increased residential proximity, and therefore increased black ethnic identity for black ethnic populations, have important implications for political resources (Segura and Rodrigues 2006; Padilla 1985). Okamoto (2003) argued that competition theory explains how ethnic groups competing for the same economic resources can increase solidarity even with the existence of salient racial and ethnic identities.

28. Residential segregation and exclusion do not automatically lead to group identification or cohesion. However, for blacks in the United States, the segregating effects do contribute to shared interactions and discriminatory practices, as well as intragroup distrust and competition for resources.

29. This strategy is complicated when black ethnic populations are competing against black American candidates. It is further complicated by the complete racial, ethnic, and even gender breakdowns of a particular district. For example, in the 2006 Brooklyn Congressional District 11 election, a black American candidate named Chris Owens, a Jewish candidate named David Yaskey, and an Afro-Caribbean candidate named Yvette Clarke all vied for the US congressional seat. District 11 is further complicated by its status as both a historically black district and a historically Afro-Caribbean district—the one from which Shirley Chisholm hails, a symbol of black electoral politics as well as Afro-Caribbean electoral successes. Yvette Clark ultimately won the seat for District 11 largely because of her ability to utilize both her racial and ethnic attachments. District 11 foreshadows the future of New York City black politics. More districts are represented by black candidates who are also of Afro-Caribbean descent. It is merely a matter of time before African candidates are elected to local and statewide office, thus creating greater complexity in the racial and ethnic political landscape, the formation of coalitions, and real versus perceived shared identities.

30. See Kinder and Dale-Riddle (2012) for a more extensive description.

31. Because Dawson did not disaggregate his African American population by ethnic distinctions, he did not discuss the extent to which social mobility differs for blacks living in the United States versus blacks who lived in the Caribbean. Much of the literature surrounding West Indian social mobility argues that upward class mobility "whitens" Caribbean people. Dawson refutes the claim that African American political solidarity breaks down due to differing class statuses and economic polarization.

32. The term "1.5 generation" refers to people who immigrated to a new country during their formative years. The label refers to the characteristics brought from their home country as well as their assimilation and socialization in the new country. Their identity is thus a hybrid of their home culture and new traditions.

33. For example, the struggles of Caribbean laborers in the 1930s and 1940s present complex interpretations of black Americans and Caribbean laborers during wartime as well as the emergence of elevated minority perceptions of Caribbean and African work ethics as compared to those of native-born blacks. More recently, black Americans and Afro-Caribbeans have struggled over limited resources in their shared communities.

34. It is important to observe that blacks with increased education and income levels are *less* inclined than blacks with dismal education and wealth to believe America is equitable and that race is a diminishing obstacle for black citizens (Hochschild 1995). The recent judicial debates over race-based affirmative action policies in academic institutions implores us to revisit the stayed notion of the color line in the United States and the inequalities, perceived for some and real for others, that still remain.

Chapter 2

1. The civil rights movement has increased class equity across race and space, thus it has dramatically affected poor white and other working-class individuals, whether they acknowledge the strides or not.

2. Africans have immigrated to the United States in significant numbers since the mid-1980s. Afro-Caribbean immigrants began migrating to the United States in small numbers in the mid-1940s.

3. For example, Shirley Chisholm, Stokely Carmichael, Marcus Garvey, and Sidney Poitier. See Irma Watkins-Owens, *Blood Relations* (1996).

4. For Nigerian and Ethiopian migration, the increase over this twenty-year period is more significant.

5. Cited from the Congressional Record, 89th Cong., 1st sess., August 25, 1965, 21812.

6. The term "Afro-American" had a brief moment in the mid-1980s (Dilday 2008).

7. All respondents were eighteen years old or older. The union does not employ individuals younger than eighteen years old.

8. That is, labor membership has provided an alternative to undocumented and low-wage jobs often obtained by immigrant groups.

9. Some scholars contend that, depending on the union organization, the practice of excluding certain marginalized groups still continue today.

10. Social activist labor unions also affect the nonmembers of the union, those who are associated with and family members of union members.

11. Although one could garner diverse data from West African livery drivers or Trinidadian child care providers in New York City, for this project, a more homogeneous class of black respondents enabled me to analyze the intraracial attitudes and opinions of interest. Because of this, I hypothesized that this group, as a consequence of class homogeneity, would have relatively consistent positions on government spending and public issues. The income levels of SSEU Local 371 respondents, however, do not represent low-income occupations, and when asked, several members identified themselves as working class or middle class. Okamoto (2003) argues that "pan-ethnic group behavior should increase when ethnic or racial groups experience high levels of occupational specialization (segmental cultural division of labor) or find themselves concentrated together in the same, low-paying occupations." She also contends that occupation specialization *within* panethnic groups will decrease the rate of panethnic collective action. This is evident in the survey population when observing the specialization of African male supervisors, which translates into decreased black unity within the union.

12. The national surveys that served as templates for the SSEU Local 37 original survey were the NES, the GSS, the National Immigrant Survey, and the National Ethnic Politics Study.

13. See appendix 2A for 1980–2008/9 data pertaining to migrants from Nigeria as the largest African group to arrive in the United States.

14. Although roughly 90 percent of the African respondents are of Nigerian descent, specific ethnic groups within the Nigerian population were not discerned.

15. For US census, totals of the ten largest African populations residing in the United States, see appendix 2A. Nigerian populations are ranked number one.
16. Forty-seven respondents indicated they were of Afro-Caribbean descent when asked their racial orientation, and forty-two respondents indicated a particular country when asked specifically about their ethnic background. Several scholars argue that, especially for ethnic groups of African ancestry or descent, racial self-labeling or racial self-designation—that is, the name one prefers to use as one's label (Speight, Vera, and Derrickson 1996: 38)—is indeed relevant (Ghee 1990; Larkey, Hecht, and Martin 1993).
17. It is important to note that although African immigrants comprise only 5 percent of New York City's black population, over the past ten years the number of Africans living in the United States has increased by 134 percent. African immigrants also comprise 6 percent of all immigrants to the United States (US Census 2010). This number does not adequately take the significant numbers of undocumented African populations living in New York City into account.
18. Scholars have noted the residential segregation of native-born and foreign-born blacks in New York City. They conclude that the close proximity of the black native and foreign-born populations in residential areas and the relative lack of nonblack housing integration also contribute to intragroup tensions (Foner 2001; Kasinitz 1992).
19. Recent studies argue that blacks are not as racially residentially segregated as in the past (Glaeser and Vigdor 2012). However, the slow "integration" numbers of blacks are largely attributed to blacks moving or being pushed out of cities and relocating in suburban areas.
20. Of the 1,500 questionnaires originally mailed to SSEU members, 155 surveys were returned due to bad addresses; 415 of the 1,345 questionnaires were completed and returned, thus the 31 percent response rate.
21. See appendix 2C for detailed survey and demographic questions.
22. As well as 1.5-generation populations.
23. A note on response bias: Scholars argue that among the several demographic factors (i.e., older age, female gender, upper-class status), people with higher education are more prone to return a postal questionnaire (Etter and Perneger 1997; Armstrong and Overton 1977). They argue that contributing to nonresponse is failure to return the questionnaire, explicit refusal, and change of address. Repeated mailings may elicit responses from busy individuals or those who dislike filling out questionnaires, but these mailings will not persuade those who object to the study. Therefore, the assumption is made that people who are interested in the subject respond more readily and who also feel they will make a favorable impression on those reading their responses (Armstrong and Overton 1977). Thus, they stated that the characteristics of nonrespondents may or may not be extrapolated from the characteristics of late respondents. They further argued that subjects who respond less readily or "late" are more like nonrespondents and have responded due to the successive waves of increased stimulus. See appendix 2D for early versus late respondents.
24. "Union leadership" refers to the president of Local 371 and members of his cabinet—that is, members who are deputy vice presidents, in charge of union outreach, political outreach, and general union operations.
25. From this point forward, both union leadership and rank-and-file members will be referred to as members, since all leadership interviewees are also members of Local 371.
26. The NES is a randomly generated, nationwide sample. The data over the twenty-year period were pooled in order to provide substantial racial and ethnic sample sizes.

Chapter 3

1. As Sawyer (2006: 103) observes, race is a particularly difficult construct to decode and understand because it is both "discursive and ideological."
2. There are other demographic and population changes that are noteworthy. Although the actual numbers of native-born blacks and foreign-born black people in the United States

has increased over the past several decades, other racial and ethnic group numbers have risen as well. People of African descent—that is, native-born and foreign-born blacks—have become the third largest group in America. Latino populations have replaced blacks as the second largest group in the country.

3. Between 1996 and 2003, the Migration Policy Institute reports that the number of immigrant wage and salary workers increased 48 percent, from 11.9 million to 17.7 million (Current Population Survey, 1996–2003 annual averages).

4. Although blacks, both native-born and foreign-born, have made economic strides, the effects of race and the susceptibility of racism are still present (Waters 1999a). Tate (1991) argues that educated blacks feel that race is most prevalent, even despite educational and financial successes. One need only observe education, housing, and urban center inequities on the local and national level to understand the limits of black inclusion and incorporation in the United States. President Ensley shared an anecdote of a union member, a city worker who was out with her boyfriend. They were both black and were stopped by police for what appeared to be no reason. He made the point of reiterating that this story took place in 2006. She showed her city identification to the police officer and was not released or given reason for the stop. She demanded to see his supervisor, and when the supervisor arrived, the supervisor assumed her to be impersonating a city employee and took her in for questioning. Because of the prevalence of race, despite economic, occupational, or educational successes, the interplay of a collective black racial identity and a specific ethnic identity presents interesting and necessary questions surrounding future coalition building possibilities.

5. According to Okamoto (2003: 816), "Organizations based on collective identities are considered to be mobilizing structures because they bring groups of potential participants together, provide social locations where mobilization may be generated, and serve as structures of communication contributing to successful collective action."

6. The vast majority of members targeted for the survey population were members of the racial and social clubs within the union.

7. President Ensley then provided an anecdote about union mine workers—Polish, Italian, and black. "They did not speak the same languages, but they found out they were being exploited and formed a union. That was the power of a union: to unite various groups of people with a common goal and interest for equality."

8. The presence of a close and highly racially interested election of 2000 might explain the high numbers of overall black voting in 2004.

9. That is, when controlling for all other demographic variables.

10. 1984–2004 NES voting by blacks in unions versus black nonunion members. NES Cumulative 1984–2004. *N*: 214 black union members, 1,536 black nonunion members.

11. There are no exact measures within the survey instrument to measure respondent attitudes toward internal union elections. However, appendix 3B presents percentages of Local 371 member feelings toward labor unions using a 100-point thermometer scale that has been condensed to a seven-point Likert scale. The data reveal that all Local 371 members had relatively warm feelings and that black members expressed the warmest feelings toward labor.

12. When using the primary data provided by the SSEU Local 371 Survey.

13. The authors view social capital as assets derived from membership in voluntary organizations (Putnam 2000).

14. That is, the social institutions best capable of promoting participation.

15. Dawson does not explicitly define or disaggregate groups of blacks in his analyses.

16. Scholars argue that citizens are more likely to vote in national elections over local elections. The question which asked survey respondents about whether they planned to vote in the 2005 mayoral election was dropped from the analysis. The first wave of the survey was distributed before the 2005 election, and the second and third waves after the 2005 election; the data therefore were not comparable and could not be used here.

17. In recent years, local New York City elections have not garnered anywhere near 50 percent of the voting eligible population.

18. It is also necessary to note the increases in voting during presidential election years. The NES voting average for black respondents in nonelection years is 55 percent, compared to 69 percent for black respondents in election years. Similarly, white voting decreased in nonelection years as well. Voting for whites was 59 percent during nonelection years, compared to 78 percent during election years.

19. See table 3.3 for SSEU Local 371 black-white voting comparisons. It is necessary to note that past national surveys and theorists have not distinguished between native-born and foreign-born blacks. Therefore, for this particular comparison of whites and blacks, I have chosen to compare individuals who self-identified as black American.

20. President Ensley was referring to SEIU Local 1199's decision to elect Dennis Rivera as president of the union from 1989 to 2007.

21. This belief supports the high levels of Local 371 black ethnic voting compared to other racial groups.

22. Table 3.6 also indicates that when aggregating the percentages of blacks who identified as strong, weak, or independent Democrats, on the national level 87 percent of black union members identified with the Democratic Party compared to 80 percent of black nonunion members.

23. The 2004 NAEP did not ask any questions directly asking respondents' partisanship. The questions in 2004 NAEP referred to particular candidates (i.e., George Bush, John Kerry, Ralph Nader, or Other).

24. The coding was as follows: 0–15 = 1; 16–30 = 2; 31–45 = 3; 46–55 = 4; 56–70 = 5; 71–85 = 6; 86–100 = 7.

25. When comparing African and Afro-Caribbean responses, 55 percent of Afro-Caribbean respondents, compared to 78 percent of African respondents, stated they had migrated from a home country with a weak or very weak political stability.

Chapter 4

1. In this chapter the SSEU Local 371 survey is the sole data source.

2. The questions used in this chapter are modeled after the New Immigrant Survey and the National Ethnic Politics Study.

3. The theoretical basis for the argument of black ethnic distinctions was previously set forth by sociologists evaluating relationships between black American and West Indian populations.

4. A research note published by Anglin and Whaley (2006) explored the relationship of racial and ethnic labels and racial socialization among college students of African descent, largely focusing on the social psychological motivations behind identification. Recent studies are currently introducing and addressing the concept of diversity within black populations in the electorate and citizenry (Nunnally 2010).

5. Again, I am cognizant of the varying degrees of diversity within black ethnic populations.

6. Much of the theorizing that guided the survey is based on the findings of the collective racial and varied ethnic identities set forth by sociologists: primarily the work of Waters, Foner, Kasinitz, and Vickerman.

7. Black Americans are also the longest-residing peoples of African descent in the United States.

8. This group identity is largely based on shared history as the United States' only nonvoluntary immigrants, the history of US-based chattel slavery, a history of segregation and Jim Crow, subsequent struggles and triumphs in the civil rights movement, and overall length of time in the United States.

9. This follows literature within the social psychology that defines "identification with a group as yielding 'a shift towards the perception of the self as an interchangeable exemplar of some social category and away from the perception of the self as a unique person'" (Penn 2008: 29).

10. Phillip Gay (1989) argues that blacks in the United States are six to seven generations culturally removed from Africa and thus speak no African language, have no relatives, have

never visited Africa, and therefore have a false and artificial sense of an African homeland or nationality, which is made up of heterogeneous nations and cultures sharing one very large continent.

11. For example, it is necessary to note the significant numbers of black Americans who responded to and marched on behalf of Diallo and Louima in the aftermath of the two incidents. One need not look too far beyond Rodney King, Amadou Diallo, and Abner Louima to see an unfortunate common bond of black male treatment by the criminal justice system in the United States.

12. Assimilationist logic posits that transnational immigrant attachments to their homeland diminish over time (Rogers 2006). Therefore, particular subethnic distinctions may decrease over time. For example, once living in the United States, Nigerians who are Ibo or Yoruba may view one another as solely Nigerian and thus having a shared ethnic identity. Whereas if these two groups were still residing in Lagos, more specific subethnic nuances would be tangible and significant.

13. By "generational effect," I mean what Schuman and Rieger (1992) define as an assumption that the behaviors and attitudes are shaped by the common experiences of a cohort.

14. In this work I prefer not to describe immigrants using the terms "first-generation" and "second-generation." There are several Afro-Caribbean immigrants who migrated to the United States when they were infants and would be considered second-generation by some scholarly disciplines, 1.5-generation in others, and first-generation by yet others. This sample population largely consists of what sociologists would classify as the 1.5 generation.

15. Morone's (1998) use of "democratic wish" is defined as the publics' ability to maintain optimism about the government structure and its ability to solve problems.

16. This is also shown in the work of Douglas Massey and Nancy Denton (1993).

17. Latino populations were not as adamant as black populations in strongly agreeing that white populations were treated fairly in this country.

18. Again, Latino respondents expressed disagreement with the statement that Afro-Caribbeans were treated fairly, at rates that more closely resembled black ethnic attitudes. And white respondents, at 41 percent, were the most likely to agree that Afro-Caribbeans were treated fairly in the United States.

19. The means and complete tables for each respective group can be found in appendix 4A.

20. It is necessary to note that 73 percent of the African respondents are male, compared to only 30 percent of native-born and 30 percent of Afro-Caribbean respondents. The optimism felt by male respondents could be linked to their belief that with hard work, economic gains would be inevitable and integration within the workforce and middle-class status would be attainable (Butcher 1994).

Chapter 5

1. Most scholars do not articulate ethnic distinctions among their African American actors: e.g., Hochschild 1995; Dawson 1994; Pinderhughes 1992. Therefore, an assumption of native-born African American status is inherent in their research.

2. The NAEP does not ask specific questions regarding increase in spending.

3. Using data over a twenty-year period is not optimal. However, Page and Shapiro (1992) argue that individuals' preferences are fairly stable over time. Also, public opinion changes in understandable ways and is often parallel across various subcategories. I chose to begin the data analysis in the 1980s, the decade when significant numbers of African immigrants arrived in the United States.

4. As a proxy for racialized questions asked in the Local 371 survey, 2006 GSS foreign-aid questions were used.

5. Although 85 percent of whites expressed a desire to increase spending on public education, the difference in levels of support compared to black ethnics could be indicative of a level of issue immunity from the labor leadership.

6. It is also important to note that these particular responses are not statistically significant.
7. In this particular instance, the psychological distinctions of "us versus them" (Kinder and Kam 2009; Winter 2006; Quadagno 1994; Massey and Denton 1993; Carmines and Stimson 1989)—that is, black versus white responses—are not as visible in union members organization of Social Security spending attitudes.
8. Latino respondents expressed attitudes supporting increased spending for the environment at similar levels compared to black American and Afro-Caribbean respondents. Similarly, Latino responses have thus far consistently mirrored black ethnic responses more closely than they have white Local 371 attitudes, which suggests some levels of possible ethnic cohesion pertaining to the spending issues present.
9. Local 371 members were also asked their opinions regarding patrolling borders against illegal immigrants. Black American respondents exhibited the least cohesive opinions with other black ethnic members. Blacks were the most likely of all Local 371 groups to support increased spending for border patrolling against illegal immigrants. Feelings of competitiveness and scarce resources continue to contribute to black American attitudes toward illegal immigration. The United States has a long history of preventing perceived "undesirable" populations from entering and incorporating into American society. Border control has been and remains an indelible fiber in the fabric of American exclusion (Andreas 2003). Fifty-four percent of black American respondents, compared to 32 and 39 percent of Afro-Caribbean and African respondents, supported increased government spending for border controls (there were no questions within the national data that asked about border patrols). An element of black American feelings of threat by foreign populations was reflected in black American fears that immigrant populations will encroach on occupational sectors and the relatively recent economic gains that have been achieved by the group.
10. See Gilens (1996) for additional discussion.
11. The 2006 GSS did not ask a specific question pertaining to spending on Africa. However, the GSS did ask a question whether the government spent too much, the same, or too little on foreign aid. Regarding overall foreign aid, foreign-born blacks were the most likely to indicate that the national government spent too little on it at 23 percent compared to 10 percent of blacks and 5 percent of whites. By contrast, 68 percent of native-born blacks believed that the national government spent too much on foreign aid, compared to 71 percent of whites and 53 percent of foreign-born blacks. In all, the majority of all respondents indicated that the government spent too much on foreign aid. The lack of support for increases in foreign-aid indicated attitudes shared by groups currently residing in the United States who reported that other countries should aid themselves. These results also indicated a desire for those resources to remain in the United States. It should be noted that in 2006 the United States was at the height of two wars, and many Americans felt that too many resources were being spent abroad.

Conclusion

1. With the exception of political scientists Reuel Rogers (2006) and Shayla Nunnally (2010), who address the nuances of race and class among native-born black Americans and Afro-Caribbeans in the United States.
2. These numbers do not include undocumented individuals living in America.
3. These debates also have implications for future studies of immigration politics debates.
4. Farley et al. (1997) argued that differences for racial residential preferences exist and that age, education, and family income were related to residential preferences for blacks.
5. Urban planning and historical literature state that blacks are the least likely to assimilate and integrate with whites in regard to housing (Freeman 2002; Wilder 2000) and that Latinos are somewhat more likely to residentially integrate with whites. However, Latinos too largely reside in relatively homogeneous residential spaces or in close proximity to blacks primarily

due to socioeconomic and class backgrounds. Scholars state that increased intergroup contact can actually lead to decreased group conflict and a possible increase in intergroup shared interests (Powers and Ellison 1995; Rothbart and John 1993). The data illustrate that groups belonging to the "out-group" share related attitudes toward the government and have increased participation rates when compared to white respondents.

For complete regression analyses of the data presented, please contact the author.

BIBLIOGRAPHY

Abramowitz, Alan I. 1994. Issue Evolution Reconsidered: Racial Attitudes and Partisanship in the U.S. Electorate. *American Journal of Political Science* 38, no. 1: 1.

Abramson, Paul R., John H. Aldrich, Phil Paolino, and David W. Rohde. 1992. "Sophisticated" Voting in the 1988 Presidential Primaries. *American Political Science Review* 86, no. 1 (March): 55–69.

Alba, Richard, and Victor Nee. 1999. Rethinking Assimilation Theory for a New Era of Immigration. In *The Handbook of International Migration: The American Experience*, edited by Charles Hirschman, Josh Dewind, and Philip Kasinitz. New York: Russell Sage Foundation.

Alba, Richard D., and Victor Nee. 2003. *Remaking the American Mainstream: Assimilation and Contemporary Immigration*. Cambridge, MA: Harvard University Press.

Allen, Richard L. 2001. A Culturally Based Conception of the Black Self-Concept. In *Transcultural Realities: Interdisciplinary Perspectives on Cross-Cultural Relations*, edited by Virginia Hall Milhouse, Molefi K. Asante, and Peter Nwosu. Thousand Oaks, CA: Sage.

Allensworth, Elaine M. 1997. Earnings Mobility of First and "1.5" Generation Mexican-Origin Women and Men: A Comparison with U.S.-Born Mexican Americans and Non-Hispanic Whites. *International Migration Review* 31, no. 2 (Summer): 386–410.

Almond, Gabriel A., and Sidney Verba. 1980. *The Civic Culture Revisited: An Analytic Study*. Boston: Little, Brown.

Alvarez, R. Michael, and Jane Junn. 2010. Assessing the Causes and Effects of Political Trust amongst U.S. Latinos. *American Politics Research* 38, no. 1: 110–41.

Andreas, Peter. 2003. Redrawing the Line: Borders and Security in the 21st Century. *International Security* 28, no. 2 (Fall): 78–111.

Anglin, Deidre M., and Arthur L. Whaley. 2006. Racial/Ethnic Self-labeling in Relation to Group Socialization and Identity in African-Descended Individuals. *Journal of Language and Social Psychology* 25, no. 4 (December): 457–63.

Apraku, Kofi Konadu. 1991. *African Emigres in the United States: A Missing Link in Africa's Social and Economic Development*. New York: Praeger.

Arenson, Karen W., and Sara Rimer. 2004. Top Colleges Take More Blacks, But Which Ones? *New York Times*, June 24.

Armstrong, J. Scott, and Terry S. Overton. 1977. Estimating Nonresponse Bias in Mail Surveys. *Journal of Marketing Research* 14, no. 3 (August): 396–402.

Arthur, John A. 2000. *Invisible Sojourners: African Immigrant Diaspora in the United States*. Westport, CT: Praeger.

Ashmore, Richard D., Kay Deaux, and Tracy McLaughlin-Volpe. 2004. An Organizing Framework for Collective Identity: Articulation and Significance of Multidimensionality. *Psychological Bulletin* 130, no. 1: 80–114.

Baicker, Katherine, et al. 2004. Who You Are and Where You Live: How Race and Geography Affect the Treatment of Medicare Beneficiaries. *Health Affairs Web Exclusive.* Retrieved June 5, 2010, from https://www.dartmouth.edu/~jskinner/documents/ BaickerKWhoyouareandWhereyoulive.pdf.

Banfield, Edward C., and James Q. Wilson. 1963. *City Politics.* Cambridge, MA: Harvard University Press.

Banton, Michael. 1983. *Racial and Ethnic Competition.* New York: Cambridge University Press.

Baptiste, Fitzroy Andre. 2003. Amy Ashwood Garvey and Afro-West Indian Labor in the U.S. Emergency Farm and War Industries' Programs of World War II, 1943–1945. *Irinkerindo: A Journal of African Migration* 2 (December). http://www.africamigration.com/archive_02/f_ baptiste.htm.

Barth, Fredrik. 1969. *Ethnic Groups and Boundaries: The Social Organization of Culture Difference.* Boston: Little, Brown.

Bashi, Vilna. 2007. *Survival of the Knitted: Immigrant Social Networks in a Stratified World.* Stanford, CA: Stanford University Press.

Bashi Bobb, V. 2001. Neither Ignorance nor Bliss: Race, Racism, and the West Indian Immigrant Experience. In *Migration, Transnationalization, and Race in a Changing New York*, edited by Héctor R. Cordero-Guzmán, Robert C. Smith, and Ramón Grosfoguel. Philadelphia: Temple University Press.

Bashi Bobb, Vilna F., and Averil Y. Clarke. 2001. Tweaking a Monolith: The West Indian Immigrant Encounter with "Blackness." In *Islands in the City: West Indian Migration to New York*, edited by Nancy Foner. Berkeley: University of California Press.

Benford, R. D. 1992. Social Movements. In *Encyclopedia of Sociology*, edited by Edgar F. Borgatta and Marie L. Borgatta. New York: Macmillan.

Bennett, Linda L. M., and Stephen Earl Bennett. 1990. *Living with Leviathan: Americans Coming to Terms with Big Government.* Studies in Government and Public Policy. Lawrence: University Press of Kansas.

Bernstein, Mary. 1997. Celebration and Suppression: The Strategic Uses of Identity by the Lesbian and Gay Movement. *American Journal of Sociology* 103, no. 3 (November): 531–65.

Bernstein, Robert, Anita Chadha, and Robert Montjoy. 2001. Overreporting Voting: Why It Happens and Why it Matters. *Public Opinion Quarterly* 65, no. 1 (Spring): 22–44.

Berry, Jeffrey M., Kent E. Portney, and Ken Thomson. 1993. *The Rebirth of Urban Democracy.* Washington, DC: Brookings Institution.

Betancur, John Jairo, and Doug Gills. 2000. *The Collaborative City: Opportunities and Struggles for Blacks and Latinos in U.S. Cities.* Garland Reference Library of Social Science, vol. 1461. New York: Garland.

Black, Earl, and Merle Black. 1987. *Politics and Society in the South.* Cambridge, MA: Harvard University Press.

Blauner, Bob. 1972. *Racial Oppression in America.* New York: Harper & Row.

Bobo, Lawrence, et al. 2001. Enduring Two-ness: Through the Eyes of Black America. *Public Perspective*, May/June, 13–16.

Bobo, Lawrence, and Franklin D. Gilliam Jr. 1990. Race, Sociopolitical Participation, and Black Empowerment. *American Political Science Review* 84, no. 2 (June): 377–93.

Bobo, Lawrence, and Vincent L. Hutchings. 1996. Perceptions of Racial Group Competition: Extending Blumer's Theory of Group Position to a Multiracial Social Context. *American Sociological Review* 61, no. 6 (December): 951–72.

Bonilla-Silva, Eduardo. 2010. *Racism without Racists: Color Blind Racism and Racial Inequality in Contemporary America.* New York: Rowman and Littlefield.

Brach, Cindy, and Irene Fraserirector. 2000. Can Cultural Competency Reduce Racial and Ethnic Health Disparities? A Review and Conceptual Model. *Medical Care Research and Review* 57, no. 4 suppl.: 181–217.

Brady, Henry E., Sidney Verba, and Kay Lehman Schlozman. 1995. Beyond SES: A Resource Model of Political Participation. *American Political Science Review* 89, no. 2 (June): 271–94.

Brewer, Marilynn. 1979. In-Group Bias in the Minimal Intergroup Situation: A Cognitive Motivational Analysis. *Psychological Bulletin* 86, no. 2: 307–24.

Brodkin, Karen. 1998. *How Jews Became White Folks and What That Says about Race in America.* New Brunswick, NJ: Rutgers University Press.

Brown, Lisa M., and Gretchen E. Lopez. 2001. Political Contacts: Analyzing the Role of Similarity in Theories of Prejudice. *Political Psychology* 22, no. 2, special issue: Psychology as Politics (June): 279–92.

Browning, Rufus P., Dale Rogers Marshall, and David H. Tabb. 2003. *Racial Politics in American Cities.* New York: Longman.

———. 1984. *Protest Is Not Enough: The Struggle of Blacks and Hispanics for Equality in Urban Politics.* Berkeley, CA: University of California Press.

Bryce-Laporte, Roy Simon. 1972. Black Immigrants: The Experience of Invisibility and Inequality. *Journal of Black Studies* 3 (September): 29–56.

Burden, Barry C. 2000. Voter Turnout and the National Election Studies. *Political Analysis* 8, no. 4: 389–98.

Butcher, Kristen F. 1994. Black Immigrants in the United States: A Comparison with Native Black and Other Immigrants. *Industrial Labor Relations Review* 42, no. 2: 265–84.

Cain, Bruce E., D. Roderick Kiewiet, and Carole J. Uhlaner. 1991. The Acquisition of Partisanship by Latinos and Asian Americans. *American Journal of Political Science* 35, no. 2 (May): 390–422.

Calderon, Jose. 1992. "Hispanic" and "Latino": The Viability of Categories for Panethnic Unity. *Latin American Perspectives* 19 (Autumn): 37–44.

Campbell, Donald. 1958. Common Fate, Similarity, and Other Indices of the Status of Aggregates of Persons Social Entities. *Behavioral Science* 3: 14–25.

Capps, Randy, Kristen McCabe, and Michael Fix. 2011. *New Streams: Black African Migration to the US.* Washington, DC: Migration Policy Institute.

Carmines, Edward G., and James A. Stimson. 1989. *Issue Evolution: Race and the Transformation of American Politics.* Princeton, NJ: Princeton University Press.

———. 1982. Racial Issues and the Structure of Mass Belief Systems. *Journal of Politics* 44, no. 1 (February): 2–20.

Cavanagh, Thomas E., and Joint Center for Political Studies (US). 1987. *Strategies for Mobilizing Black Voters: Four Case Studies.* Washington, DC: Joint Center for Political Studies.

Chandra, Kanchan. 2006. What Is Ethnic Identity and Does It Matter? *Annual Review of Political Science* 9: 397–424.

Cho, Wendy K. Tam. 1999. Naturalization, Socialization, Participation: Immigrants and (Non) voting. *Journal of Politics* 61, no. 4 (November): 1140–55.

Chowdhury, Abdur. 1991. A Casual Analysis of Defense Spending and Economic Growth. *Journal of Conflict Resolution* 35, no. 1 (March): 80–97.

Clark, William A. V., and Sarah A. Blue. 2004. Race, Class and Segregation Patterns in U.S. Immigrant Gateway Cities. *Urban Affairs Review* 39, no. 6: 667–88.

Coleman, William D. 1988. *Business and Politics: A Study of Collective Action.* Kingston, Ontario: McGill-Queen's University Press.

Collier, M. J., and M. Thomas. 1988. Cultural Identity: An Interpretive Perspective. In *Theories in Intercultural Communication,* edited by Young Yun Kim, and William B. Gudykunst. New York: Sage; published in cooperation with the Speech Communication Association, Commission on International and Intercultural Communication.

Conover, Pamela Johnston. 1988. The Role of Social Groups in Political Thinking. *British Journal of Political Science* 18, no. 1 (January): 51–76.

———. 1984. The Influence of Group Identifications on Political Perception and Evaluation. *Journal of Politics* 46, no. 3 (August): 760–85.

Conover, Pamela Johnston, and Stanley Feldman. 1984. How People Organize the Political World: A Schematic Model. *American Journal of Political Science* 28, no. 1 (February): 95–126.

Converse, Philip E. 1972. Change in the American Electorate. In *The Human Meaning of Social Change,* edited by Angus Campbell and Philip E. Converse. New York: Russell Sage Foundation.

———. 1964. The Nature of Belief Systems in Mass Publics. In *Ideology and Discontent*, edited by David Ernest Apter, 206–61. New York: Free Press.

Cordero-Guzman, Hector R., and Ramon Grosfoguel. 2000. The Demographic and Socio-Economic Characteristics of Post-1965 Immigrants to New York City: A Comparative Analysis by National Origin. *International Migration* 38, no. 4: 41–79.

Cordero-Guzmán, Héctor R., Robert C. Smith, and Ramón Grosfoguel. 2001. *Migration, Transnationalization, and Race in a Changing New York*. Philadelphia: Temple University Press.

Cornell, Stephen E., and Douglas Hartmann. 1998. *Ethnicity and Race: Making Identities in a Changing World*. Thousand Oaks, CA: Pine Forge.

Cregan, Christina. 2005. Can Organizing Work? An Inductive Analysis of Individual Attitudes toward Union Membership. *Industrial and Labor Relations Review* 58, no. 2: article 7.

Dahl, Robert. 1961. *Who Governs?: Power and Democracy in an American City*. New Haven, CT: Yale University Press.

Danigelis, Nicholas L. 1977. A Theory of Black Political Participation in the United States. *Social Forces* 56, no. 1 (September): 31–47.

Davies, B., and R. Harre. 1983. Positioning: The Discursive Production of Selves. *Journal for the Theory of Social Behavior* 20: 43–63.

Davies, Gareth, and Martha Derthick. 1997. Race and Social Welfare Policy: The Social Security Act of 1935. *Political Science Quarterly* 112, no. 2: 217–35.

Davis, Christine J. 1998. The Principle of Benefit and Burden. *Cambridge Law Journal* 57, no. 3 (November): 522–53.

Dawson, Michael C. 2012. Racial Tragedies, Political Hope, and the Tasks of American Political Science. *Perspectives on Politics* 10, no. 3 (September): 669–73.

———. 2001. *Black Visions: The Roots of Contemporary African-American Political Ideologies*. Chicago: University of Chicago Press.

———. 1994. *Behind the Mule: Race and Class in African-American Politics*. Princeton, NJ: Princeton University Press.

Dawson, Michael C., and Cathy Cohen. 2002. Problems in the Study of Race. In *Political Science: The State of the Discipline III*, edited by Ira Katznelson and Helen V. Milner. New York: W. W. Norton.

de la Garza, Rodolfo O. 1992. *Latino Voices: Mexican, Puerto Rican, and Cuban Perspectives on American Politics*. Boulder, CO: Westview.

de la Garza, Rodolfo O., and Jeronimo Cortina. 2008. Get Me to the Polls on Time: Latino Mobilization and Turnout in the 2000 Election. In *New Race Politics: Understanding Minority and Immigrant Politics*, edited by Jane Junn and Kerry Haynie. New York: Cambridge University Press.

de la Garza, R., and Louis DeSipio. 1998. Interests Not Passions: Mexican American Attitudes toward Mexico and Issue Shaping U.S.-Mexico Relations. *International Migration* 32 (Summer): 412–22.

de la Garza, Rodolfo O., Jerry L. Polinard, Robert D. Wrinkle, and Longoria Tomás. 1991. Understanding Intra-ethnic Attitude Variations: Mexican Origin Population Views of Immigration. *Social Science Quarterly* 72, no. 2: 379–87.

de la Garza, Rodolfo O., and Muserref Yetim. 2003. The Impact of Ethnicity and Socialization on Definitions of Democracy: The Case of Mexican Americans and Mexicans. *Mexican Studies / Estudios Mexicanos* 19, no. 1 (Winter): 81–104.

Deaux, Kay. 2006. *To Be an Immigrant*. New York: Russell Sage Foundation.

———. 1996. Social Identification. In *Social Psychology: Handbook of Basic Principles*, edited by E. Tory Higgins and Arie W. Kruglanski, 777–98. New York: Guilford.

Deaux, Kay, Nida Bikmen, Alwyn Gilkes, Ana Ventuneac, Yvanne Joseph, Yasser Payne, and Claude Steele. 2007. Becoming American: Stereotype Threat Effects in Afro-Caribbean Immigrant Groups. *Social Psychology Quarterly* 70, no. 4: 384–404.

Delaney, John Thomas, Marick F. Masters, and Susan Schwochau. 1988. Unionism and Voter Turnout. *Journal of Labor Research* 9, no. 3: 221–36.

DeSipio, Louis. 1996. *Counting On the Latino Vote: Latinos as a New Electorate.* Charlottesville: University Press of Virginia.

Deutsch, Morton. 1985. *Distributive Justice: A Social-Psychological Perspective.* New Haven, CT: Yale University Press.

DeVos, G. A. 1984. Ethnic Pluralism: Conflict and Accommodation. In *Ethnic Identity Cultural Continuities and Change,* edited by George A. DeVos. Chicago: University of Chicago Press.

Diamond, Larry Jay, and Marc F. Plattner. 1994. *Nationalism, Ethnic Conflict, and Democracy.* Baltimore: Johns Hopkins University Press.

Dilday, K. A. 2008. Back to Black. *New York Times,* February 27.

Djamba, Yanyi. 1999. African Immigrants in the United States: A Socio-Demographic Profile in Comparison to Native Blacks. *Journal of Asian and African Studies* 34, no. 2: 210–15.

Dodoo, F. Nii-Amoo. 1997. Assimilation Differences among Africans in America. *Social Forces* 76, no. 2 (December): 527–46.

———. 1991a. Blacks and Earnings in New York State. *Sociological Spectrum* 11, no. 2: 203–12.

———. 1991b. Immigrant and Native Black Workers' Labor Force Participation in the United States. *National Journal of Sociology* 5: 1–17.

———. 1991c. Minority Immigrants in the U.S.: Earnings Attributes and Economic Success. *Canadian Studies in Population* 18: 42–55.

Dovi, Suzanne. 2002. Preferable Descriptive Representatives: Will Just Any Woman, Black, or Latino Do? *American Political Science Review* 96, no. 4 (December): 729–43.

Du Bois, W. E. B. 1899. *Fourth Conference for the Study of the Negro Problems.* Atlanta University.

———. 1929. Immigration Quote. *Crisis.* August.

———. 1993 [1903]. *The Souls of Black Folk.* New York: Knopf.

Dyer, Ervin. 2003. West Pennsylvania Proves to Be a Land of Opportunity for African Immigrants. *Post Gazette,* March 16.

Edelman, Murray. 1993. Contestable Categories and Public Opinion. *Political Communication* 10, no. 3: 231–42.

Edwards, Brent Hayes. 2003. *The Practice of Diaspora: Literature, Translation and the Rise of Black Internationalism.* Cambridge, MA: Harvard University Press.

Eismeier, Theodore J. 1982. Public Preferences about Government Spending: Partisan, Social, and Attitudinal Sources of Policy Differences. *Political Behavior* 4, no. 2: 133–45.

Elder, Charles D., and Roger W. Cobb. 1983. *The Political Uses of Symbols.* New York: Longman.

Elliott, Evel, et al. 1997. Political and Economic Development of Individual Support for Environmental Spending. *Journal of Environmental Management* 51, no. 1 (September): 15–27.

Epstein, David, and Sharyn O'Halloran. 1999. Measuring the Electoral and Policy Impact of Majority-Minority Voting Districts. *American Journal of Political Science* 43, no. 2 (April): 367–95.

Espiritu, Yen Le. 1992. *Asian American Panethnicity: Bridging Institutions and Identities.* Philadelphia: Temple University Press.

Etter, Jean Francois, and Thomas V. Perneger. 1997. Analysis of Non-response Bias in a Mailed Health Survey. *Journal of Clinical Epidemiology* 50, no. 10 (October): 1123–28.

Farley, Reynolds, Elaine Fielding, and Maria Krysan. 1997. The Residential Preferences of Blacks and Whites: A Four-Metropolis Analysis. *Housing Policy Debate* 8, no. 4: 763–800.

Fearon, James D., and David D. Laitin. 1996. Explaining Interethnic Cooperation. *American Political Science Review* 90, no. 4 (December): 715–35.

Fears, Darryl. 2003. Disparity Marks Black Ethnic Groups, Report Says. *Washington Post,* March 9.

Fernandez, Raquel, and Richard Rogerson. 1996. Income Distribution, Communities, and the Quality of Public Education. *Quarterly Journal of Economics* 111, no. 1: 135–64.

Fields, Barbara. 1982. Ideology and Race in American History. In *Region, Race, and Reconstruction: Essays in Honor of C. Vann Woodward*, edited by C. Vann Woodward, J. Morgan Kousser, and James M. McPherson. New York: Oxford University Press.

Fine, Michelle, and Cheryl Bowers. 1984. Racial Self-Identification: The Effects of Social History and Gender. *Journal of Applied Social Psychology* 14: 136–46.

Foner, Nancy. 2001. *Islands in the City: West Indian Migration to New York*. Berkeley: University of California Press.

———. 1987. The Jamaicans: Race and Ethnicity among Migrants in New York City. In *New Immigrants in New York*, ed. Nancy Foner. New York: Columbia University Press.

Foner, Phil. 1950. *The Life and Writings of Frederick Douglass*. Vol. 2. New York: International.

Freeman, Lance. 2002. Does Spatial Assimilation Work for Black Immigrants in the U.S.? *Urban Studies* 39, no. 11: 1983–2003.

Fuchs, Ester R. 1992. *Mayors and Money: Fiscal Policy in New York and Chicago*. Chicago: University of Chicago Press.

Fuchs, Ester R., Lorraine C. Minnite, and Robert Y. Shapiro. 2001. Social Capital, Political Participation, and the Urban Community. In *Social Capital and Poor Communities*, edited by Susan Saegert et al. New York: Russell Sage Foundation.

Gamson, William A. 1968. *Power and Discontent*. Homewood, IL: Dorsey.

Gans, H. 1989. Symbolic Ethnicity: The Future of Ethnic Groups and Cultures in America. *Dissent* 2, no. 1: 1–20.

Garcia, J. A. 1982. Ethnic Identification, Consciousness, and Identity: Explanations of Measurement and Inter-relationships. *Hispanic Journal of Behavioral Sciences* 4, no. 3 (September): 295–314.

Garcia, John A., and Rodolfo O. de la Garza. 1985. Mobilizing the Mexican Immigrant: The Role of Mexican American Organizations. *Western Political Quarterly* 38, no. 4: 551–64.

Garcia Coll, Cynthia T. 1992. *Cultural Diversity: Implications for Theory and Practice*. Wellesley, MA: The Stone Center, Wellesley College.

Gates, Henry L. 1997. *Thirteen Ways of Looking at a Black Man*. New York: Vintage Books.

Gates, H. L., Jr. 1989. What's in a Name? Some Meanings of Blackness. *Dissent* 36: 487–95.

Gay, Claudine. 2004. Putting Race in Context: Identifying the Environmental Determinants of Black Racial Attitudes. *American Political Science Review* 98, no. 4 (November): 547–62.

———. 2002. Spirals of Trust? The Effect of Descriptive Representation on the Relationship between Citizens and Their Government. *American Journal of Political Science* 46, no. 4 (October): 717–32.

Gay, Phillip. 1989. A Vote against Use of African-American. *Los Angeles Times*, April 2.

Ghee, K. L. 1990. The Psychological Importance of Self-Definition. *Journal of Black Psychology* 17: 75–93.

Gilens, Martin. 1999. *Why Americans Hate Welfare: Race, Media, and the Politics of Antipoverty Policy*. Chicago: University of Chicago Press.

———. 1996. "Race Coding" and White Opposition to Welfare. *American Political Science Review* 90, no. 3: 593–604.

Giles, Michael W., and Arthur Evans. 1985. External Threat, Perceived Threat and Group Identity. *Social Science Quarterly* 66, no. 1: 50.

Glaeser, Edward, and Jacob Vigdor. 2012. *The End of the Segregated Century: Racial Separation in America's Neighborhoods, 1980–2012*. New York: Manhattan Institute.

Goff, Phillip A., Claude M. Steele, and Paul G. Davies. 2008. The Space between Us: Stereotype Threat and Distance in Interracial Contexts. *Journal of Personality and Social Psychology* 94, no. 1 (January): 91–107.

Goldberg, David Theo. 1990. The Social Formation of Racist Discourse. *In Anatomy of Racism*, ed. David Theo Goldberg. Minneapolis: University of Minnesota Press.

Gonzales, John Moreno. 2003. The Hispanic Color Divide. *Newsday*, July 15.

Gordon, April. 1998. The New Diaspora- African Immigration to the United States. *Journal of Third World Studies* 15, no. 1 (Spring): 79–103.

Gordon-Larsen, Penny, Melissa C. Nelson, Phil Page, and Barry M. Popkin. 2006. Inequality in the Built Environment Underlies Key Health Disparities in Physical Activity and Obesity. *Pediatrics* 117, no. 2: 417–24.

Goren, Paul. 2003. Race, Sophistication, and White Opinion on Government Spending. *Political Behavior* 25, no. 3 (September): 201–20.

Greeley, Andrew M. 1972. Political Attitudes among American White Ethnics. *Public Opinion Quarterly* 36, no. 2 (Summer): 213–20.

Greer, Christina. 2008. Black Ethnicity: Identity, Political Participation, and Policy. PhD diss., Columbia University.

Gronke, Paul. 1992. Overreporting the Vote in the 1988 Senate Election Study: A Response to Wright. *Legislative Studies Quarterly* 17, no. 1 (February): 113–29.

Grosfoguel, R., and Hector Cordero-Guzman. 1998. Social Capital, Context of Reception and Transnationalism: Recent Approaches to International Migration. *Diaspora* 7, no. 3: 351–68.

Guinier, Lani, and Gerald Torres. 2002. *Miner's Canary*. Cambridge, MA: Harvard University Press.

Gurin, Patricia. 2004. *Defending Diversity: Affirmative Action at the University of Michigan*. Ann Arbor: University of Michigan Press.

Gurin, Patricia, and Edgar G. Epps. 1975. *Black Consciousness, Identity, and Achievement: A Study of Students in Historically Black Colleges*. New York: Wiley.

Guterbock, Thomas M. 1980. *Machine Politics in Transition: Party and Community in Chicago*. Chicago: University of Chicago Press.

Guterbock, Thomas M., and Bruce London. 1983. Race, Political Orientation, and Participation: An Empirical Test of Four Competing Theories. *American Sociological Review* 48, no. 4: 439–53.

Halter, Marilyn. 1993. *Between Race and Ethnicity: Cape Verdean American Immigrants, 1860–1965*. Urbana: University of Illinois Press.

Hanks, Lawrence J. 1987. *The Struggle for Black Political Empowerment in Three Georgia Counties*. Knoxville: University of Tennessee Press.

Hannan, Michael T. 1979. National Development and the World System. In *National Development and the World System: Educational, Economic, and Political Change, 1950–1970*, edited by John W. Meyer and Michael T. Hannan. Chicago: University of Chicago Press.

Harris, Frederick. 2012. *The Price of the Ticket*. New York: Oxford University Press.

Hecht, Michael L., Mary Jane Collier, and Sidney A. Ribeau. 1993. *African American Communication: Ethnic Identity and Cultural Interpretation*. Newbury Park, CA: Sage.

Hechter, Michael. 2000. *Containing Nationalism*. New York: Oxford University Press.

Hero, Rodney. 1992. *Latinos and the US Political System: Two-Tiered Pluralism*. Philadelphia: Temple University Press.

Hesse, Barnor. 2007. Racialized Modernity: An Analytics of White Mythologies. *Ethnic and Racial Studies* 30, no. 4: 643–63.

Ho, Christine. 1991. *Salt-Water Trinnies: Afro-Trinidadian Immigrant Networks and Non-assimilation in Los Angeles*. New York: AMS.

Hochschild, Jennifer L. 2012. Race and Cities: New Circumstances Imply New Ideas. *Perspectives on Politics* 10, no. 3 (September): 647–58.

———. 2005. Looking Ahead: Racial Trends in the United States. *Daedalus* 134, no. 1: 70–81.

———. 1995. *Facing Up to the American Dream: Race, Class, and the Soul of the Nation*. Princeton, NJ: Princeton University Press.

Hochschild, J., and R. Rogers. 2000. Race Relations in a Diversifying Nation. In *New Directions: African Americans in a Diversifying Nation*, edited by James S. Jackson. Ann Arbor: University of Michigan.

Hochschild, Jennifer L., Vesla M. Weaver, and Traci R. Burch. 2012. *Creating a New Racial Order: How Immigration, Multiracialism, Genomics, and the Young Can Remake Race in America*. Princeton, NJ: Princeton University Press.

Holt, Thomas C. 2000. *The Problem of Race in the Twenty-first Century*. Cambridge, MA: Harvard University Press.

Hood, M. V. III, Irwin L. Morris, and Kurt A. Shirkey. 1997. "!Quedate o Vente!": Uncovering the Determinants of Hispanic Public Opinion toward Immigration. *Political Research Quarterly* 50, no. 3 (September): 627–47.

Huckfeldt, R. Robert, and Carol W. Kohlfeld. 1989. *Race and the Decline of Class in American Politics*. Urbana: University of Illinois Press.

Huddy, Leonie. 2004. Contrasting Theoretical Approaches to Intergroup Relations. *Political Psychology* 25, no. 6 (December): 947–67.

Hunt, April. 2002. Black Immigrants Feel No Racial Kinship in U.S. *Orlando Sentinel*, April 28.

Ignatiev, Noel. 1995. *How the Irish Became White*. New York: Routledge.

Itzigsohn, Jose, and Carlos Dore-Cabral. 2000. Competing Identities? Race, Ethnicity and Panethnicity among Dominicans in the United States. *Sociological Forum* 15, no. 2: 225–47.

Jackson, Byran O. 1987. The Effects of Racial Group Consciousness on Political Mobilization in American Cities. *Western Political Quarterly* 40, no. 4 (December): 631–46.

Jackson, Byran O., Elisabeth R. Gerber, and Bruce E. Cain. 1994. Coalitional Prospects in a Multi-racial Society: African-American Attitudes toward Other Minority Groups. *Political Research Quarterly* 47, no. 2 (June): 277–94.

Jackson, Jennifer V., and Mary E. Cothran. 2003. Black versus Black: The Relationships among African, African American, and African Caribbean Persons. *Journal of Black Studies* 33, no. 5 (May): 576–604.

Jacobson, Matthew Frye. 2001. Becoming Caucasian: Vicissitudes of Whiteness in American Politics and Culture. *Identities: Global Studies in Culture and Power* 8, no. 1: 83–104.

Jacoby, William G. 2000. Issue Framing and Public Opinion on Government Spending. *American Journal of Political Science* 44, no. 4 (October): 750–67.

———. 1994. Public Attitudes toward Government Spending. *American Journal of Political Science* 38, no. 2 (May): 336–61.

James, Winston. 1999. *Holding Aloft the Banner of Ethiopia: Caribbean Radicalism in Early Twentieth-Century America*. New York: Verso.

Jennings, James. 1992. *Race, Politics, and Economic Development: Community Perspectives*. New York: Verso.

Johnson, Valerie C. 2002. *Black Power in the Suburbs: The Myth or Reality of African-American Suburban Political Incorporation*. Albany: State University of New York Press.

Johnson, Violet Showers. 2008. "What, Then, Is the African American?": African and Afro-Caribbean Identities in Black America. *Journal of American Ethnic History* 28, no. 1 (Fall): 77–103.

Jones-Correa, Michael. 1998a. *Between Two Nations: The Political Predicament of Latinos in New York City*. Ithaca, NY: Cornell University Press.

———. 1998b. Different Paths: Gender, Immigration, and Political Participation. *International Migration Review* 32, no. 2 (Summer): 326–49.

Jones-Correa, Michael, and David Leal. 1996. Becoming Hispanic: Secondary Pan-ethnic among Latin American Origin Population in the U.S. *Hispanic Journal of Behavioral Science* 18: 214–54.

Junn, Jane. 1999. Participation in Liberal Democracy: The Political Assimilation of Ethnic Minorities in the U.S. *American Behavioral Scientist* 42, no. 9: 1417–38.

———. 2007. From Coolie to Model Minority: U.S. Immigration Policy and the Construction of Racial Identity. *DuBois Review* 4, no. 2 (Fall): 355–73.

Junn, Jane, and Kerry Haynie. 2008. *New Race Politics in America*. New York: Cambridge University Press.

Junn, Jane, Taeku Lee, S. Karthick Ramakrishnan, and Janelle Wong. 2011. Asian American Public Opinion. In *Oxford Handbook of the Presidency and the Media*, edited by Robert Y. Shapiro and Lawrence Jacobs. New York: Oxford University Press.

Junn, Jane, and Natalie Masuoka. 2008a. Asian American Identity: Shared Racial Status and Political Context. *Perspectives on Politics* 6, no. 4: 729–40.

———. 2008b. Identities in Context: Politicized Racial Group Consciousness among Asian American and Latino Youth. *Applied Developmental Science* 12, no. 2 (April): 93–101.

Junn, Jane, and Simran Singh. 2009. Examining the Link between Issue Attitudes and News Source: The Case of Latinos and Immigration. *Political Behavior* 31, no. 1: 1–30.

Kalmijn, Matthijs. 1996. The Socioeconomic Assimilation of Caribbean American Blacks. *Social Forces* 74, no. 3 (March): 911–30.

Kasinitz, Philip. 1992. *Caribbean New York: Black Immigrants and the Politics of Race.* Ithaca, NY: Cornell University Press.

Kasinitz, Philip, and Jan Rosenberg. 1996. Missing the Connection: Social Isolation and Employment on the Brooklyn Waterfront. *Social Problems* 43, no. 2 (May): 180–96.

Kasinitz, Philip, Juan Battle, and Ines Miyares. 2001. Fade to Black?: The Children of West Indian Immigrants in South Florida. In *Ethnicities: Coming of Age in Immigrant America*, edited by Alejandro Portes and Ruben Rumbaut, 267–300. Berkeley: Russell Sage Foundation and the University of California Press.

Katz, Michael, Matthew J. Creighton, Daniel Amsterdam, and Merlin Chowkwanyun. 2010. Immigration and the New Metropolitan Geography. *Journal of Urban Affairs* 32, no. 5 (December): 523–47.

Katznelson, Ira. 1981. *City Trenches: Urban Politics and the Patterning of Class in the United States.* New York: Pantheon.

Keefe, Susan E., and Amado M. Padilla. 1987. *Chicano Ethnicity.* Albuquerque: University of New Mexico Press.

Keely, Charles B. 1971. Effects of the Immigration Act of 1965 on Selected Population Characteristics of Immigrants to the United States. *Demography* 8, no. 2 (May): 157–69.

Kelley, Robin D. G. 1999a. But a Local Phase of a World Problem: Black History's Global Vision, 1883–1950. *Journal of American History*: 1045–77.

———. 1999b. People in Me: "So, What Are You?" *Colorlines* 1, no. 3 (Winter): 5.

Kim, Claire Jean. 2003. *Bitter Fruit: The Politics of Black-Korean Conflict in New York City.* New Haven, CT: Yale University Press.

Kinder, Donald R., and Allison Dale-Riddle. 2012. *The End of Race: Obama, 2008, and Racial Politics in America.* New Haven, CT: Yale University Press.

Kinder, Donald R., and Cindy Kam. 2009. *Us against Them: Ethnocentric Foundations of American Opinion.* Chicago: University of Chicago Press.

Kinder, Donald R., and Lynn M. Sanders. 1996. *Divided by Color: Racial Politics and Democratic Ideals.* Chicago: University of Chicago Press.

Kriesi, Hanspeter. 1995. *New Social Movements in Western Europe: A Comparative Analysis.* Minneapolis: University of Minnesota Press.

Kusi, Newmark. 1994. Economic Growth and Defense Spending in Developing Countries. *Journal of Conflict Resolution* 38, no. 1 (March): 152–59.

Ladd, Everett Carll, and Charles D. Hadley. 1978. *Transformations of the American Party System: Political Coalitions from the New Deal to the 1970s.* New York: Norton.

Ladd, Everett Carll, Marilyn Potter, Linda Basilick, Sally Daniels, and Dana Suszkiw. 1979. The Polls: Taxing and Spending. *Public Opinion Quarterly* 43, no. 1 (Spring): 126–35.

Landry, Bart. 1987. *The New Black Middle Class.* Berkeley: University of California Press.

Langbein, Soss, and A. Metelko. 2003. Why Do White Americans Support the Death Penalty? *Journal of Politics* 65, no. 2: 397–421.

Larkey, L. K., M. L. Hecht, and Judith Martin. 1993. What's in a Name? African American Ethnic Identity Terms and Self-Determination. *Journal of Language and Social Psychology* 12, no. 4: 302–17.

Lau, Richard R., Richard A. Smith, and Susan T. Fiske. 1991. Political Beliefs, Policy Interpretations, and Political Persuasion. *Journal of Politics* 53, no. 3 (August): 644–75.

Lee, Taeku. 2011. *Why Americans Don't Join the Party: Race, Immigration, and the Failure (of Political Parties) to Engage the Electorate.* Princeton, NJ: Princeton University Press.

Lee, Taeku, S. Karthick Ramakrishnan, and Ricardo Ramirez, eds. 2006. *Transforming Politics, Transforming America: The Civic and Political Incorporation of Immigrants in the United States.* Charlottesville: University of Virginia Press.

Leege, David C. 2002. *The Politics of Cultural Differences: Social Change and Voter Mobilization Strategies in the Post-New Deal Period.* Princeton, NJ: Princeton University Press.

Leighley, Jan E. 2001. *Strength in Numbers?: The Political Mobilization of Racial and Ethnic Minorities.* Princeton, NJ: Princeton University Press.

Leighley, Jan E., and Jonathan Nagler. 2007. Unions, Voter Turnout, and Class Bias in the U.S. Electorate, 1964–2004. *Journal of Politics* 69, no. 2: 430–41.

Leighley, Jan E., and Arnold Vedlitz. 1999. Race, Ethnicity, and Political Participation: Competing Models and Contrasting Explanations. *Journal of Politics* 61, no. 4 (November): 1092–1114.

Leslie, Lourdes Medrano, and David Peterson. 2002. Africans Struggle to Make a New Home. *Star Tribune*, October 6.

Levi, Margaret. 2003. Organizing Power: The Prospects for an American Labor Movement. *Perspectives on Politics* 1, no. 1 (March): 45–68.

Lieberman, Robert. 2008. *Shaping Race Policy: The United States in Comparative Perspective.* Princeton, NJ: Princeton University Press.

———. 1998. *Shifting the Color Line: Race and the American Welfare State.* Cambridge, MA: Harvard University Press.

Lieberson, Stanley, and Arnold R. Silverman. 1965. The Precipitants and Underlying Conditions of Race Riots. *American Sociological Review* 30, no. 6: 887–98.

Lien, Pei-te, M. Margaret Conway, and Janelle Wong. 2004. *The Politics of Asian Americans: Diversity and Community.* New York: Routledge.

Lock, Shmuel T., Robert Y. Shapiro, and Lawrence R. Jacobs. 1999. The Impact of Political Debate on Government Trust: Reminding the Public What the Federal Government Does. *Political Behavior* 21, no. 3 (September): 239–64.

Logan, John R. 2003, July. How Race Counts for Hispanic Americans. Retrieved June 15, 2006, from http://mumford1.dyndns.org/cen2000/BlackLatinoReport/BlackLatino01.htm.

London, Bruce, and Michael W. Giles. 1987. Black Participation: Compensation or Ethnic Identification? *Journal of Black Studies* 18, no. 1 (September): 20–44.

Maier, Mark. 1987. *City Unions: Managing Discontent in New York City.* New Brunswick, NJ: Rutgers University Press.

Mampilly, Zachariah. 2011. *Rebel Rulers: Insurgent Governance and Civilian Life during War.* Ithaca, NY: Cornell University Press.

Mansbridge, Jane. 2003. Rethinking Representation. *American Political Science Review* 97, no. 4: 515–28.

———. 1999. Should Blacks Represent Blacks and Women Represent Women? A Contingent "Yes." *Journal of Politics* 61, no. 3 (August): 628–57.

Martin, Ben L. 1991. From Negro to Black to African American: The Power of Names and Naming. *Political Science Quarterly* 106, no. 1 (Spring): 83–107.

Martinez, Michael D. 2003. Comment on "Voter Turnout and the National Election Studies." *Political Analysis* 11, no. 2: 187–92.

Mashaw, Jerry, and Theodore Marmor. 1994. Conceptualizing, Estimating, and Reforming Fraud, Waste, and Abuse in Healthcare Spending. *Yale Journal of Regulation* 11: 455–94.

Massey, Douglas S., and Nancy A. Denton. 1993. *American Apartheid: Segregation and the Making of the Underclass.* Cambridge, MA: Harvard University Press.

———. 1988. The Dimensions of Residential Segregation. *Social Forces* 67, no. 2: 281–315.

Master, Bob. 1997. A New Political Strategy for American Unions. *Working USA*, September/October, 22.

McAdam, Doug. 1988. *Freedom Summer.* New York: Oxford University Press.

McAdam, Doug, John D. McCarthy, and Mayer N. Zald. 1996. *Comparative Perspectives on Social Movements: Political Opportunities, Mobilizing Structures, and Cultural Framings.* New York: Cambridge University Press.

McClosky, Herbert, and John Zaller. 1984. *The American Ethos: Public Attitudes toward Capitalism and Democracy*. Cambridge, MA: Harvard University Press.

McDonald, Michael P. 2003. On the Overreport Bias of the National Election Study Turnout Rate. *Political Analysis* 11, no. 2: 180–86.

Meier, Kenneth J., and Joseph Stewart Jr. 1991. Cooperation and Conflict in Multiracial School Districts. *Journal of Politics* 53, no. 4: 1123–33.

Meriwether, James Hunter. 2002. *Proudly We Can Be Africans: Black Americans and Africa, 1935–1961*. Chapel Hill: University of North Carolina Press.

Migration Policy Institute. 2004. *Immigrant Union Members: Numbers and Trends*. Fact Sheet No. 7. May.

Milbrath, Lester W. 1965. *Political Participation: How and Why Do People Get Involved in Politics?* Chicago: Rand McNally.

Milbrath, Lester W., and Madan Lal Goel. 1977. *Political Participation: How and Why Do People Get Involved in Politics?* Chicago: Rand McNally.

Miller, Arthur H., Patricia Gurin, Gerald Gurin, and Oksana Malanchuk. 1981. Group Consciousness and Political Participation. *American Journal of Political Science* 25, no. 3 (August): 494–511.

Minnite, Lorraine. 2009. Lost in Translation? A Critical Reappraisal of the Concept of Immigrant Political Incorporation. In *Bringing Outsiders In: Transatlantic Perspectives on Immigrants Political Incorporation*, edited by Jennifer Hochschild and John Mollenkopf, 48–59. Ithaca, NY: Cornell University Press.

Model, Suzanne. 1995. West Indian Prosperity: Fact or Fiction? *Social Problems* 42, no. 4 (November): 535–53.

———. 1991. Caribbean Immigrants: A Black Success Story? *International Migration Review* 25, no. 2 (Summer): 248–76.

Mollenkopf, J. H. 1999. Urban Political Conflicts and Alliances: New York and Los Angeles Compared. In *Handbook of Immigration: The American Experience*, edited by Charles Hirschman, Philip Kasinitz, and Josh Dewind. New York: Russell Sage Foundation.

Mollenkopf, John H., and Manuel Castells. 1991. *Dual City: Restructuring New York*. New York: Russell Sage Foundation.

Morone, James A. 1998. *The Democratic Wish: Popular Participation and the Limits of American Government*. New Haven, CT: Yale University Press.

Muller, Edward N. 1977. Behavioral Correlates of Political Support. *American Political Science Review* 71, no. 2 (June): 454–67.

Myrdal, Gunnar. 1944. *An American Dilemma: The Negro Problem and Modern Democracy*. Vol. 2. New York: Harper and Row.

Nelson, Dale C. 1979. Ethnicity and Socioeconomic Status as Sources of Participation: The Case for Ethnic Political Culture. *American Political Science Review* 73, no. 4 (December): 1024–38.

Nelson, Thomas E., and Donald R. Kinder. 1996. Issue Frames and Group-centrism in American Public Opinion. *Journal of Politics* 58, no. 4 (November): 1055–78.

Nelson, Thomas E., Zoe M. Oxley, and Rosalee A. Clawson. 1997. Toward a Psychology of Framing Effects. *Political Behavior* 19, no. 3 (September): 221–46.

Nie, Norman H., Jane Junn, and Kenneth Stehlik-Barry. 1996. *Education and Democratic Citizenship in America*. Chicago: University of Chicago Press.

Nunnally, Shayla. 2012. *Trust in Black America: Race, Discrimination, and Politics*. New York: New York University Press.

———. 2010. Linking Blackness or Ethnic Othering? *Du Bois Review* 7, no. 2 (September): 335–55.

Obama, Barack. 2008. New Hampshire Primary speech. January 8.

Oboler, Suzanne. 1992. The Politics of Labeling: Latino/a Cultural Identities of Self and Others. *Latin American Perspectives* 19, no. 4 (Autumn): 18–36.

Ogbaa, Kalu. 2003. *The Nigerian Americans*. Westport, CT: Greenwood.

Okamoto, Ding G. 2003. Toward a Theory of Panethnicity: Explaining Asian American Collective Action. *American Sociological Review* 68, no. 6: 811–42.

Olsen, Marvin E. 1970. Social and Political Participation of Blacks. *American Sociological Review* 35, no. 4 (August): 682–97.

Olzak, Susan. 1992. *The Dynamics of Ethnic Competition and Conflict*. Stanford, CA: Stanford University Press.

Omi, Michael, and Howard Winant. 1994. *Racial Formation in the United States: From the 1960s to the 1990s*. New York: Routledge.

Osajima, Keith. 1998. Pedagogical Considerations in Asian American Studies. *Journal of Asian American Studies* 1, no. 3: 269–92.

———. 1985. *Latino Ethnic Consciousness: The Case of Mexican Americans and Puerto Ricans in Chicago*. Notre Dame, IN: University of Notre Dame Press.

Padilla, Felix. 1984. On the Nature of Latino Ethnicity. *Social Science Quarterly* 65: 651–64.

Page, Benjamin I., and Robert Y. Shapiro. 1992. *The Rational Public: Fifty Years of Trends in Americans' Policy Preferences*. Chicago: University of Chicago Press.

Parham, Thomas A., and Janet E. Helms. 1981. The Influence of Black Students' Racial Identity Attitudes on Preferences for Counselor's Race. *Journal of Counseling Psychology* 28, no. 3: 250–57.

Patterson, Orlando. 1989. Toward a Study of Black America. *Dissent*, Fall.

Penn, Elizabeth. 2008. Citizenship v. Ethnicity: The Role of Institutions in Shaping Identity Choice. *Journal of Politics* 70: 1–18.

Perlmann, Joel, and Roger Waldinger. 1997. Second Generation Decline? Children of Immigrants, Past and Present—A Reconsideration. *International Migration Review* 31, no. 4 (Winter): 893–922.

Petersen, William. 1971. *Japanese Americans: Oppression and Success*. New York: Random House.

Petrocik, John R. 1996. Issue Ownership in Presidential Elections, with a 1980 Case Study. *American Journal of Political Science* 40, no. 3 (August): 825–50.

Pettigrew, Thomas F. 1963. Actual Gains and Psychological Losses: The Negro American Protest. *Journal of Negro Education* 32, no. 4 (Autumn): 493–506.

Philpot, Tasha, and Hanes Walton. 2007. One of Our Own: Black Female Candidates and the Votes Who Support Them. *American Journal of Political Science* 51: 49–62.

Pinderhughes, Dianne M. 1997a. An Examination of Chicago Politics for Evidence of Political Incorporation and Representation. In *Racial Politics in American Cities*, edited by Rufus P. Browning, Dale Rogers Marshall, and David H. Tabb. New York: Longman.

———. 1997b. Voting Rights Policy and Redistricting: An Introductory Essay. In *Race and Representation: The National Political Science Review*, edited by Georgia Anne Persons. New Brunswick, NJ: Transaction.

———. 1995. Black Interest Groups and the 1982 Extension of the Voting Rights Act. In *Blacks and the American Political System*, edited by Huey Perry and Wayne Parent. Gainesville: University Press of Florida.

———. 1992. Divisions in the Civil Rights Community. *PS: Political Science and Politics* 25, no. 3 (September): 485–87.

Pitkin, Hanna. 1967. *The Concept of Political Representation*. Berkeley: University of California Press.

Piven, Frances Fox, and Richard A. Cloward. 1988. *Why Americans Don't Vote*. New York: Pantheon.

Poe, Juanita. 2003. Being Latin and Black: Afro-Latinos Grapple with Labels in U.S. *Atlanta Journal Constitution*, August 6.

Portes, Alejandro. 1995. *The Economic Sociology of Immigration: Essays on Networks, Ethnicity, and Entrepreneurship*. New York: Russell Sage Foundation.

Portes, Alejandro, and Rubén G. Rumbaut. 2001. *Legacies: The Story of the Immigrant Second Generation*. New York: Russell Sage Foundation.

———. 1990. *Immigrant America: A Portrait*. Berkeley: University of California Press.

Portes, Alejandro, and Alex Stepick. 1993. *City on the Edge: The Transformation of Miami*. Berkeley: University of California Press.

Powers, Daniel A., and Christopher G. Ellison. 1995. Interracial Contact and Black Racial Attitudes: The Contact Hypothesis and Selectivity Bias. *Social Forces* 74, no. 1 (September): 205–26.

Price, Melanye. 2009. *Dreaming Blackness: Black Nationalism and African American Public Opinion.* New York: New York University Press.

Price, Melayne, and Gloria Hampton. 2010. Linked Fates, Disconnected Realities: The Post–Civil Rights African American Politics. In *Perspectives on Race, Ethnicity, and Religion*, edited by Valerie Martinez-Ebers and Manochehr Dorraj. New York: Oxford University Press.

Price, Vincent, and John Zaller. 1993. Who Gets the News? Alternative Measures of News Reception and Their Implications for Research. *Public Opinion Quarterly* 57, no. 2 (Summer): 133–64.

Purdie-Vaughns, Valerie, Claude. M Steele, Paul G. Davies, Ruth Ditlmann, and J. Randall Crosby. 2008. Social Identity Contingencies: How Diversity Cues Signal Threat or Safety for African Americans in Mainstream Institutions. *Journal of Personality and Social Psychology* 94, no. 4 (April): 615–30.

Putnam, Robert D. 2000. *Bowling Alone: The Collapse and Revival of American Community.* New York: Simon & Schuster.

Pye, Lucian W., and Sidney Verba. 1965. *Political Culture and Political Development.* Princeton, NJ: Princeton University Press.

Quadagno, Jill 1999. Creating a Capital Investment Welfare State: The New American Exceptionalism? *American Sociological Review* 64: 1–11.

Radcliff, Benjamin, and Patricia Davis. 2000. Labor Organization and Electoral Participation in Industrial Democracies. *American Journal of Political Science* 44, no. 1 (January): 132–41.

Ramakrishnan, S. Karthick. 2005. *Democracy in Immigrant America: Changing Demographics and Political Participation.* Stanford, CA: Stanford University Press.

Regalado, Jaime A. 1997. The Political Incorporation of L.A.'s Communities of Color: A Critical Assessment. In *Pursuing Power: Latinos and the Political System*, edited by F. Chris Garcia. Notre Dame, IN: University of Notre Dame Press.

Reid, Ira De Augustine. 1969. *The Negro Immigrant, His Background, Characteristics, and Social Adjustment, 1899–1937.* New York: Arno.

Rimer, Sara, and Karen Arenson. 2004. Top Colleges Take More Blacks, but Which Ones? *New York Times*, June 24.

Rivera-Batiz, Francisco L. 1983. The Economics of the "To and Fro" Migrant: Some Welfare-Theoretical Considerations. *Scandinavian Journal of Economics* 85, no. 3: 403–13.

Rivera-Batiz, Francisco L., and Carlos Enrique Santiago. 1996. *Island Paradox: Puerto Rico in the 1990s.* New York: Russell Sage Foundation.

Robinson, Chauncy. 2002. Can African Americans and Hispanics Form a Coalition in Atlanta? *Mundo Hispanico*, June 6.

Rochefort, David A., and Roger W. Cobb. 1994. *The Politics of Problem Definition: Shaping the Policy Agenda.* Lawrence: University Press of Kansas.

Roediger, David R. 1991. *The Wages of Whiteness: Race and the Making of the American Working Class.* New York: Verso.

Rogers, Reuel Reuben. 2006. *Afro-Caribbean Immigrants and the Politics of Incorporation: Ethnicity, Exception, or Exit.* New York: Cambridge University Press.

———. 2000. Afro-Caribbean Immigrants, African Americans, and the Politics of Group Identity. In *Black and Multiracial Politics in America*, edited by Yvette M. Alex-Assensoh and Lawrence J. Hanks, 15–59. New York: New York University Press.

Rosenstone, Steven J., and John Mark Hansen. 1993. *Mobilization, Participation, and Democracy in America.* New York: Macmillan.

Rothbart, Myron, and Oliver P. John. 1993. Intergroup Relations and Stereotype Change: A Social Cognitive Analysis and Some Longitudinal Findings. In *Prejudice, Politics, and the American Dilemma*, edited by Paul M. Sniderman, Philip Tetlock, and Edward G. Carmines. Stanford, CA: Stanford University Press.

Rothstein, Richard. 2004. Social Class Leaves Its Imprint. *Education Week* 23, no. 37: 40–41.

Rumbaut, Ruben G. 1997. Assimilation and Its Discontents: Between Rhetoric and Reality. *International Migration Review* 31, no. 4 (Winter): 923–60.

Sanders, Arthur. 1988. Rationality, Self-Interest, and Public Attitudes on Public Spending. *Social Science Quarterly* 69: 311–24.

Santoro, Wayne A., and Gary M. Segura. 2011. Generational Status and Mexican American Political Participation: The Benefits and Limitations of Assimilation. *Political Research Quarterly* 64, no. 1: 172–84.

Sassen, Saskia. 1991. *The Global City: New York, London, Tokyo*. Princeton, NJ: Princeton University Press.

———. 1988. *The Mobility of Labor and Capital: A Study in International Investment and Labor Flow*. New York: Cambridge University Press.

Sawyer, Mark Q. 2006. *Racial Politics in Post-Revolutionary Cuba*. New York: Cambridge University Press.

Schiller, Nina, et al. 1995. From Immigrant to Transmigrant: Theorizing Transnational Migration. *Anthropology Quarterly* 68, no. 1 (January): 48–63.

Schneider, Anne, and Helen Ingram. 1993. Social Construction of Target Populations: Implications for Politics and Policy. *American Political Science Review* 87, no. 2 (June): 334–47.

———. 1990. Behavioral Assumptions of Policy Tools. *Journal of Politics* 52, no. 2 (May): 510–29.

Schnur, James A. 1993. Caught in the Crossfire: African Americans in Florida's System of Labor during WWII. *Journal of the Tampa Historical Society* 19 (November): 47–52.

Schön, Donald A., and Martin Rein. 1994. *Frame Reflection: Toward the Resolution of Intractable Policy Controversies*. New York: Basic Books.

Schuman, Howard, and Cheryl Rieger. 1992. Historical Analogies, Generational Effects, and Attitudes toward War. *American Sociological Review* 57, no. 3 (June): 315–26.

Sears, David O., and Jack Citrin. 1985. *Tax Revolt: Something for Nothing in California*. Cambridge, MA: Harvard University Press.

Sears, David O., and Carolyn L. Funk. 1990. Self-interest in Americans' Political Opinions. In *Beyond Self-interest*, edited by Jane J. Mansbridge. Chicago: University of Chicago Press.

See, Kathleen O'Sullivan, and William J. Wilson. 1989. Race and Ethnicity. In *Handbook of Sociology*, edited by Neil J. Smelser. Newbury Park, CA: Sage.

Segura, G. M. 2005. Who Are We? *Perspectives in Politics* 3, no. 3: 640–42.

Segura, Gary M., and Helena Alves Rodrigues. 2006. Comparative Ethnic Politics in the United States: Beyond Black and White. *Annual Review of Political Science* 9: 375–95.

Seidman, G. 1994. *Manufacturing Militance: Workers' Movements in Brazil and South Africa, 1970–1985*. Berkeley: University of California Press.

Seligson, Mitchell A., and John A. Booth. 1979. *Politics and the Poor*. New York: Holmes & Meier.

Shapiro, Robert Y., Kelly D. Patterson, Judith Russell, and John T. Young. 1987. A Report: Employment and Social Welfare. *Public Opinion Quarterly* 51, no. 2 (Summer): 268–81.

Shapiro, Robert Y., and Tom W. Smith. 1985. The Polls: Social Security. *Public Opinion Quarterly* 49, no. 4: 561–72.

Shaw, Todd. 2009. *Now Is the Time! Detroit Black Politics and Grassroots Activism*. Durham, NC: Duke University Press.

Sherman, Jeffrey W., Steven J. Stroessner, Frederica R. Conrey, and Omar A. Azam. 2005. Prejudice and Stereotype Maintenance Processes: Attention, Attribution, and Individuation. *Journal of Personality and Social Psychology* 89, no. 4 (October): 607–22.

Shingles, Richard D. 1981. Black Consciousness and Political Participation: The Missing Link. *American Political Science Review* 75, no. 1 (March): 76–91.

Sigelman, Lee, and Steven A. Tuch. 1997. Metastereotypes. *Public Opinion Quarterly* 61, no. 1 (Spring): 87–101.

Sipress, Joel M. 1997. Relearning Race: Teaching Race as a Cultural Construction. *History Teacher* 30, no. 2 (February): 175–85.

Smith, Robert C. 1996. Mexicans in New York City: Membership and Incorporation of New Immigrant Groups. In *Latinos in New York: Communities in Transition*, edited by Gabriel Haslip-Viera and Sherrie L. Baver. Notre Dame, IN: University of Notre Dame Press.

Smith, Robert C., Héctor R. Cordero-Guzmán, and Ramón Grosfoguel. 2001. Introduction: Migration, Transnationalization, and Race in a Changing New York. In *Migration, Transnationalization, and Race in a Changing New York*, edited by Héctor R. Cordero-Guzmán, Robert C. Smith, and Ramón Grosfoguel. Philadelphia: Temple University Press.

Smitherman, Geneva. 1991. "What is Africa to Me?": Language, Ideology, and African American. *American Speech* 66, no. 2 (Summer): 115–32.

———. 1989. The Dynamics of Biracial Coalitions: Crossover Politics in Los Angeles. *Western Political Quarterly* 42, no. 2: 333.

Sonenshein, Raphael J. 1986. Biracial Coalition Politics in Los Angeles. *Political Science* 19, no. 3: 582–90.

Soss, Joe. 2002. *Unwanted Claims: The Politics of Participation in the U.S. Welfare System*. Ann Arbor: University of Michigan Press.

Sowell, Thomas. 1994. *Race and Culture: A World View*. New York: Basic Books.

———. 1984. *Civil Rights: Rhetoric or Reality?* New York: W. Morrow.

Speight, Suzette L., Elizabeth M. Vera, and Kimberly B. Derrickson. 1996. Racial Self-Designation, Racial Identity, and Self-Esteem Revisited. *Journal of Black Psychology* 22: 37–52.

Spilerman, Seymour. 1970. The Causes of Racial Disturbances: A Comparison of Alternative Explanations. *American Sociological Review* 35, no. 4: 627–49.

Steele, Claude M. 1997. A Threat in the Air: How Stereotypes Shape Intellectual Identity and Performance. *American Psychologist* 52, no. 6: 613–29.

Steele, Claude M., Steven J. Spencer, and Joshua Aronson. 2002. Contending with Group Image: The Psychology of Stereotype and Social Identity Threat. *Advances in Experimental Social Psychology* 34: 379–440.

Stepick, Alex, et al. 2001. Shifting Identities and Intergenerational Conflict: Growing Up Haitian in Miami. In *Ethnicities: Children of Immigrants in America*, edited by Ruben G. Rumbaut and Alejandro Portes. Berkeley: University of California Press.

Stimson, James A. 1991. *Public Opinion in America: Moods, Cycles, and Swings*. Boulder, CO: Westview.

Stokes, Atiya Kai. 2003. Latino Group Consciousness and Political Participation. *American Politics Research* 31, no. 4 (July 1): 361–78.

Sundquist, James L. 1973. *Dynamics of the Party System: Alignment and Realignment of Political Parties in the United States*. Washington, DC: Brookings Institution.

Swain, Carol Miller. 1993. *Black Faces, Black Interests: The Representation of African Americans in Congress*. Cambridge, MA: Harvard University Press.

Swarns, Rachel L. 2004a. "African-American" Becomes a Term for Debate. *New York Times*, August 29.

———. 2004b. Hispanics Resist Racial Group by Census. *New York Times*, October 24.

Tajfel, Henry, and John Turner. 2001. An Integrative Theory of Intergroup Conflict. In *Intergroup Relations: Essential Readings*, edited by Michael A. Hogg and Dominic Abrams. Philadelphia: Psychology Press.

Takougang, Joseph. 1995. Recent African Immigrants to the United States: A Historical Perspective. *Western Journal of Black Studies* 19, no. 1: 50–57.

Tam Cho, Wendy K. 1999. Naturalization, Socialization, Participation: Immigrants and (Non-) Voting. *Journal of Politics* 61, no. 4: 1140–55.

———. 1995. Asians-A Monolithic Voting Bloc? *Political Behavior* 17, no. 2 (June): 223–49.

Tate, Katherine. 2004. *Black Faces in the Mirror*. Princeton, NJ: Princeton University Press.

———. 1993. *From Protest to Politics: The New Black Voters in American Elections*. Cambridge, MA: Harvard University Press.

———. 1991. Black Political Participation in the 1984 and 1988 Presidential Elections. *American Political Science Review* 85, no. 4 (December): 1159–76.

Taylor, Ronald L. 1979. Black Ethnicity and the Persistence of Ethnogenesis. *American Journal of Sociology* 84, no. 6 (May): 1401–23.

Tedin, Kent L., and Richard W. Murray. 1994. Support for Biracial Political Coalitions among Blacks and Hispanics. *Social Science Quarterly* 75, no. 4: 772–89.

Tesler, Michael, and David Sears. 2010. *Obama's Race: The 2008 Election and the Dream of a Post-Racial America*. Chicago: University of Chicago Press.

Thompson, J. Phillip. 2005. *Double Trouble: Black Mayors, Black Communities, and the Call for a Deep Democracy*. New York: Oxford University Press.

Tilly, Charles. 1990. Transplanted Networks. In *Immigration Reconsidered: History, Sociology, and Politics*, edited by Virginia Yans-McLaughlin. New York: Oxford University Press.

Torres, Andrés. 1995. *Between Melting Pot and Mosaic: African Americans and Puerto Ricans in the New York Political Economy*. Philadelphia: Temple University Press.

Torres, Andres, and Frank Bonilla. 1993. Decline within Decline: The New York Perspective. In *Latinos in a Changing U.S. Economy: Comparative Perspectives on Growing Inequality.* edited by Rebecca Morales and Frank Bonilla. Newbury Park, CA: Sage.

Torres, Carlos Alberto. 1995. State and Education Revisited: Why Educational Researchers Should Think Politically about Education. *Review of Research in Education* 21: 255–331.

Torres, Kim C., and Camille Z. Charles. 2004. Metastereotypes and the Black-White Divide: A Qualitative View of Race on an Elite College Campus. *Du Bois Review* 1: 115–49.

Tuan, Mia. 1999. *Forever Foreigners or Honorary Whites?: The Asian Ethnic Experience Today*. New Brunswick, NJ: Rutgers University Press.

Turnball, Rutherford, and Ann Turnball. 1998. *Free Appropriate Education: The Law and Children with Disabilities*. Denver: Love Publishing.

Uhlaner, Carole J. 1989. Rational Turnout: The Neglected Role of Groups. *American Journal of Political Science* 33, no. 2 (May): 390–422.

Uhlaner, Carole J., Bruce E. Cain, and D. Roderick Kiewiet. 1989. Political Participation of Ethnic Minorities in the 1980s. *Political Behavior* 11, no. 3 (September): 195–231.

Verba, Sidney, and Lucian W. Pye. 1978. *The Citizen and Politics: A Comparative Perspective*. Stamford, CT: Greylock.

Verba, Sidney, and Kay Lehman Schlozman. 1977. Unemployment, Class Consciousness, and Radical Politics: What Didn't Happen in the Thirties. *Journal of Politics* 39, no. 2 (May): 291–323.

Verba, Sidney, Kay Lehman Schlozman, and Henry E. Brady. 2004. Political Equality: What Do We Know About It? In *Social Inequality*, edited by Kathryn Neckerman, 729–67. New York: Russell Sage.

Verba, Sidney, Kay Lehman Schlozman, Henry Brady, and Norman H. Nie. 1993. Race, Ethnicity and Political Resources: Participation in the United States. *British Journal of Political Science* 23, no. 4 (October): 453–97.

———. 1972. *Participation in America: Political Democracy and Social Equality*. New York: Harper & Row.

Verba, Sidney, et al. 1971. *Caste, Race, and Politics: A Comparative Study of India and the United States*. Beverly Hills, CA: Sage.

Vickerman, Milton. 1999. *Crosscurrents: West Indian Immigrants and Race*. New York: Oxford University Press.

Von Eschen, Penny. 1997. *Race against Empire: Black Americans and Anti-colonialism, 1937–1957*. Ithaca, NY: Cornell University Press.

Waldinger, Roger David. 1996. *Still the Promised City?: African-Americans and New Immigrants in Postindustrial New York*. Cambridge, MA: Harvard University Press.

Warren, Christopher L., John F. Stack Jr., and John G. Corbett. 1986. Minority Mobilization in an International City: Rivalry and Conflict in Miami. *Political Science* 19, no. 3: 626–35.

Warren, Dorian. 2005. A New Labor Movement for a New Century?: The Incorporation of Marginalized Workers in U.S. Unions. PhD diss., Yale University.

Waters, Mary C. 2001. *Black Identities: West Indian Immigrant Dreams and American Realities*. Cambridge, MA: Harvard University Press.

———. 1999. West Indians and African Americans at Work: Structural Difference and Cultural Stereotypes. In *Sociodemographic Aspects of Immigration for African Americans*, edited by Frank D. Bean and Stephanie B. Rose. New York: Russell Sage Foundation.

———. 1998. Multiple Ethnic Identity Choices. In *Beyond Pluralism: The Conception of Groups and Group Identities in America*, edited by Wendy F. Katkin, Ned Landsman, and Andrea Tyree, 28–46. Urbana: University of Illinois Pres.

———. 1994. Ethnic and Racial Identities of Second-Generation Black Immigrants in New York City. *International Migration Review* 28, no. 4 (Winter): 795–820.

———. 1990. *Ethnic Options: Choosing Identities in America*. Berkeley: University of California Press.

Watkins-Owens, Irma. 1996. *Blood Relations: Caribbean Immigrants and the Harlem Community, 1900–1930*. Bloomington: Indiana University Press.

Welch, Susan. 1985. The "More for Less" Paradox: Public Attitudes on Taxing and Spending. *Public Opinion Quarterly* 49, no. 3 (Autumn): 310–16.

West, Cornel. 1990. The Cultural Politics of Difference. In *Out There: Marginalization and Contemporary Cultures*, edited by Russell Ferguson, Martha Gever, Trinh T. Minh-ha, and Cornel West. Cambridge, MA: MIT Press.

Williams, David R., and Pamela Braboy Jackson. 2005. Social Sources of Racial Disparities in Health. *Health Affairs* 24, no. 2: 325–34.

Wilson, James Q. 1974. *Political Organizations*. New York: Basic Books.

Wilson, William J. 1996. *When Work Disappears: The World of the New Urban Poor*. New York: Knopf.

———. 1987. *The Truly Disadvantaged: The Inner City, the Underclass, and Public Policy*. Chicago: University of Chicago Press.

———. 1980. *The Declining Significance of Race: Blacks and Changing American Institutions*. Chicago: University of Chicago Press.

Winant, Howard. 1994. *Racial Conditions: Politics, Theory, Comparisons*. Minneapolis: University of Minnesota Press.

Winter, Nicholas. 2006. Beyond Welfare: Framing and the Racialization of White Opinion on Social Security. *American Journal of Political Science* 50, no. 2 (April): 400–420.

Wolfinger, Raymond E., and Steven J. Rosenstone. 1980. *Who Votes?* New Haven, CT: Yale University Press.

Wong, Cara. 2010. *Boundaries of Obligation in American Politics: Geographic, National, and Racial Communities*. New York: Cambridge University Press.

Wong, Janelle. 2006. *Democracy's Promise: Immigrants and American Civic Institutions*. Ann Arbor: University of Michigan Press.

Yun, Grace, ed. 1989. *A Look beyond the Model Minority Image: Critical Issues in Asian America*. New York: Minority Rights Group.

Zaller, John. 1992. *The Nature and Origins of Mass Opinion*. New York: Cambridge University Press.

INDEX

affirmative action
    agreement strength about, 96–97, 96t
    definition of, 95
    white treatment compared to, 97
Africa, 86, 183n12
Africa aid spending, 134–5, 134t
    black Americans on, 115, 117–18, 130,
        135, 135t
Africans
    on affirmative action, 95–97, 96t
    on Africa aid spending, 135, 135t
    on African treatment, 100–101, 100t
    Afro-Caribbeans compared to, 81
    on Afro-Caribbean treatment, 99–100, 99t
    age of, 150t
    ambition of, 107
    for American Dream, 86–87
    American Dream generational effects for,
        87–92, 88t
    attitude towards, 171t
    on black Americans' treatment, 98t, 99
    on blame, 102–3, 102f, 112, 133
    against border patrols, 184n9
    census on, 140, 184n2
    citizenship of, 165, 165t
    class of, 150t
    on defense spending, 126, 126t
    education of, 133, 149t
    elevated minority for, 108–9, 109t, 111
    on environmental spending, 128t
    exit option of, 20, 176n8
    gender of, 133
    hard work by, 101, 104–7, 105t, 170t–171t
    on health care spending, 122t
    home country return for, 20, 139, 176n8
    home country stability of, 75, 77, 92, 167t,
        182n25
    immigration of, 12, 20, 39, 42t, 147t, 175n2,
        176n8, 179n2
    income of, 149t–150t
    on labor thermometer, 163t
    lazy vs. hardworking, 170t–171t
    Local 371 voting, presidential elections, 66t,
        69, 69t
    in New York City, 48, 180n17
    occupational threats to, 109–10, 110t
    optimism of, 106–7

    as political candidates, 141
    political participation of, 113, 141
    on poor people, 174t
    on public education spending, 120t–121t
    on Social Security spending, 124, 124t
    on spending on immigrants, 130–31, 131t
    on success from hard work, 107–8, 107t,
        183n20
    term use of, 43–44
    union and nonunion party identification for,
        73, 74t, 75, 76t, 77
    on welfare, 173t
    on welfare spending, 132–33, 133t
    on white treatment, 93–95, 94t
African Americans. See also black Americans
    Afro-Caribbeans compared to, 19–20, 31,
        81, 85
    American Dream generational effects
        compared to, 90–91
    blending of, 23
    group identity , 32–33, 178n31
    definition of, 11–12, 140–42
    names for, 42–44
African and Afro-Caribbean immigrants
    advancement of, 40, 179n3
    black Americans compared to, 62, 111–12,
        181n12
    increases in, 39–41, 42t, 179n2, 179n4
    location of, 41–42
African treatment, 100–101, 100t
Afro-Americans, 179n6
*Afro-Caribbean Immigrants and the Politics of
    Incorporation* (Rogers), 82
Afro-Caribbeans. See also African and Afro-
    Caribbean immigrants
    on affirmative action, 95–97, 96t
    on Africa aid, 119
    on Africa aid spending, 135, 135t
    African Americans compared to, 19–20
    on African treatment, 100, 100t
    age of, 150t
    for American Dream, 86–87, 102,
        111–12
    American Dream generational effects for,
        88–92, 88t
    America raised, 88–89, 88t
    attitude towards, 171t

Printed in Australia
AUHW022144161122
371463AU00004B/6